The History and Religious Heritage of

OLD CAIRO

Its Fortress, Churches, Synagogue, and Mosque

Gawdat Gabra, Gertrud J.M. van Loon, Stefan Reif, and Tarek Swelim

Edited by Carolyn Ludwig and Morris Jackson

Photographs by Sherif Sonbol

A Ludwig Publishing Edition
The American University in Cairo Press
Cairo • New York

All photographs are by Sherif Sonbol, except photographs on pages: 27, 82 top, 90 top, 109 right, 113 bottom, 114, 115, 126, 130–31 top, 140, 141 top, 170, 171, 172, 173, 200 top left, 216 left, 231, 234, 253, 279 top right (Carolyn Ludwig); 38 center and bottom (Mark Kroll); 16–17, 28, 29, 31, 32, 33, 124, 141 bottom, 146–47, 230, 232–33, 238 bottom, 239–41, 254, 255, 277 bottom, 278, 279 (Hannah Sonbol); 252 (reproduced courtesy of Dr. Samir Simaika); 253 bottom, 255, 256–65, 266–67 top (Boulos Isaac); 266 bottom (Tarek Swelim).

Postcards on page 98 are reproduced courtesy of the Rare Books and Special Collections Library, the American University in Cairo. Painting of Girgis al-Guhari by Michele Rigo on page 136 is reproduced by permission of Réunion des Musées Nationaux/Art Resource, NY. Painting by Jean-Léon Gerome on page 311 is reproduced by permission of the Metropolitan Museum of Art in New York/Art Resource NY.

A special thanks to Dr. Ben Outhwaite, head of the Genizah Research Unit at Cambridge University Library, for his generous support with images from the Cairo Genizah.

Maps on pages 270 and 272 and plan on page 281 are by Ola Seif.

This flexibound edition published in 2016 by
The American University in Cairo Press
113 Sharia Kasr el Aini, Cairo, Egypt
420 Fifth Avenue, New York, NY 10018
www.aucpress.com

Published by arrangement with Ludwig Publishing, Inc.
545 South Figueroa Street, Suite 1233, Los Angeles, CA 90007

Dar el Kutub No. 22456/15
ISBN 978 977 416 769 0

Dar el Kutub Cataloging-in-Publication Data

Ludwig, Carolyn
    The History and Heritage of Old Cairo: Its Fortress, Churches, Synagogue, and Mosque/ Gawdat Gabra [et.al.]; edited by Carolyn Ludwig.—Cairo: The American University in Cairo Press, 2016
        p. cm.
            ISBN 978 977 416 769 0
            1. Cairo (Egypt)—Description and travel.   2. Egypt—Antiques—Description and travel
        I. Loon, Gertrud van (jt. auth.)
        II. Reif, Stefan (jt. auth.)
        III. Swelim, Tarek (jt. auth.)
        IV. Ludwig, Carolyn (ed.)
            913.2

1 2 3 4 5   20 19 18 17 16

Designed by Morris Jackson
Printed in China

To the memory of

Ibrahim al-Guhari *(?–1795), Egypt's minister of finance, who restored many of Egypt's churches and is buried in Old Cairo*
Shelomo Dov Goitein *(1900–85), a great scholar whose life's work on the Cairo Genizah documents reveals the tolerance that Old Cairo has enjoyed for many centuries*
Ahmed Kadry *(1931–90), chairman of the Egyptian Antiquities Organization (1981–87), who gave serious attention and care to the monuments of Old Cairo*

CONTENTS

PREFACE

Carolyn Ludwig

The Golden Rule

FROM THE TORAH
You shall not take vengeance, nor bear any grudge against the sons of your people, but you shall love your neighbor as yourself.
— Leviticus 19:18

FROM THE BIBLE
In everything, therefore, treat people the same way you want them to treat you, for this is the Law and the Prophets.
— Matthew 7:12

FROM THE HADITH
None of you [truly] believes until he wishes for his brother what he wishes for himself.
— The Prophet Muhammad
(from Imam al-Nawawi's
Forty Hadith)

"DO UNTO OTHERS AS YOU WOULD HAVE THEM DO UNTO YOU." The Golden Rule appears in Judaism, Christianity, and Islam. The premise originated in ancient Egypt, however, long before the appearance of the three great Abrahamic faiths. *Maat* was the ancient Egyptian concept of truth, balance, order, law, morality, and justice, and the earliest surviving records indicating that *Maat* was the norm for nature and society, in this world and the next, can be traced back to the Old Kingdom in pyramid texts (ca. 2780–2250 BCE). It seems appropriate, therefore, that *The History and Religious Heritage of Old Cairo* should celebrate the shared history and heritage of Judaism, Christianity, and Islam in the land that gave birth to *Maat*.

The History and Religious Heritage of Old Cairo, written by expert scholars in their field, is a rich and stunning documentation of religious harmony and mutually beneficial coexistence between the three monotheistic religions.

In the individual sections of this book the reader discovers the struggles and sacrifices that went into building the places of worship that were to play such a central role in the daily lives of so many people. We are hugely fortunate to have had these sacred places bequeathed to us, for the stories they tell give us hope that we can live and work together in peace as did the people of Old Cairo. Through modern communication worldwide, there are fewer excuses not to understand and live by the Golden Rule.

INTRODUCTION
Gawdat Gabra

NYONE WHO KNEW OLD CAIRO BEFORE THE BEGINNING OF THE 1980s will certainly appreciate all that has been achieved there since. Today Old Cairo is one of the most important sites in the city and is visited by Egyptians and foreigners alike. When I joined the Coptic Museum in 1976, I was struck by its old-fashioned methods of exhibition and lighting, primitive showcases and flooring, and lack of the simplest museum facilities. The museum and the beautiful old churches of this neighborhood, which preserve the atmosphere of medieval times, suffered from terrible infrastructure problems, among them an antiquated municipal sewage system, a high groundwater level, and dust generated by the traffic on unpaved streets. During my first year at the museum, I had to devote part of my time to work in the 'Technical Section' under the director general of the Egyptian Antiquities Organization (EAO), Ahmed Kadry, one of the three great men to whom this volume is dedicated. I seized the opportunity to bring the incredible state of this important site to his attention.

I left the museum for a time to study Coptology in Münster, Germany, and I returned to a happy surprise: Significant improvements had been made to the Coptic Museum and a number of the monuments of Old Cairo, including the restoration of some pillars and walls in the Fortress of Babylon that support the Hanging Church. The entire New Wing of the Coptic Museum and the upper floor of the Old Wing had been renovated, and new methods of exhibition had been introduced. President Hosni Mubarak opened the restored museum and the Hanging Church (al-Mu'allaqa) on 8 March 1984.

The following year, I was appointed director of the Coptic Museum. In this position and as a member of the Permanent Committee for Islamic and Coptic Antiquities I bore a responsibility to the entire site, which I knew still deserved more attention and development. At that time, Old Cairo was shabby and dilapidated. Any attempt at landscaping to beautify the area would fail, however, owing to the antiquated sewage system, which had not yet been replaced and which was often in need of repair. The rising groundwater levels endangered the South Gate, the quay, and an inner court of the Fortress of Babylon, as well as the crypt that is believed to have provided refuge for the Holy Family. Moreover, a weekly livestock market offering sheep, goats, and fowl for sale added to the miserable atmosphere.

Working at a number of pharaonic sites had taught me that promoting tourism is always an effective means of attracting the attention of the authorities, and thereby leading to further development of the site. My starting point in Old Cairo was the renovated Coptic Museum with its collection of Coptic art—the largest and most significant in the world—which was presented in an attractive setting: *mashrabiyas*, decorative timbered ceilings in the Old Wing, gazebos in the garden, and a refreshing fountain, along with facilities such as a gift shop and a fine cafeteria shaded by surrounding trees. After only a few annual marketing campaigns, the number of tourists increased more than tenfold, from eight thousand in 1984 to eighty-four thousand in 1988; attendance rates were second only to the Egyptian Museum.

Since the early twentieth century, the Coptic Museum, the churches surrounding it, and Fustat, with the Mosque of 'Amr, have not only shared the same neighborhood, they have also been united by initiatives to protect and promote the entire area.[1] Advocacy targeting government officials and efforts to raise their awareness of the condition and importance of the site have been effective in securing vital changes to the neighborhood's infrastructure.

In 1986 work began on the construction of a bridge to link the busy thoroughfare of Corniche al-Nil to Fustat. The resulting increase in traffic, however, would endanger all the monuments in Old Cairo, including the Coptic Museum. Ahmed Kadry, chairman of the EAO, therefore invited minister of communication Soliman Metwalli to make an inspection tour of the site in the hope of persuading the government to abandon the bridge project. The effort was successful and construction halted. The minister admired the museum, and later he responded positively to requests for improvements to the transport and communications infrastructure, ordering the renovation of the adjacent Mari Girgis metro station and facilitating the installation of two public telephones in the museum garden.

In 1986, when the deterioration of the Church of Sts. Sergius and Bacchus *(Abu Sarga)* made restoration imperative, a working group comprising university professors of engineering and related fields, experts from the construction industry, and members of the Permanent Committee for Islamic and Coptic Antiquities conducted a thorough investigation of the entire area. Their findings confirmed the long-known causes of the problem: the rising groundwater levels and pressure from the sewage. During the project to salvage the church, a number of reused limestone blocks were found under its northern wall. One of them, which depicts a Nile god, must have belonged to a temple of considerable size erected by Ptolemy V (204–180 BC), very probably in the district of contemporary Old Cairo.[2] Work continued in the late 1980s to strengthen the walls of the Old Wing of the Coptic Museum, where, providentially, all the foundations had been reinforced just a few months before the earthquake of 1992.[3]

It was President Anwar Sadat who, after signing the historic Camp David treaty between Egypt and Israel on 26 March 1979, proposed the creation of an interfaith center on Mount Sinai that should include a synagogue, a church, and a mosque. Moreover, he himself expressed the desire to be buried there and suggested that the American people might like to contribute to establish such a center. About $50,000 was collected toward the project in the United States.[4] After Sadat's assassination on 6 October 1981 and his burial in Cairo, people began to consider Old Cairo, in which Jews, Christians, and Muslims had coexisted for many centuries, an appropriate alternative site to house the proposed interfaith center.[5] Between 1985 and 1989, as work progressed on the restoration of the Ben Ezra Synagogue, American and Canadian delegations—regularly accompanied by a representative of the Canadian or the American Embassy— came to my office to discuss the possibilities of the development of the entire site, the future of tourism there, and where in Old Cairo an interfaith center could be established. Well acquainted with the very complex circumstances of the site and the need to accommodate the interests of many private as well as bureaucratic and governmental authorities (the municipality of Old Cairo, the Coptic patriarchate, the Greek Orthodox Church, the Greater Cairo Sewage Authority, and the EAO), I proposed the creation of a master plan for Old Cairo as an imperative initial step. While the interfaith center has not yet been realized, the "Old Cairo Master Plan" was drawn up through a collaborative process initiated in 1999 by the American Research Center in Egypt (ARCE), a project in which I gladly participated. The Master Plan is a unique document that can serve as a guide for the development of the area, covering nearly all the key issues, from archaeology and landscaping to infrastructure and architectural conservation.

In recent decades, the amount of scholarly information about Old Cairo has increased significantly. When the number of tourists visiting the site came to the attention of the Faculty of Tourism at Helwan University, a course on Coptic Civilization was added to the curriculum. There was a pressing need for a reliable illustrated guide to the Coptic Museum and the churches of Old Cairo. I therefore compiled *Cairo: The Coptic Museum and Old Churches*, which was published by the Egyptian International Publishing Company-Longman in English in 1993; it has since been translated into Arabic, German, French, Italian, and Russian.[6] The publication in the 1990s of the first studies of Old Cairo based on archaeological investigations greatly increased the information available on the Fortress of Babylon, the historical monuments within it, and its surroundings.[7]

The tragic earthquake that struck Egypt in 1992 seriously affected the monuments of Old Cairo, especially the Hanging Church and the adjacent Old Wing of the Coptic Museum. The collection of the museum's Old Wing objects had to be evacuated and the structure supported by scaffolding.[8] The situation was so serious that a parliamentary committee, accompanied by the secretary general of the Supreme Council of Antiquities (SCA), Mohammed Bakr, investigated the Coptic Museum and the Hanging Church. Bakr promised to secure the funding necessary to save the endangered monuments of Old Cairo.

Conservation efforts embarked on a new phase at the turn of the twenty-first century, with a huge project undertaken by the American Research Center, and funded by USAID, to lower the groundwater levels at the sites of significant historic buildings. The five-year project was successfully completed in 2005, and there is no doubt that Old Cairo will continue to benefit from this vital improvement for decades to come. Subsequently, the SCA restored and renovated the Coptic Museum and a number of buildings in its vicinity, including the famous Hanging Church, the crypt of the Holy Family, the Wedding Hall, and the Convent of St. George. During the renovation of the Coptic Museum, all its holdings had to be evacuated, including the very fragile niches from the monasteries of Sts. Jeremiah of Saqqara and Apollo of Bawit, which are beautifully decorated and among the most valuable treasures of Coptic art. Zahi Hawass, secretary general of the SCA, supported my suggestion that ARCE be entrusted with the restoration of these niches, which they have successfully completed. President Hosni Mubarak officially opened the fully renovated museum on 25 June 2006; the following year, the American University in Cairo Press published a book on the museum's artistic treasures and the churches of Old Cairo and a corresponding smaller-format illustrated guide.[9]

In the decade and a half I spent at the Coptic Museum, no archaeologist was as devoted to Old Cairo as Peter Sheehan. He participated in a number of projects there in the 1990s, and in the last decade has compiled and carefully studied a huge amount of invaluable material about this historic neighborhood. His unique approach covers the history of the entire site, from the earliest evidence of culture to the present day. Sheehan's exceptional achievement is the discovery of the relationship between the Canal of Trajan and the Babylon Fortress and the historic buildings within. He has shown how the canal influenced the establishment of the new Islamic capitals to the north of the fortress. This book has benefited greatly from Sheehan's *Babylon of Egypt: The Archaeology of Old Cairo and the Origins of the City*, published in 2010 by the American University in Cairo Press.

Jews, Christians, and Muslims lived together in Old Cairo for many centuries in a wonderful atmosphere of tolerance, making this unique site ideal for studying the coexistence of the three 'Abrahamic' faiths in medieval times.[10] Scholars have long considered Hellenistic Egypt, Islamic Spain, and Renaissance Italy to be 'golden ages' in Jewish history; I propose adding Fatimid and Ayyubid Old Cairo to this list. The Cairo Genizah documents show that here, Jewish, Christian, and Muslim merchants were partners and their families dwelled alongside each other as neighbors. Egypt's oldest synagogue still stands in Old Cairo, where the city's most ancient Christian churches were built. Old Cairo is also the site of Egypt's oldest Islamic capital, Fustat, and the most ancient mosque in Africa.

When Carolyn Ludwig proposed a book on Old Cairo, we agreed on a provisional title—"The Jewish, Christian, and Islamic Heritage of Old Cairo"—to reflect the shared history of the site and recall the idea of the interfaith center proposed by Anwar Sadat. I invited three respected specialists to collaborate in the preparation of this volume. Stefan Reif, professor emeritus of Medieval Hebrew Studies and director of the Genizah Research Unit at Cambridge University, kindly agreed to provide the chapter on the Jewish legacy of Old Cairo. Gertrud J.M. van Loon of the KU Leuven (Catholic University of Leuven), an expert on Egypt's Christian art who is particularly familiar with the churches of Old Cairo, addresses the site's Christian heritage. And Tarek Swelim, who earned his doctorate at Harvard University specializing in Egypt's early Islamic art and architecture, is responsible for the texts on Fustat and the Mosque of 'Amr. I, meanwhile, have contributed the chapters on the Fortress of Babylon and the Coptic Museum. A grant of the Brigitte and Martin Krause Foundation enabled me to use the library of the Institute of Egyptology and Coptology of Münster University in Germany. We have all benefited from Sherif Sonbol's exceptional skill as a photographer and from Morris Jackson's talent as a book designer. Without the support, patience, and enthusiasm of Mrs. Ludwig, this volume could not have been realized. We hope that laypersons, students, and scholars will benefit from both the text and the illustrations, and we trust that this volume reflects the spirit of interfaith collaboration and trust that once characterized Old Cairo, and that we hope will be strengthened.

N

PLAN OF OLD CAIRO

showing

1 Babylon
2 Mosque of 'Amr ibn al-'As
3 Monastery of St. Mercurius
4 Churches to the South
   of the Fortress
5 Ben Ezra Synagogue
6 Coptic Museum

River Nile

CHRONOLOGY OF EVENTS

89–119 CE	Canal dug by Trajan
98–117	Public practice of Christianity declared capital offense
284–305	Reign of Diocletian—severe persecution of Christians; and the building of the Fortress of Babylon
311	Christianity accepted by Emperor Constantine the Great
313	Edict of Milan—freedom of religion declared throughout the Roman Empire
325	Council of Nicea—Nicean Creed
341	Pagan rites forbidden
379–95	Emperor Theodosius declares Christianity the official religion of the empire
431	Council of Ephesus—rift between the bishop of Alexandria and the sees of Constantinople, Antioch, and Rome
451	Council of Chalcedon—creates schism with Egyptians over the nature of Christ
476	Fall of Rome
6th Century	Church of St. Mercurius built *(Dayr Abu Sayfayn)*
619	Persians invade and occupy Egypt—many monasteries destroyed
622	Muhammad's flight from Mecca to Medina, marking the beginning of the Islamic Era
639–42	*al Mu'allaqa* (Hanging Church) built
	Fustat established as Muslim capital city after Arab Conquest
642	'Amr ibn al-'As Mosque built
After Arab Conquest	*al-Mu'allaqa* (Hanging Church) built
Late 7th Century	Church of Sts. Sergius and Bacchus *(Abu Sarga)* built
	Church of St. George (Coptic) built
	Church of Sts. Cyrus and John (now St. Barbara) built
861	Nilometer
9th Century	Purchase of land for a synagogue
11th Century	Building of Ben Ezra Synagogue
13th–14th Century	Wedding Hall *(Qa'at al-'Irsan)* near the Coptic Church of St. George
15th Century	Rebuilding of Ben Ezra Synagogue
18th Century	Rebuilding or restoration of most of the churches in the fortress
	Dayr Abu Sayfayn and the churches to the south of the fortress
	Icon painters Yuhanna al-Armani and Ibrahim al-Nasikh play a leading role in the refurbishing of churches
1832–71	Workshop of icon painter A[na]stasi al-Qudsi al-Rumi

End 19th Century	Large-scale restoration and rebuilding of the Hanging Church
	Demolition of part of the fortress walls
	Start of involvement of the Comité de conservation des monuments de l'art arabe in the restoration of churches in and around the fortress
1904	Greek Orthodox Church of St. George burnt down
1908	Coptic Museum founded; opened 1910
1909	Consecration of rebuilt Greek Orthodox Church of St. George
1912–13	Building of the new Convent of St. Mercurius *(Abu Sayfayn)*

For the Church of the Virgin "Pot of Basil" *(Qasriyat al-Rihan)*, the Chapel of St. George in the Convent of St. George, the Greek Orthodox Church of St. George, the Church of St. Shenute *(Dayr Abu Sayfayn)*, the Church of the Virgin "al-Damshiriya," the Church of the Virgin near Babylon of the Steps, and the Churches of St. Theodore, Sts. Cyrus and John, and St. Michael al-Qibli, no reliable date for the original building can be given.

THE FORTRESS OF BABYLON IN OLD CAIRO

Gadwat Gabra

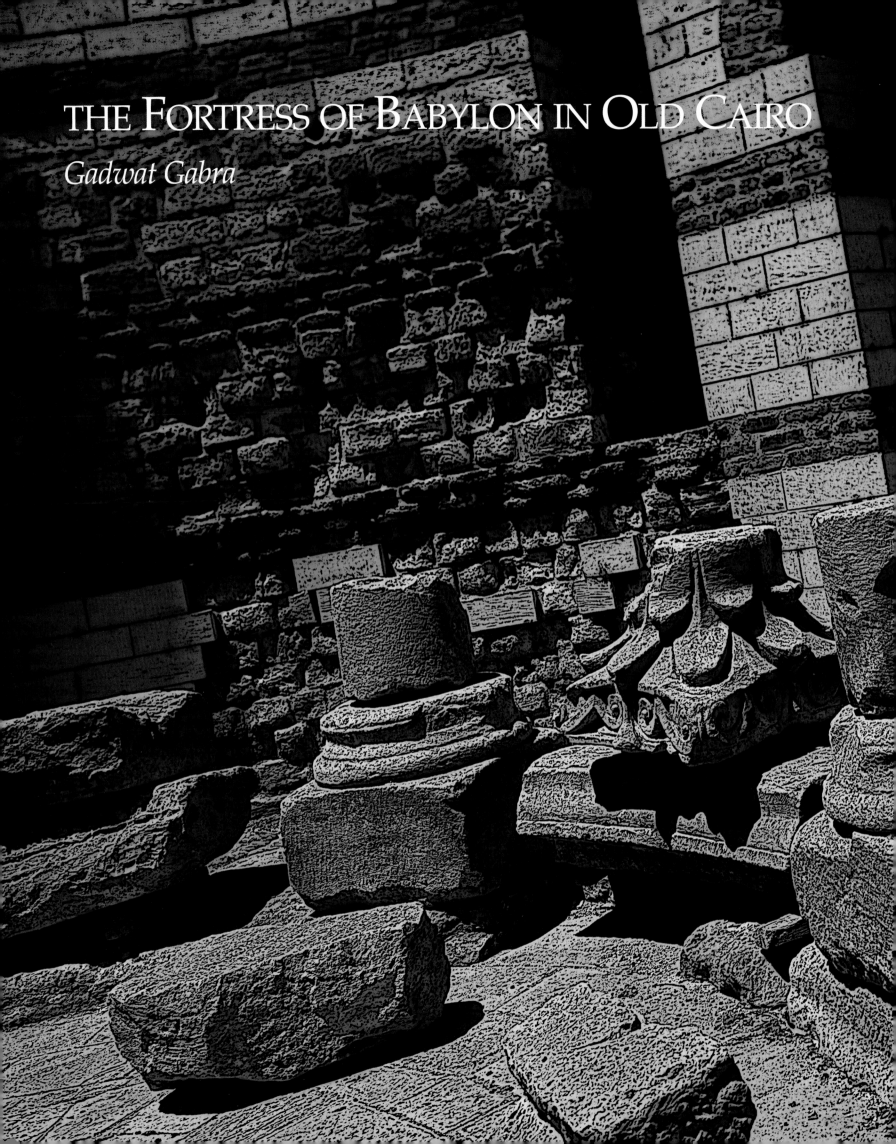

THE FORTRESS OF BABYLON IN OLD CAIRO

CAIRO, OR RATHER GREATER CAIRO, the largest city in Africa and in the Middle East, is an aggregate of the great cultural centers that successive civilizations founded at the apex of the Nile Delta. The earliest were predynastic settlements dating from the fourth millennium before Christ, founded in Maadi[1] and Helwan,[2] two suburbs of present-day Cairo.

Visitors to Cairo are encouraged to see not only the famous and imposing pharaonic monuments on the western bank of the Nile at Giza—the pyramids and the sphinx—but also to enjoy its Jewish, Christian, and Islamic legacies. This great heritage lies on the eastern bank of the Nile, where a number of national capitals were established.

Medieval sources differentiate between Old Cairo (Fustat Misr or simply Misr, colloquially pronounced Masr)[3] and Cairo (al-Qahira), which scholars call 'Historic' or 'Medieval' Cairo. While 'Historic' Cairo was founded in 969 by Gawhar al-Siqilli, commander of the Fatimid troops,[4] Old Cairo boasts a longer history. Many pharaonic monuments were discovered in Old Cairo in the area that belonged to the southernmost part of the thirteenth district of Lower Egypt. Ancient Egyptian texts mention two localities associated with this area, which was both strategically important and symbolically significant due to the junction of the Nile Valley and the Delta. Identification and localization of both sites are therefore often discussed together.

One, called Kher-Aha (the Scene of Battle, or the Battlefield), was connected with the mythological conflict between the Egyptian gods Horus and Seth. The majority of scholars identify it with Old Cairo or Babylon, in which still stands the famous fortress bearing that name.[5] The name 'Babylon' derives from the contemporaneous Greek vocalization of the ancient Egyptian name for the site, Pr-Hapi-n-Iwnw (Nile House of Heliopolis).[6] According to recent archaeological investigations, Kher-Aha may designate the whole east-bank area of cemeteries south of Heliopolis.[7]

The other locality mentioned by ancient Egyptian texts is Pr-Hapi (the House of the Nile). Ancient Egyptian sources consider this site to be the beginning of the Nile in Lower Egypt and to mark the border between Upper and Lower Egypt. It is generally accepted that Pr-Hapi was situated in Athar al-Nabi, about two kilometers south of Old Cairo.[8] It is possible, however, that it was located farther south, at Helwan.[9] Pr-Hapi housed a Nilometer to measure the height of the annual flood, and it was the harbor of Heliopolis, to which it was connected by a canal.

Both Kher-Aha and Pr-Hapi were scenes of the great Heliopolitan Nile festivals. They grew in importance during the Greco-Roman era after the fortunes of the famous city of Heliopolis began to decline in the late period (664–332 BCE).[10] Heliopolis, one of the most significant ancient Egyptian cultural cities, associated with astronomy and solar theology, was largely destroyed by the Persian invasions of 525 and 343 BCE. When Strabo visited the city in the late first century, he found it partly abandoned; many of its remaining obelisks and statues had been moved to Alexandria and Rome when Egypt was under Roman rule. Today, museums around the world display ancient monuments from Heliopolis,[11] but the site itself is occupied by modern buildings. Few of its historic treasures remain in situ. A standing obelisk of King Senusert I (ca. 1918–1875 BCE) in present-day Matariya, which borders the southwestern part of modern Heliopolis, reminds us of the area's former glory; other remnants have been found in northeastern

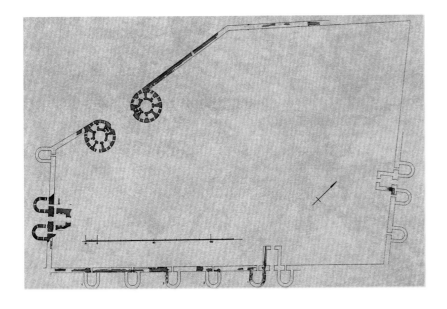

The general plan of the visible remains of the Fortress according to Grossmann, Le Quesne, and Sheehan (1994). Since the construction of the fortress the course of the Nile has moved about 400 meters to the west. The plan of the fortress features an irregular five-sided layout, occupying an area of around three hectares.

The first precise ground plan of the fortress showing the building within it appeared in Alfred Butler's The Ancient Coptic Churches of Egypt (1884, vol. 1, plan facing p. 155).

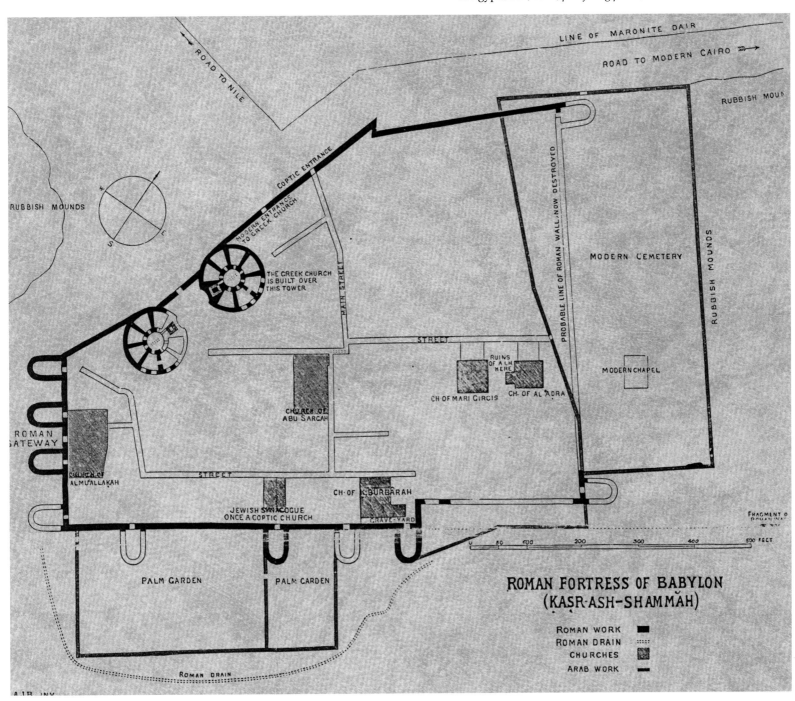

ROMAN FORTRESS OF BABYLON
(KAṢR·ASH·SHAMMĂH)

ROMAN WORK
ROMAN DRAIN
CHURCHES
ARAB WORK

The Greek Orthodox Church of St. George is built on the northern tower of the former river gate that was on the Trajanic Canal and harbor of the Fortress of Babylon.

neighborhoods of Cairo like Ain Shams and Arab al-Tawil. The migration of these artifacts across the city results from the practice of reusing stone from the ancient buildings of the Heliopolitan district, including Pr-Hapi and Kher-Aha, to construct newer edifices in Fustat and Medieval Cairo.[12]

Ancient and modern historians connect Emperor Trajan (98–117) with the construction of the Fortress of Babylon and a canal running from there to the Red Sea. The Alexandrian geographer, astronomer, and astrologer Claudius Ptolemaeus (ca. 90–ca. 168), known as Ptolemy, refers to the canal—which started in Babylon and connected the Nile and the Red Sea—as the "River of Trajan." It was Herodotus who first mentioned such a canal around the mid-fifth century BCE. He stated that King Necho II (610–595 BCE) commissioned its construction, but did not carry it out after being influenced by an oracle that only foreigners would benefit from the canal. Later, the Persian ruler Darius I (522–486 BCE) completed the canal.[13] Pliny the Elder (23–79) records that the canal was never finished; Sesostris and after him Darius had completed the cutting of the canal but the work had finally been undertaken by Ptolemy II (283/282–246 BCE). However, the latter did not continue the project when he found that the level of the Red Sea was three cubits higher than that of the land of Egypt.[14]

Four stelae show that a navigable route from the Nile to the Red Sea existed, at the latest, in the reign of Darius I. This was accomplished by a canal connecting Bubastis, the Timsah Lake, the Bitter Lakes, and the Red Sea.[15] Ptolemy II commissioned the re-excavation of this canal. There is no evidence that the canal was in use at the end of the Ptolemaic period and the beginning of the early Roman period. It should also be noted that the long-distance trade of the Red Sea port of Berenike flourished in the first century and in the mid-fourth to fifth centuries of our era. Since roads from Coptos and Edfu connected Berenike and the Nile Valley,[16] it is plausible to infer that Berenike prospered when the canal was not functioning.

The archaeological investigations carried out by Peter Sheehan between 1999 and 2005 have clearly shown that it was Emperor Trajan (98–115) who moved the canal south to Babylon and ordered the construction of a stone harbor that incorporated the mouth of the canal. Portions of the huge walls that formed the two sides of the canal entrance have been documented under the Church of Sts. Sergius and Bacchus (*Abu Sarga*) and the Coptic Church of St. George. This canal survived in Cairo until the modern period as al-Khalig al-Misri, which had to be filled in 1896 as a precaution to avoid the spread of cholera.[17]

It is not surprising that Emperor Diocletian (284–305) chose the entrance to the canal as the location for an imposing military fortress that came to be known as the Fortress of Babylon. The canal went out of use again at some time between the reign of Diocletian and the Arab conquest of Egypt in 641.[18] In the seventh century, however, the Arabs re-excavated the canal and moved its entrance farther north in order to accommodate the new buildings of Fustat, the first Islamic capital of Egypt. It appears that the canal had to be re-excavated immediately after the Arabs settled in Fustat in order to provide Arabia with Egyptian corn.[19]

The canal may have been purposely blocked either during the Umayyad and Abbasid conflict around 750 or by the Abbasid caliph al-Mansur in 767 or 768 to stop the flow of provisions into the hands of rebels in al-Madina.[20] According to medieval sources, there was an additional fortification at the southern part of the island of Roda connected to the Fortress of Babylon by a bridge.[21] The latter may have been destroyed during the Fatimid invasion of Egypt.[22]

It is not a coincidence that the oldest archaeological materials found in situ in Old Cairo conform to the early history of the canal in the seventh and sixth centuries BCE, at the very time when Egypt's trade greatly increased in both the Mediterranean and the Near East. The canal continued to influence the

21

An underground corridor beneath the Greek Orthodox Church of St. George in the north tower of the Fortress wall.

topography of Cairo, especially the successive capitals of Egypt on the east bank north of the Fortress of Babylon. Moreover, the canal had a crucial impact on the position of religious buildings throughout Old Cairo, in particular those within the fortress. Among the key findings of the recent archaeological excavation of the Fortress of Babylon are remnants of the massive stone river-walls that formed the harbor and the entrance to the Canal of Trajan. A seventh-century chronicle from John of Nikiou, a Coptic bishop, attributes to the Roman Emperor Trajan the creation of a canal that connected the Nile and the Red Sea and began in Babylon, as well as the foundation of a fortress named Babylon of Egypt:

> *And Trajan came to Egypt and built a fortress with a strong impregnable tower, and he brought water into it in abundance and he named it Babylon in Egypt. Nebuchadnezzar the king of the Magi and Persians was the first to build its foundations and to name it the fortress of Babylon. This was the epoch when he became its king by the ordinance of God, when he drove the Jews into exile after the destruction of Jerusalem, and also when they stoned to death a prophet of God at Thebes in Egypt, and added sin to sin. And Nebuchadnezzar came to Egypt with a numerous army and made a conquest of Egypt, because the Jews had revolted against him, and he named "the Fortress" Babylon after the name of his own city. And Trajan moreover added some buildings to the fortress and other parts in it. And he dug also a small canal—sufficiently large to convey water from the Gihon to the city Clysma. And he put this water into connexion [sic] with the Red Sea, and he named this canal Trajan after his own name.[23]*

John of Nikiou was neither the first historian nor the last to associate the Fortress of Babylon with Trajan. In the last decade of the twentieth century, however, fieldwork carried out by the German Archaeological Institute in Cairo, the Canadian Center of Architecture (Montreal),[24] and the German and British excavations[25] considerably increased our information about the fortress. These excavations revealed the general layout of the western side with the two towers, the eastern side, northern extremity, southern gate, 'barracks,' and a number of buildings within the fortress, possibly including a fortified imperial palace. They also established that the Fortress of Babylon dates from the time of Emperor Diocletian, a century and a half after Trajan, although the legends that attribute the fortress to Trajan have continued to influence scholars.[26]

In fact the reign of Diocletian saw a series of major administrative, financial, and military reforms that affected the entire Roman Empire and created new conditions for Egypt in particular.[27] Diocletian subdivided the old provinces in order to exert stricter control and develop economic resources. In Egypt he introduced a bipartite division, in which the Thebaid was detached from the province of Aegyptius. Taxation was the primary means by which foreign rulers fiscally exploited the Egyptians. The taxation system introduced by Diocletian, which ignored the influence of Nile flooding in its taxation of the peasants, led to their impoverishment and eventually to the formation of a very wealthy and powerful class of local magnates and big landowners.[28] Under Diocletian, Egypt was no longer an isolated currency zone and its coinage was integrated into the rest of the empire. A result of the reform was that the mint of Alexandria lost the privilege of striking its own currency.[29] The oppressive taxation and the difficulties in administration[30] resulted in revolts during the 290s. The most serious revolt occurred in Alexandria in 297; Diocletian lost control of the great city and was to besiege it for eight months in order to retake it. After reconquering Alexandria, the emperor traveled southward and fortified the island of Philae. The Dodekaschoenos south of Aswan was relinquished and the frontier was returned to the first cataract. A fortress and palace were constructed in Nag' al-Hagar, about fifteen kilometers north of Aswan,[31] and also in Luxor.[32] Diocletian's defense policy is summarized by the fifth-century historian Zosimus as follows: "By the foresight of Diocletian, the frontiers of the Roman Empire were everywhere studded with cities and forts and towers . . . and the whole army was stationed along them so that it was impossible for the barbarians to break through, as the attackers were everywhere withstood by an opposing force."[33]

The South Tower and the entrance to the corridor leading to the Hanging Church (al-Mu'allaqa). *The church's belfries and the Coptic Museum can be seen in the background.*

Diocletian visited a second time four years later, just before his final attempt to destroy the increasingly influential and organized Christian movement in the 'Great Persecution.'[34] It is well known that this campaign so traumatized the Egyptians that they made Diocletian's accession to the throne in 284 the starting point of their Coptic calendar (Era of the Martyrs: *Anno Martyrum*).[35] Somewhat ironically, Diocletian was the last Roman emperor to visit Egypt, and in his imposing Fortress of Babylon stand some of the oldest churches in Cairo. With these and the artifacts in the Coptic Museum, Diocletian's fortress and the surrounding area became one of the most important centers of Christianity in Egypt.

Although the Fortress of Babylon has sustained considerable damage over the years, and indeed was nearly ruined in the nineteenth century, it ranks among the most significant Roman military structures still extant.[36] It is very probable that Diocletian oversaw the erection of the fortress during his visit to Egypt. His aim was to enclose the mouth of Trajan's canal to the Red Sea, with its early Roman harbor, within an imposing fortress that would dominate the land route to Lower Egypt as well.

Since the construction of the fortress, the course of the Nile has moved about four hundred meters to the west. The plan of the fortress features an irregular five-sided layout, occupying an area of around three hectares (p. 19). The first precise ground plan of the fortress that shows the enclosed building appeared in Alfred Butler's *The Ancient Coptic Churches of Egypt* (p. 19). Apparently, no buildings dating from before Diocletian's time were incorporated within the fortress except for the remains of the Trajanic riverside walls. The huge Diocletianic fortress was well designed to accommodate the necessary military and administrative manpower. Four sides of the fortress feature bastions; the western side does not, but instead boasts two round towers about twenty-eight meters in diameter, which are unique in the military architecture of the Roman period. The gateway leading to the Coptic Museum stands between the towers, and the Greek Orthodox Church of St. George is built on the northern one, whose interior makes up a considerable part of the church (pp. 20–22). The main function of these massive round towers was to defend the mouth of the canal. Three stories high, they are built of three regular layers of fired bricks alternated with five limestone layers. This building technique, known as *opus mixtum*,

Inner court of the southern gate. The staircase leads up to the Coptic Museum's old wing courtyard.

OPPOSITE:
Looking out through the south gate courtyard.

OPPOSITE INSET:
Light shining through the floor beams from the Hanging Church (al-Mu'allaqa) *above.* The church's suspension beams laid over the Fortress walls lead to the popular name: 'Hanging' or 'Suspended Church.'

The South Gate is a magnificent construction of limestone flanked by two U-shaped projecting towers that lead to an inner court and a second gateway.

The barrel vault of the South Gate towers' entrance is surmounted by a pediment that encloses a niche. The latter may have contained a statue. The Hanging Church (al-Mu'allaqa) can be seen on top of the Fortress walls.

was used in most walls of the fortress, including the curtain wall. Each story consists of eight (p. 28) roughly trapezoidal rooms radiating from an inner core. It is probable that one of these towers contained a Nilometer. The towers also contain a number of semicircular niches; in Roman times, these might have been occupied by imperial statues to create an imposing entrance, which must have been controlled by a huge gate (pp. 23, 28).

The south gate (p. 26) is a magnificent limestone construction flanked by two U-shaped projecting towers that lead to an inner court (p. 24) and a second gateway. The latter can be reached from the Old Wing of the Coptic Museum. The semicircular arched niches in these towers were possibly occupied by statues of the Tetrarchs (p. 26). The barrel vault of the gate's entrance is surmounted by a pediment that encloses a niche, which also might have contained a statue. It is above this gate and the upper portion of its towers that the Hanging Church (al- Mu'allaqa) was built (pp. 25, 26). The upper parts of the U-shaped towers flanking the south gate were added after the time of Diocletian, unlike the façade of the gate itself. The few reused blocks with Greco-Roman bas-reliefs in the south gate, as well as the discovery of many ancient Egyptian monuments within the fortress,[37] indicate that earlier buildings were quarried to erect it (pp. 32, 33). Scholars in Napoleon's 1798 expedition and a number of nineteenth-century travelers documented the Fortress of Babylon as it then appeared. Their records show how terrifying the huge façade of the south gate would have appeared to anyone who thought to attack the fortress. They also, however, highlight the sad damage that the structure had sustained in just a few decades.[38]

LEFT:
The three-story towers are built of three regular layers of fired bricks alternated with five limestone layers. This building technique, known as opus mixtum, *has been used in most of the walls of the Fortress, including the curtain wall.*

RIGHT:
The Southern Tower or Museum Tower entrance leads to the Coptic Museum. The main function of the huge round towers, which are built around a central core, was to defend the entrance of the canal.

The rear wall of the Coptic Museum and the Hanging Church stand in the southeast angle of the fortress. This area has become known as al-Muqawqas, and it is largely occupied by later structures; tomb chapels in a Coptic cemetery there, for instance, date from the nineteenth and twentieth centuries. Although only a small part of the eastern curtain wall has survived, much of its height—10.5 meters at the highest point, and thus nearly the full height of the wall—has been preserved within the Muqawqas area. The Ben Ezra Synagogue, in which the famous Genizah documents were found, lies to the north of this area. Roman barracks east of the synagogue are arranged in blocks.

Archaeological observations and the study of the architecture of the Fortress of Babylon suggest that it once had six gates: two in the northern wall, and one or two in each of the eastern and western walls. It is almost certain that the remains of a fifth U-shaped tower north of the Muqawqas area would once have flanked the eastern gate of the fortress.

Excavations of the Muqawqas area and the south gate's eastern tower have unearthed artifacts dating from the fifth to the eleventh centuries, including rich troves of pottery: amphorae, cooking bowls, and plates diverse in shape, material, and provenance, with the decorated glazed wares of special importance for further studies. The coins found in the area cover a period of more than a thousand years, from the fourth to the fourteenth centuries. In contrast, there is comparatively little material dating from the period between the construction of the fortress around 300 and the Arab invasion of Egypt in 641.

Wooden gear of the press.

LEFT:
Lower part of the Fortress with newly restored press that may have been used to produce olive oil or to grind grains.

When the Arabs seized the fortress in 641 and settled in the site, they moved the canal entrance to the north to prepare the site for the construction of the new Islamic capital, Fustat. It was around this time that people began to inhabit the area immediately to the west of the round towers. Babylon must have been a considerable city long before the Arab occupation, since its bishop Cyrus participated in the Council of Ephesus in 449.[39] But although his cathedral cannot have been the only church in Babylon at that time, there is no evidence within the fortress of churches that predate the Arab conquest of Egypt. Thus the magnificent fifth- and sixth-century wooden pieces found in the churches of St. Sergius and St. Barbara, which were probably founded around 700, must have been moved there from churches built in an earlier period, perhaps in the Fustat area before the Arab settlement there. This applies too to the elaborate marble column capital with a looped cross that has been brought from Fustat to the Coptic Museum.[40]

The Arab takeover of the Fortress of Babylon—whether or not it was achieved by force[41]—was a decisive factor in their conquest of Egypt. It seems, however, that the new rulers of Egypt preferred to live outside the fortress in the newly founded city of Fustat, and thus the population within the fortress continued to be largely non-Muslim. In early and medieval Islamic sources, the fortress is sometimes called Qasr al-Sham' (the Palace of the Candles), a name that al-Maqrizi (d. 1442) suggests came from the Persians' illumination of the fortress towers with innumerable candles.[42]

The heritage of the Fortress of Babylon, or Qasr al-Sham', extends through three millennia and thus deserves more attention than it has so far received. Its importance for the history of Judaism, Christianity, and Islam in Egypt cannot be overestimated.

ABOVE:
A long carved stone, re-used from a pharaonic building, showing a traditional scene of a ruler in front of a god.

OPPOSITE:
The few reused blocks with Greco-Roman bas-reliefs in the South Gate and the discovery of many ancient Egyptian monuments within the fortress indicate that earlier buildings were quarried to erect the South Gate.

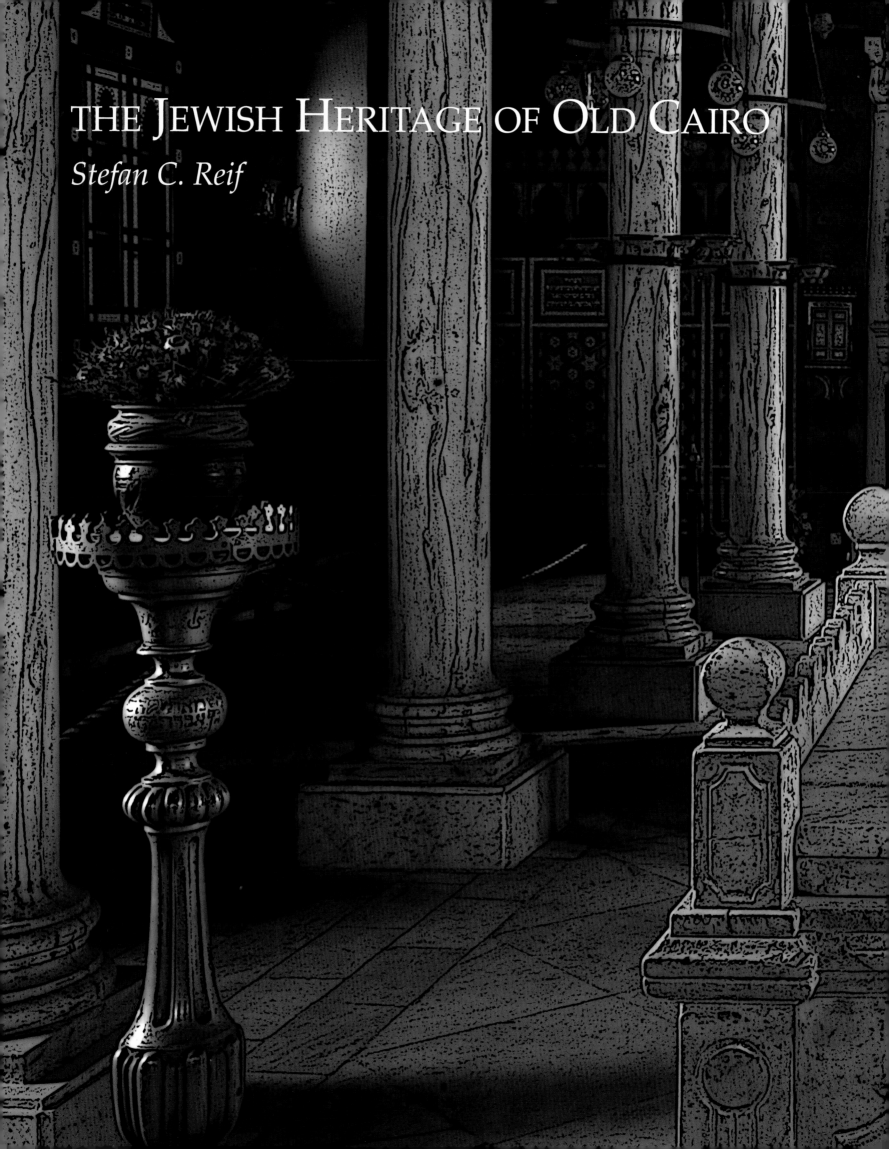

THE JEWISH HERITAGE OF OLD CAIRO

Stefan C. Reif

THE JEWISH HERITAGE OF OLD CAIRO

Earlier History

Jewish connections with Egypt are thousands of years old and are documented in some of the earliest records relating to both peoples. It seems that in the mists of hoary antiquity there are shadowy figures from the Eastern Mediterranean that flit in and out of pharaonic history. Whether we choose to call them Hebrews or Jews, and whether we classify their tales as chronicles, theology, or myth, the members of the group that ultimately embraced and propagated the ideas of Judaism constantly harked back to their youthful flirtations with Egypt. The figures of Abraham, Isaac, and Jacob, whom they saw as their founding fathers, had adventures with Egyptian kings, while the leader Moses, whom they admired and respected above all others, had been reared as an Egyptian prince and bore an Egyptian name. The rulers of the kingdoms of Samaria and Judah, like their predecessor Solomon, son of David, enjoyed treaties as well as confrontations with great pharaohs, and the Hebrew prophets were often obsessed with their powerful neighbors to the southwest. At times they railed against them, their lifestyle, and their politics; on other occasions they saw them as a bulwark against the incursions into the Syro-Palestinian areas being made by the Mesopotamian kingdoms to the east. When the Babylonians sacked Jerusalem and destroyed its institutions, the Judahite prophet Jeremiah was taken to Egypt and spent the remainder of his life preaching his religious message to compatriot exiles there.

In the fifth pre-Christian century, a Jewish garrison at Elephantine, an island on the Nile to the west of Aswan, protected the Egyptian border with Nubia and left us the records of its life and religion.[1] It had its own temple, and records indicate that some three centuries later there was another Jewish temple at Leontopolis (in Lower Egypt), also apparently in competition with the better-known building in Jerusalem.[2] When pharaonic rule gave way to the Greek hegemony imposed on the Near East by Alexander of Macedon and the generals who succeeded him, the settlements along the Nile that culminated in the great city of Alexandria proved no less attractive to Jews seeking broader and more cosmopolitan circles in which to operate. Their brightest thinkers absorbed the language, literature, and ideas of the Classical world in the days before and after the reign of the famous Cleopatra and created a form of their religion—Hellenistic Judaism—that was destined to leave its mark on many aspects of rabbinic literature and to make a major impact on the evolution of Christian theology.

Greek thought patterns and culture continued to thrive in Classical and Byzantine Egypt, and the Jewish community in that area continued to develop its own brand of Jewish ideology and religious practice. This was not always approved by its counterparts in the Palestinian homeland nor in the emerging Babylonian diaspora centers, but there are traces of some grudging admiration. Though personally pious, learned, and abstemious, the second-century rabbinic teacher, Judah ben Ilai, nevertheless spoke of the massive, well- attended, and beautiful synagogue in Alexandria as "the glory of Israel."[3] So large was the building that one of the synagogue officials had reputedly to wave a flag when it was time to respond 'Amen.' This description of the synagogue must relate to a period before the Jewish revolt of 115–17 against the Romans in Egypt, Cyrene, and Cyprus, since this had led to a punitive campaign by Trajan in which thousands of Alexandrian Jews were killed.[4]

Islamic Conquest

With the Christianization of the Roman Empire in the fourth century, the lot of Jews in Egypt, Syria, and Palestine undoubtedly deteriorated. It is not therefore surprising that they took the side of the Persians during their invasions of Egypt in the sixth and seventh centuries. This created animosity toward Jews on the part of some Christians, and the Byzantine emperor Heraclius, representative of a crumbling regime, ordered the forced conversion of the Jewish communities in or around 633. A Judaeo-Arabic Genizah text provides an account of the favorable response of the Jews in Jerusalem to the conquest of the city by 'Umar ibn al-Khattab. He successfully mediated between the Jews and the Christians on the matter of Jewish resettlement in the Holy City and about where precisely in the city they would reside. A similar situation appears to have obtained in Egypt. Interestingly, there were Christians as well as Jews, each for their own reasons, who welcomed the conquering Arab armies that, after some military fits and starts, succeeded in gaining control of the whole of Egypt by 641.[5]

The period from that date until Egypt came under the control of the Fatimid dynasty in 969 was not well documented until the discovery and scholarly exploitation of the Genizah manuscripts (see the description of the contents of these manuscripts on pages 49–71). With the aid of these fragmentary but exciting and informative texts, patches of historical fog have begun to clear from those three centuries, and it is now possible to trace some aspects of Jewish communal development in Egypt, as well as in the various neighboring countries, especially Palestine, prior to the arrival of the crusaders. Either with the invading Muslims or in their wake, Jewish émigrés from other centers took up residence in Egypt. It is not unlikely that their numbers increased with the arrival of immigrants from Babylonia at the beginning of the Iraqi Abbasid takeover from the Syrian Umayyads in 750. The settlements of the Jews ultimately spread into many smaller towns as well as into the larger cities, and they soon had a formidable presence in the first Muslim city to be established in Egypt, that is, Fustat. This name derived from either the Arabic, meaning 'tent,' or the Greek, yielding the sense of 'fortified camp,' and the city became the initial place of residence of the Arab governors.

It was not a virgin site but, given its position on the east bank of the Nile at the head of the Delta, had long been of strategic importance and the obvious place for a fortress. There had been a settlement there in pre-Christian times that gloried in the unlikely name of Babylon, either, more romantically, because some Babylonians had once settled there or, more realistically, through some linguistic corruption (see, in this volume, Gabra's chapter on the Fortress of Babylon). In the third and fourth centuries, Roman walls and towers had been added as part of a building project undertaken during visits to Egypt between 296 and 302 by the emperor Diocletian with the aim of strengthening its defensive capabilities.[6] Fustat Misr, as the Muslims came to call it, enjoyed the status of Egypt's capital city for well nigh half a millennium, and it still had an important part to play in the lives of the Jews of the area for some considerable time afterward.

The Ben Ezra Synagogue

Jewish history being what it has been, there are few places in the world where one can point to a site that hosts a synagogue and claim that it has been there for more than a few hundred years. Yet the area still today occupied by the newly restored Ben Ezra Synagogue in Fustat has certainly functioned as a Jewish religious center for almost a thousand years, and it may even be the case that there was a Jewish presence there as early as the ninth century. If, as now seems clear, the Umayyad and Abbasid periods saw the expansion of the Christian communities and the construction of impressive places of worship in Fustat, one should not rule out the possibility that there was also a synagogue in that area to accommodate the earliest Jewish settlers (or resettlers). As in so many other cases of important sites, there are the traditional tales relating to the history of the Ben Ezra site and the duller, less romantic, but probably more scientifically sound version of what transpired.

First, the romance. The tale goes that in 882, Ahmed ibn Tulun, the governor of Egypt, anxious to acquire funds for his military plans, demanded such a high tribute from the Coptic patriarch Michael that the Christian leader was forced to sell the Church of St. Michael to the Jews, who promptly converted it into a synagogue. Hence the beginning of the synagogal site that was in much later times given the name of Ben Ezra. Alas, there are difficulties with this explanation of events. First, there is some confusion as to whether the Jews bought one synagogue or two and whether St. Michael's was involved. Second, the archaeological evidence appears to indicate that lying deep beneath the current Ben Ezra Synagogue are foundations of an earlier synagogue, rather than a church, and that such foundations incorporated earlier Roman remains.[7] Furthermore, if Jews did settle in Fustat before the ninth century, perhaps they built an early synagogue there, rather than purchasing and renovating a church. In the Genizah collections, there are Greek documents that go back to the sixth century and rabbinic and Judeo-Arabic items that may date from two or more centuries earlier than the classical Genizah period of the tenth to the thirteenth centuries.[8] Perhaps this indicates a presence of Jews, synagogues, and communal officials already at that time amassing documents classified as *genizah*.

Exterior views of the entrance side of the
restored Ben Ezra Synagogue, functioning
as a Jewish religious center for almost a
thousand years. There is some evidence that
there was a Jewish presence in Old Cairo as
early as the ninth century. According to one
record, the land for the synagogue was
purchased in 882 by Abraham ibn Ezra of
Jerusalem for 20,000 dinars. Photographs
left and below by Mark Kroll.

OPPOSITE:
The aron ha-kodesh, holy ark, is the
repository for the Torah scrolls when not
in use. The wood-and-gilded ark serves
as the focus for one's prayers. Two
tablets are inscribed with the Ten
Commandments. Above the ark is the
ner tamid representing the eternal light
(Exodus 27:20–21).

The keter or atarah, the crown of silver at the top of the Torah, emphasizes that "the Torah is a crown for Israel." The rimmonim, finials, adorn the rollers. The Torah, now written on the finest quality paper, used to be written on goat skins by a trained scribe, and it had to be written with no mistakes or it could not be used. The sefer, the box covering the Torah, is made of wood and adorned with silver.

OPPOSITE:
Interior of the Ben Ezra Synagogue, with a view of mastaba, bima, and haykal. When the mastaba in the foreground was restored, a large marble stone was found underneath. It is believed that this is the stone on which Moses sat when he came out of Pharaoh's palace to pray, asking God to intercede with the Pharaoh. This is one of the reasons this site was chosen for building the synagogue.

Intricate patterns cover the central
ceiling of the Ben Ezra Synagogue.
Beautiful stained-glass windows
can barely be seen on the sides
above the painted arches.

RIGHT:
One of the geometrically designed
panels painted on the ceiling under
the balcony.

One of the most recognizable emblems of Judaism, a Star of David, is ornately and beautifully carved in gypsum that adorns a marble cabinet.

The newest building of the Ben Ezra complex, the annex, is used to house a permanent exhibition concerning the history, discovery, and study of the Genizah texts once stored in this synagogue. The annex was built by the contractor who worked on the underground water project and was responsible for shattering the previous annex that stood in front of the synagogue. In 2005, by request of the Cairo Jewish Community, it was rebuilt on land owned by the Community which had been purchased in 1933.

LEFT:
A side and back view of the synagogue. A row of stained-glass windows graces the façade of the building. At one time the Nile flowed where the synagogue stands today. Tradition says that this is where the baby Moses was found in the reeds by Pharoah's daughter. Centuries later, after the synagogue was built, the vault in the basement was used as a mikvah for purification.

The well, built in later years, is used as a wishing well.

Exterior view of the library located behind the synagogue.

The library contains approximately 3000 books, prayer books, and other publications. Many people who emigrated in the 1950s left their books with the Community Center. Later, in the 1980s, scholars were brought in to sort the material and arrange the collection into three libraries: one at Shaar Hashamayim Synagogue, one at the Karaite Synagogue, and one here at the Ben Ezra Synagogue, which was inaugurated in 1997 by Mrs. Esther Weinstein, first woman president of the Cairo community. Photograph courtesy of Carmen Weinstein.

Fatimid Success

Whenever the origins of the Fustat Jewish community are to be dated, there is no doubt that the pinnacle of its power, productivity, and overall comfort was reached during the period of Fatimid hegemony from 969 to 1171. Though Shi'i Isma'ili in their Muslim allegiance, the new rulers often had a broad enough outlook to advance their political and economic status in the Mediterranean area, to encourage trade as far as India and East Asia, and to involve Christians and Jews in carrying out their plans, as well as encouraging them to run their own communities. As a result of this degree of tolerance, and with the influx of coreligionists from the Holy Land (especially in the crusader period) and from Tunisia and other parts of the Maghreb, the Jews of Egypt generally thrived economically and culturally and were able to expand and consolidate their religious and communal institutions. It was indeed in about 1040 that the Ben Ezra synagogue was rebuilt in a most impressive fashion. In the Fatimid period it was known as Kanisat al-Yerushalmiyin or Kanisat al-Shamiyin, after the Palestinian Jews who possibly founded or refounded it, or were among its early occupants, while from the fifteenth century onward it was known as Kanisat Eliyahu, after the prophet Elijah. Its later name of Ben Ezra may in some way be related to the tradition that the synagogue possessed a Torah scroll written by Ezra the Scribe in biblical times. The head of the Egyptian Jewish community in the Fatimid period held the title of *nagid*, which gave him an aristocratic if not royal status and the opportunity of representing his people at the Egyptian court. Early in that period, the Egyptian communities still owed allegiance to the religious authorities of 'Eretz Yisra'el, as they knew it, but the decline of that community during the crusader military successes and the loss of many of its Jewish inhabitants meant that by the twelfth century the situation had been reversed, and Fustat/Cairo stood at the helm of all Jewish progress in the Egyptian, Syrian, and Palestinian areas.

But life was never a picnic for religious minorities in the Middle Ages, even if, or perhaps because, they enjoyed in the Islamic world the protected status of *dhimmi*.[9] Some rulers, either out of personal animosity or in an effort to curry favor with religious hardliners, took measures to persecute the Christians and the Jews. Caliph al-Hakim (996–1021), for instance, ordered them to wear marks of identification and forbade them to ride horses or purchase slaves. At one time, he even decreed forcible conversion and the destruction of synagogues and churches.[10] Despite these setbacks, outbreaks of famine and epidemic disease, and other disasters, especially during the reign of al-Mustansir (1036–94), the whole population of Fustat did manage to bounce back and to maintain its overall standards until the city was finally eclipsed by its parvenu neighbor to the northeast, Cairo, which underwent a metamorphosis from small suburb to large and powerful new capital. This was, to an extent, a reflection of the decline of Egyptian sea power, the narrower horizons of the Ayyubid and Mamluk (Sunni orthodox) regimes, and the consequent weakening of Fustat's role in commerce and politics. The family of the great Jewish sage, physician, and philosopher, Moses Maimonides (1138–1204), continued to reside there for two more generations but then followed the general exodus to Cairo of those who were not too poverty-stricken to make the move.

Mamluk and Ottoman Developments

Given the more narrow-minded approach of the Mamluks in the thirteenth and fourteenth centuries, persecution of the Jews and Christians became more commonplace and led to their economic decline, a reduction in their populations, and their inability to maintain the cultural standards of the Fatimid period. During Mamluk rule, there were numerous instances of military and economic disaster, as well as serious outbreaks of disease. The fifteenth century brought additional trials for the Jews, including false accusations, torture, and forced conversion, and their famous synagogue in Fustat was badly neglected and even suffered a devastating fire. In 1473, however, they were finally authorized to rebuild it, and it arose again, grander and more beautiful than before.[11]

The Tunisian Jewish element had meanwhile come to dominate their local religious brethren, as well as those who had come from Palestine and Babylonia, but the situation changed again in the early sixteenth century when the new Ottoman rulers, at least early in their period of power, eased the plight of the non-Muslims, encouraged immigration, and opted for the development of technical, military, and political know-how. The Jews who had been expelled from Christian Spain arrived in significant numbers and effected a tripartite division of the rabbinic community into *Musta'rabin*, the native Arabic-speaking faction; *Maghribyin*, that is, those who had their origin farther west in North Africa; and *Sefaradim*, the refugees from the persecutions in Spain and Portugal. It was the last-mentioned group that succeeded in imposing its traditions on the Egyptian Jewish community as it emerged from the Middle Ages into the early modern period. It also oversaw improvements in status, conditions, and standards of Jewish learning. There are numerous Genizah texts that testify to lively correspondence between the Jewish communities of places such as Jerusalem and Safad with their counterparts in Egypt, often in an attempt to attract financial support for institutions and individuals in the impecunious Jewish homeland.

As is, however, well-known, Ottoman rule, in Egypt and elsewhere, from the end of the sixteenth century to the nineteenth century was often characterized by financial extortion, court intrigue, political corruption, and arbitrary execution. This state of affairs brought more poverty, persecution, and ignorance. It was Napoleon who began a process of major change. His expedition to the Orient and its numerous ramifications, followed in the nineteenth century by the emergence of Egypt as a kingdom independent of Ottoman Turkey, and the reforms of Muhammad 'Ali, meant that the country found itself the recipient of the advantages and disadvantages of colonial interest and power. With the construction of the Suez Canal and the attendant economic expansion, Cairo emerged as an important modern capital, and its population, which became considerably more cosmopolitan, almost tripled in the course of the century. The number of Jewish inhabitants, which had stood at about four thousand, made a similar, proportional increase over the period, although by that time no more than a handful of Jewish families were resident in Fustat, or Misr al-'Atiqa (or al-Qadima), as it had come to be called. With the exception of the occasional outburst of animosity, the situation greatly improved for the Jews, who again developed into a vibrant and confident community—one that could even negotiate the transfer of its Genizah texts for close study in academic institutions of the West.

The Notion of *Genizah*

Before more reference is made to the contents of what has come to be known as the Cairo Genizah, it will now undoubtedly be helpful for some explanation to be offered of what precisely this institution was and how it has come to play such an important role in rewriting the history of the Jewish community in and around Cairo from the Abbasid to the Ottoman and even British periods. The Hebrew root g-n-z, from which the word *genizah* is derived, first occurs in late sections of the Hebrew Bible, in reference to the storage of valuable items. The root, probably of Persian origin, is attested not only in Hebrew and Aramaic but also more widely in Semitic languages with the meanings 'hide,' 'store,' and 'bury.' In the rabbinic literature of the first few Christian centuries, it is used to describe special treasures stored away by God, such as the Torah and the souls of the righteous.

In Jewish religious law *(halakhah)*, which proscribes the obliteration of the name of God on the basis of its interpretation of Exodus 20:7 and Deuteronomy 12:4, *genizah* describes the removal from circulation of some item that is or has at some stage been regarded as sacred, whether legitimately or illicitly, and is now ruled inappropriate for ritual use. Such items may include controversial religious texts, materials once used in worship, capricious transcriptions of the four-letter Hebrew name of God (tetragrammaton), or artifacts about whose sacred status there is irresolvable doubt. As synagogal ritual became more institutionalized, it became customary for communities to set aside a *bet genizah*, or simply *genizah*, into which could be consigned Hebrew Bible texts that were damaged or worn, as well as other Hebraica, including works regarded as heretical, that contained biblical verses or references to God. There they would await the natural process of disintegration.

In antiquity and in the early medieval period, it is likely that numerous *genizot* were amassed in many areas of Jewish settlement. Sadly, however, the survival rate of such *genizot* has not proved impressive, the ravages of time and climate on the one hand and the vicissitudes of Jewish history on the other either ensuring a return to dust, or denying later generations adequate knowledge of where a search for surviving *genizot* might even commence. Fortunately, however, in the case of medieval Fustat/Cairo, the first stage of consignment into the synagogue *genizah* appears not to have been followed by removal to a cave or burial place, with the result that the study of Jewish history and literature has been greatly enriched.

The Cairo Genizah

The long survival of the Jewish community on the same site in Fustat; the dry climate of Egypt; the central importance of the city to Muslim, Christian, and Jewish history for a number of centuries; and the reluctance of the Jewish communal leaders to take any action in the matter of its *genizah*, other than to expand its contents with all forms of the written word—all these factors contributed to the survival there of a collection of some two hundred thousand fragmentary Jewish texts that is at least as significant as the Dead Sea Scrolls.[12] For generation after generation Egyptian Jews appear to have collected, from homes and institutions in and around Cairo, texts that were no longer appropriate for circulation; thousands of them were consigned to the *genizah* of what later came to be known as the Ben Ezra Synagogue.

In a move that was to make its collection unique in terms of world culture and history, the Jewish community of Fustat/Cairo chose to preserve much of the written word that passed through its hands, regardless of its religious status. There thus came to be amassed all manner of ephemera that had more to do with the daily activities of ordinary folk than with the ideology of rabbis and scholars. In an age that certainly predated the concern for the preservation of archives, the explanation for their behavior may be that they saw Hebrew letters, or even any texts written by or about Jews, as either intrinsically sacred or bearing a degree of holiness because of the frequent occurrence therein of references to God, the Hebrew Bible, or other religious subjects. The peak of this archival activity, if it may anachronistically be described as such, was reached between the tenth and thirteenth centuries, precisely when the community reached the zenith of its social, economic, and cultural achievements.

Some texts from what became known to scholars as the Cairo Genizah were transferred by synagogue officials to dealers and visitors in the second half of the nineteenth century. Famous libraries in St. Petersburg, Paris, London, Oxford, New York, and Philadelphia acquired major collections, but it was Solomon Schechter who obtained communal permission to remove 140,000 items to Cambridge University Library in 1897.[13] Smaller collections found their way to a number of other libraries around the world.

The Genizah texts are written in various languages—especially Hebrew, Arabic, and Aramaic—mainly on vellum/parchment and paper, but also on papyrus and cloth. They represent the most important discovery of new material for every aspect of scientific Hebrew and Jewish studies in the Middle Ages. As a result of the conservation, decipherment, and description done for over a century, but particularly in recent years and at Cambridge, previous ignorance has been dispelled and theories drastically modified. The question now to be addressed is precisely what was the cultural level of the Jewish communities of the eastern Mediterranean countries in general and of that in Fustat/Cairo in particular during the medieval period. On the basis of the Genizah documents, what may now be said about their learning, their literacy, and their education; about their daily lives, religious groupings and relationships, and leading personalities; and about their religious heritage and what they contributed to its preservation and transmission?

Literacy

Under the direct influence of their authoritative communities and leaders in Babylonia and Palestine, the Jewish communities of the Islamic world, including Egypt, made considerable progress in Jewish literacy in the pre-medieval period. Texts were edited, literature was analyzed, and religious guidance was formulated even for the less educated. According to Rabbinic Judaism, communion with God could be achieved through the learning process, with the rabbi as teacher (and not as priestly mediator) and the Hebrew Bible and the Talmud as the reference works. Hebrew was an essential element of common Jewish life, and not exclusively the language of an intellectual elite.

The Genizah texts testify to the Jewish adoption of a new medium. The Hebrew codex (bound volume) apparently made its appearance in the eighth century, presumably under the influence of Islam, which had borrowed it from the Christian and Classical worlds. Within three centuries, it became the standard medium for textual transmission. The contents of scrolls as well as collections of oral traditions were copied on to codices, to which later generations added their own notes. In the new format, these works acquired greater authority, were copied and disseminated in the extensive Islamic world, and encouraged greater interest in popular as well as advanced study. There clearly existed a large enough body of literate Jews to make the whole exercise worthwhile.

With similar developments taking place among the Muslims, Jews gradually replaced papyrus with vellum/parchment as the primary material for the transcription of texts, and ultimately replaced that with paper. Studies of Genizah fragments are gradually revealing how the whole scribal process developed from a primitive to a fairly sophisticated level. As the process reached its zenith, pride was taken in producing particularly beautiful codices of the Hebrew Bible.

In the Jewish communities of North Africa in the ninth and tenth centuries, texts were widely copied and circulated and extensive libraries, comprising various languages, were amassed and sold. Such libraries, built by individuals as well as communities, included not only the classical Jewish sources, but also the newest commentaries on the one hand and more general learning on the other. By copying and disseminating these libraries, the Maghrebi Jews introduced a wide variety of literature to other communities and thereby influenced their cultural achievements. The impressive contents of the Cairo Genizah owe much to the volumes that the Jewish refugees from Tunisia brought to the Egyptian center.

Interior of the Ben Ezra Synagogue circa 1911.

Letter of thanks from the University of Cambridge to the Jewish Community in Cairo for the gift of the Genizah collection, 1898.

Solomon Schechter at work in Cambridge University Library, 1898. In 1897, he obtained the permission of the Cairo Jewish community to remove 140,000 items to Cambridge University Library. Smaller collections found their way to a number of other libraries around the world.

FOLLOWING PAGES:

The Cairo Genizah is a collection of some two hundred thousand fragmentary Jewish texts that is at least as significant as the Dead Sea Scrolls. The Jewish community of Fustat/Cairo chose to preserve much of the written word that passed through its hands, even though its content had more to do with the daily activities of ordinary folk than with the ideology of rabbis and scholars.

Jewish prayer for the twelfth-century Imam, al-Amir bi-'ahkam Allah, T-S NS 110.26.

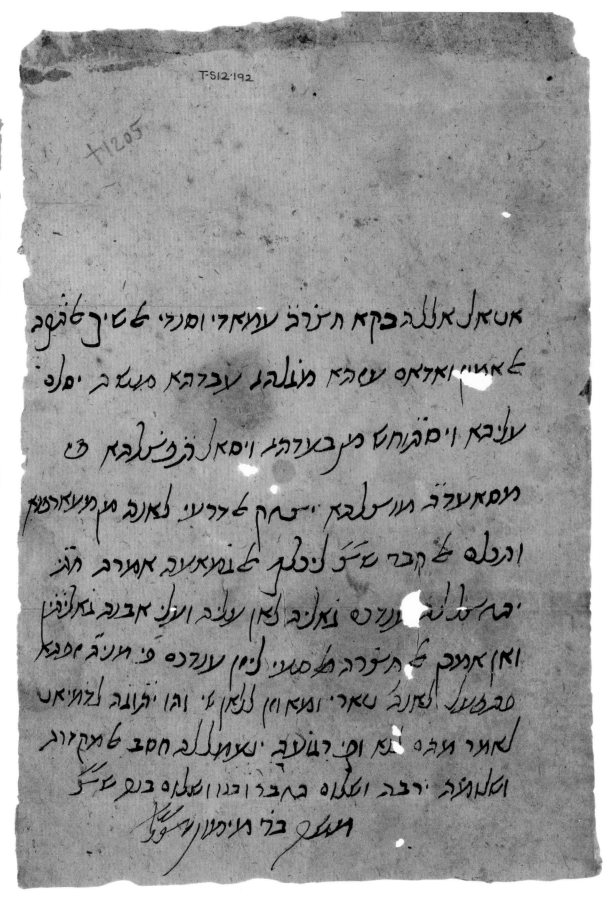

Moses Maimonides, a preeminent medieval Jewish philosopher, was one of the greatest Torah scholars and physicians in the Middle Ages. Although his writings on Jewish law and ethics were met with opposition during his lifetime, he is now acknowledged to be one of the foremost rabbinical arbiters and philosophers in Jewish history.

Letter from Moses Maimonides (1138–1204), with his signature at the end, T-S 12.192.

Qur'anic teachings in Hebrew script, T-S Ar.51.62.

Jewish teachings about Jesus, T-S NS 164.26.

Petition to the eleventh-century Fatimid caliph concerning murder on the Nile, T-S Ar.42.158

Virgin Mary liturgy in Syriac, T-S AS 213.20.

وأخذ عليها عهدًا ألّا تفشي سرّه إلى الأسد

إلى غيره وجعلت ذلك لها ما خبّرها أُسامح مروءة

كليلة ودمنة واقرأ ردّمنا قلّ أصحابنا إلا

أقبلت حتّى دخلت على أسدٍ فرأته مكتئبًا حزينًا

فلمّا عاينت ذلك عرفت أنّه ليتركّ ذلك الأسد

قتل شتربة الأسد وأمّه

Medieval Arabic tales, T-S Ar.51.60
This is part of a medieval collection of tales, *Kalila wa-dimna. The animals in the illumination are described as a lioness and a lion cub, and the story is about how a jackal spoiled the friendship between a lion and an ox.*

וישראיין יאו ויחיטו טחיטר בול מולם
אן פי צבלד ופי יהמאאק וחיצור דן
בהם גמאינה מן ליהוד תס אנ
אמדהת בבנם קודס ותטיפ
רעווגר ויזרא עורהט פיכול וקד פכל
מא אנבשטב אדהדין לשיוך
לאוהריבן ט יחרד שיוזו בן שהתר
שראן בינך לעלמא וחז ד לא מורעיע
שיאן יבנשיא פאמר ביאן יבנא יבור
קודב ויבני עלי יצבות קוב
ולא בטדהב ובי הדאורסולי
ליהוד ליפגור ישאס וגי פהט
מן ראקטהס עומר בשעירבל שדד
יקולו ומנש יכון עדה יקוס טנוקלי
ל יקודם פדכלו יעצומר קטורל
ובכס יאמור אמיר למומניך באץ
יפוקלו ליי הדיא יבולד מן טאיתה
יהוד וקט עתמ מא יקולו פנומכס
תם אזכולכו אנהת ובעד הדיא אקו

Judaeo-Arabic text concerning Jewish resettlement in Jerusalem after the Muslim conquest of the Holy Land, T-S Ar.6.1

OPPOSITE:
Synagogal music recorded by a twelfth-century convert to Judaism from Christianity, Obadiah the Proselyte, T-S K5.41

בָּרוּךְ הַגֶּבֶר אֲשֶׁר יבטח ב... וְהָיָה יוי מִבְטַחוֹ :

בְּטַח אֶל יוי בְּכָל לִבֶּךָ וְאֶל בִּינָתְךָ אַל תִּשָּׁעֵן :

בְּכָל דְּרָכֶיךָ דָעֵהוּ ... וְישׁר אוֹרְחוֹתֶי...

אַשְׁרֵי אָדָם מָצָא חָכְמָה וְאָדָם יָפִיק תְּבוּנָה :

הנה אַשְׁרֵי אֱנוֹשׁ יוֹכִיחֶנּוּ אֱלוֹהַ וּמוּס שרי אל תמאס:

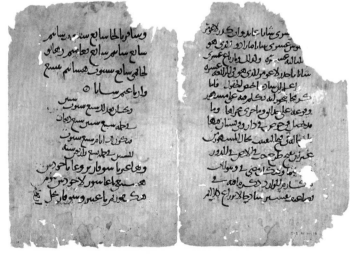

אל על עקצין מיכאל רבן רבך על קרעתיך
גבי שמיא על מתעתיך אלהא אסריך
ואנא טעין לך : לוא לאו לחיויא דבראך
מלכא דבר אך אלאה אדים אסריאל גנתא
דעדן איגינתא דעדן : ⊙ לעקרה ⊙
דלא ילדה כת בי עם בציון ישב בירושלם
בכו לא תבכה חנן יחנך לקול זעקך כשמעתו
ענך בשם יי עבתך הנדך והדרך אלחונניה
חיאליסיס שומך אמונה אזמר לך אשיר לך
אנא נשחנך והחיוו נאן נאן נאו נאונאו נאונאו נאו
נאו נאו כתנביתיה בטס נהוי להון בנן ב
ברוך מגן אברהס > ⌇ ⌇ ⌇ ⌇ ⌇ ⌇ >

לאיתתא דלא תפל כת במגלת יעבי ותרל
בדרעה דשמלא נאן נאן נאו נאו נאו נאו אונאו
אונאו נאו נאיא יא ינהי והיויו ויו נאו אמנא
אמן תעלית ⊙   לאתתא דמקשיא
למילד ⊙

נדגדיאל וצפצפיאל קנקניאל ממליא לנריאל
לוחיאל מישאל ברביאל תנאל אתון קדישיא
מלאכיה הוו בסעדי הוו לי חיי לי נחיי והבו לי
גבורא דנפתח תרעא הדין בשם ברכיאל
דקאיס וממונה על רקיע השלישי בשם
ספסקיאל דקאיס וממונה על רקיע החמשי
בשם חוריאל דקאיס וממונה על רקיע
הרביע בשם ברוכיאל דקאיס וממונה
על רקיע החמישי בשם סעריאל דקאיס
וממונה על רקיע הששי אתון מלאכיה
קדישיא פתחונלי תרע הדין נהך קופר ב
ברינגלך ותאמר האיפם וקא כי הנה הלכן
משד מיצריס תקבצעם מף תקברס מחמד
לכספס קמוש יירשס חנת באהליהס

בשם רבא אמר (רבא אמר רבתא בברתא)
בשמא רבא אמר   בבתא רבתא מנזוף
די אלהא חייא דיעזיז קליה אספהוס
בדרקום איומא לה עד ז זמנן ⊙
לעקרב

Magic amulet, T-S K1.19.

Hebrew text of Leviticus 25:8 in Arabic script, T-S Ar.41.18.

Marriage document of Karaite bride with Rabbanite groom in 1082, T-S 24.1

Check given by Abu Zikri Kohen in the twelfth century,
T-S Ar.30.184

It is remarkable that a bibliophile who was having a bookcase made prepared a delightful text in praise of such an item of furniture and its educational importance, with the apparent intention of having it engraved on the front:

> *I, the bookcase, say to you: Open up my contents regularly and learn from them.*
> *I, the bookcase, because of my contents, am greatly superior to all other containers.*
> *They contain stores of silver and gold and precious items that cannot save you from fiery damnation.*
> *I, the bookcase, contain treasure from Eden's tree of knowledge, Israel's special inheritance.*
> *How can chaff be compared to the grain which it contains?*[14]

On the linguistic front, Hebrew was used for the statutory prayers and for the composition of liturgical poetry. It remained the 'holy tongue' and left a particularly strong linguistic legacy within communities that were closely influenced by the Palestinian Jewish homeland. There was, however, constant tension about whether the biblical or the rabbinic variety of Hebrew was the authoritative form for post-biblical works, as well as persistent competition from its two sister languages, Aramaic and Arabic. Aramaic was restricted to a more scholarly role, being used for the Talmud, for commentaries and codes, and for Jewish religious law. Some of the earliest prayers survived in Aramaic because they had been composed in what had been a popular language, while some of the latest liturgical material was written in Aramaic because that gave it a high level of intellectual sophistication. In many ways, the use of Aramaic among the Jews of that period resembles that of Latin among medieval Christian scholastics, its function having evolved from a vernacular used by the majority into an almost esoteric medium for the intellectually initiated. Thanks to the early texts now available from the Cairo Genizah, it has proved possible to trace the historical development of Jewish Aramaic and to correct many corrupted texts.

Arabic was of course the dominant language of the huge Islamic empire of the Genizah period and the vernacular of its Jews and Christians. The Jews chose to use it with Hebrew and not Arabic script. This Arabic, currently called Judaeo-Arabic, preserves more vernacular forms and later dialectical features than classical Muslim Arabic, and is also characterized by the occurrence of many Hebrew, as well as some Aramaic, words and phrases. It was Judaeo-Arabic that was chosen for biblical commentary and translation; for studies of rabbinic literature and Jewish religious law; and to provide grammatical, liturgical, and philosophical guidance. Folklore and belles-lettres are well represented, and there are important works in the fields of science and medicine. Among the more mundane items are letters, accounts, lists, and legal documents. But the Jews were trilingual. Mundane letters were written in Hebrew, poems were composed in Aramaic, rubrics for the Hebrew prayers were couched in Judaeo-Arabic, and Hebrew vowel-points were attached to Judaeo-Arabic texts. Sometimes the same work was composed in both Hebrew and Judaeo-Arabic. Some generations of Karaites preferred Arabic, while others reverted to Hebrew, usually in an effort to make a polemical religious point. In addition to Judaeo-Arabic, although in much more limited number, the Genizah researcher encounters texts in other Jewish languages such Judaeo-Greek, Judaeo-Spanish, Judaeo-German (Yiddish), and Judaeo-Persian.

Greek left its mark in the medieval period within the Islamic empire and at its edges, in such places as Egypt, Asia Minor, and the Greek archipelago. It is therefore not surprising to find Genizah fragments written in Judaeo-Greek. The contents of a recently published set of Greek Jewish texts from the Genizah are sufficiently varied to permit the assumption that what is being uncovered here is a mere remnant of a linguistic phenomenon that was once extensive and significant. Bible interpretation, Talmudic discussion, Passover ritual, marriage documents, business agreements, and personal correspondence are all represented. There is even a letter from a husband to his wife complaining about the miseries he is undergoing during his travels, and another from a mother to her son cajoling him to come and fetch her from Alexandria to Fustat.

Leading Jews brought an outstanding Jewish intellectual tradition from al-Andalus—as they called Muslim Spain—to North Africa and Egypt, and it is powerfully represented in the Cairo Genizah. Although that Jewish culture, from the 'golden age of Spanish Jewry,' bequeathed much that is still practiced and enjoyed in modern Judaism, it was essentially absorbed into the Muslim–Jewish symbiosis characteristic of Arab lands. After the reconquest of Spain by the Christians, a new expression of Spanish Jewish civilization got under way, this time conveyed in Judaeo-Spanish. After the expulsion from Spain in 1492 of those Jews who preferred not to convert to Christianity, the émigrés did everything they could to impose it wherever they settled; the evidence of their activity in Egypt and the surrounding area is clearly to be found among the Cairo Genizah fragments written in Judaeo-Spanish, which date mainly from the fifteenth to the seventeenth century. The range of the literature represented among these manuscript remnants is wider than that of the Judaeo-Greek items emanating from the same source, and more akin to those written in Judaeo-Arabic, although the numbers are far smaller. Some texts provide translations and commentaries on biblical, rabbinic, and liturgical texts. There are intriguing collections of ballads, songs, and proverbs. The scientific, medical, and folkloristic fields are well represented, and some fragments relate to astrology and the calendar. Above all, there are personal letters written by and about Sefaradi Jews on their Mediterranean wanderings. Money is lent; charity is sought; travel instructions are given; and family matters are discussed.

If Jewish motherly emotions are recorded in Judaeo-Arabic and in Judaeo-Spanish, it is hardly surprising that they are also to be found in Judaeo-German form, that is, in Yiddish. What is perhaps surprising is that such a language is also to be found in the Genizah at all, but when one recalls that there was a substantial Ashkenazi community in Jerusalem in the sixteenth century, the occurrence is more easily explained. Members of that community sometimes made their way to Egypt to seek their fortune, or at least a basic livelihood, and it was natural for them to correspond with their families in Yiddish. We are fortunate in having a number of such letters written in 1567 by Rachel Zussmann to her son Moshe, who was working in Cairo as a religious scribe.

As far as Judaeo-Persian is concerned, there is no full list of Genizah items in this language, but from the preliminary findings it is clear that there were Jews who were using that dialect for mundane and literary texts a thousand years ago. Various literary compositions and documents have surfaced, including two Karaite commentaries on Daniel and fragments of grammatical writings. Perhaps it was the Karaite Jews of Egypt and Palestine who brought the language with them when they emigrated there from the East.

It was not without good reason that the Arabs referred to the Jews (as to the Christians) as *ahl al-kitab*, 'the people of the book.' The literary output and linguistic competence just described presuppose an almost obsessive concern with the written word. While that concern had its origins in the biblical period, it had to a large extent been transferred to the area of oral transmission in Talmudic and immediately post-Talmudic times insofar as the rabbinic traditions were concerned. Only with the passion of the rabbinic authorities to establish their whole ideology and practice as central and definitive did it return to its original form, or even to an extension of that form. The Rabbanites were anxious to refute the accusation made by such theological opponents as the Karaites that their oral traditions were a travesty of the original, sacred scripture, prone to error and alterations. They therefore embraced the written medium once again and used it to publicize an ever- expanding variety of works that adopted the latest ideas to defend and promote their own theological position. It is still unknown to what extent the wider availability of such texts can be assumed to correspond to a broadly based knowledge of them on the part of what may be referred to as the Jewish masses.

What then can be said about the extent of Jewish literacy some eight centuries ago? The evidence from the Genizah convincingly demonstrates that written material of a great variety of content existed in the Jewish community in and around Fustat/Cairo from the tenth to the thirteenth centuries. In the region of at least two hundred thousand manuscript fragments—the majority of them dating from those centuries—yielding a total of two or three times that number of individual leaves, have survived the ravages of time and the elements to excite the interest of the modern researcher. One may therefore confidently assume that the original hoard deposited in the Ben Ezra Synagogue was greatly in excess of that number and itself represented only a portion of what was actually produced in the communities in and around the Egyptian capital. Also relevant to the discussion is the fact that Fustat/Cairo was not renowned for being the most scholarly or literate of the Jewish societies of the period. Indeed, much of this material emanated from circles that were not primarily concerned with scholarship, religion, or science. Its particular value lies in the fact that it represents what has been referred to as 'counter-history' rather than the views of the leadership, and as such it provides ample testimony to the whole gamut of education, from the elementary to the advanced, and from children's alphabetical exercises to adults' guest lectures. Most of the male community achieved at least the most basic level of reading and writing Hebrew; a few more educated members became familiar with more difficult biblical and rabbinic texts. Fathers sometimes give teachers clear instructions about their children's Jewish education.

Generally, competence in Arabic itself (rather than Judaeo-Arabic) was required only by those in contact with the Muslim world. Interestingly, even when preparing a text for ultimate transmission outside the Jewish community, the writer would prepare a draft in Judaeo-Arabic. Once this was deemed satisfactory, the relevant Arabic text could be drawn up, perhaps by a professional, and dispatched as necessary.

Classes in various subjects took place in the synagogue, in the communal study center, at the teacher's residence, or in the pupil's home, and they were conducted by a professional teacher. The fees were generally paid by the parents; if the parents lacked the means or the children were orphans, the community met the cost.

Reinforcement of these lessons, or education in wider religious practice, was the task of the father in the synagogue and of either or both parents in the domestic setting. Scrap paper was used for practice; and since copies of books were expensive, one text was often used for the whole class. Pupils therefore had to acquire the ability to read the text from whatever angle at which they might be seated in relation to the script. Alphabet primers were among the few items of Hebrew literature that attracted illumination, presumably with the intention of exciting the interest of the budding scholars; individual wooden boards were also in use.

Girls did not automatically receive such an education, but occasionally there were parents who made such arrangements for them, usually for biblical studies. Some succeeded so well that they became professional teachers themselves, while others developed skills as calligraphers. In one sad little manuscript, a father bewails the loss of just such a daughter, mournfully remembering her intellect, her knowledge of the Torah, and her piety, and poignantly recalling the lessons he used to give her. The fact that there are a number of letters in which wives are directly addressed by their husbands, as against others in which a male colleague is requested to pass on written information by word of mouth to the writer's spouse, appears to demonstrate that women were not universally illiterate. There are also some letters and documents apparently written by female hands. One mother was so anxious that her daughter should receive a sound education that she made a deathbed request in a letter to her sister written in her own hand.

Those boys who advanced to higher levels of learning developed a more educated hand, and the range of styles recorded among the Genizah texts begins at the primitive and advances to the most expert. Some young men spent many years at Talmudic centers of learning both at home and abroad, maintained by communal and individual subscriptions. Adults who were engaged in making a living nevertheless devoted time, sometimes daily, to studying the traditional texts of biblical and rabbinical works with friends, or attending courses given by local scholars or lectures delivered by specially invited authorities. Even if Fustat/Cairo was better known among the communities of the Jewish world for its economic activity than for its academic prowess, there are still clear indications in the Genizah of a fairly high level of literacy.

By the middle of the classical Genizah period, then, literacy for the Jews of the communities living under Islam constituted a fairly complex and sophisticated level of education for a broad section of the community in a variety of Jewish and non-Jewish subjects. By this time, too, their Jewish brethren in Christian Europe were following their lead and had established a sound base for a later flowering of Hebrew and Jewish letters in that center that was to have important cultural consequences for the modern Western world. The paradox is that while these Jewish centers to the north flourished, so their counterparts to the south, for various reasons, failed in later centuries to maintain the levels they had once attained in the medieval world.

Daily Life

Jewish daily life in medieval Fustat, as documented in the Genizah texts, makes fascinating reading. As in earlier Talmudic times, marrying into the aristocracy meant for the Jewish parent the opportunity of securing a son-in-law with outstanding Jewish knowledge. In order to make such a match equally attractive in other aspects, there were Cairene families who were willing to look as far afield as Lebanon (600 kilometers), Iraq (1,300 kilometers), Yemen (2,400 kilometers) or even Spain (3,350 kilometers). Often the young couple had little opportunity to become acquainted before the marriage. Sometimes the prospective bride and groom were not separated geographically but by religious allegiance. Before the rabbinic authorities demurred, marriages took place between the Rabbanite Jews, who looked to the Talmud as their authority, and their Karaite counterparts, who followed only the letter of the biblical law. In those cases, each side agreed not to offend the religious susceptibilities of the other.

Within the Rabbanite community itself there were women who insisted on unusual conditions before they agreed to marry. What was important to many in a community that countenanced polygyny was the right to be the exclusive wife. Among the Palestinian Jewish women, but not their Babylonian counterparts, it was an accepted practice to insist on the right to demand a divorce for no reason other than incompatibility, that is, in the event that the wife simply no longer cared for her husband and that she was willing to forfeit her alimony. Some women were concerned about protecting the inheritance rights of their children by an earlier marriage, while for others the matter of a fine funeral, or a beautifully illuminated marriage contract *(ketubbah)*, was paramount. Other, more unfortunate, women were delighted to have the opportunity to marry at all. In a case brought before the grandson of Maimonides, a woman whose future husband had rescued her from captivity agreed that he should retain the right to have other wives. She felt obligated to him for having paid the ransom to her captors and was obviously aware that her bargaining position had been weakened by the fact that they had raped her, and a number of other Jewish women, during captivity.

Not all women functioned only as housewives. Some provided simple medical services, while others specialized in wholesale dealing, in the sale of flour, in the teaching of embroidery, in book sales, or in the making of perfumes. One of the most remarkable, known as Wuhsha (Désirée), or Karima (dear one), daughter of Ammar, was independently minded enough to make her own way in the commercial world, to fight for her financial rights in business deals, and to build up a large fortune as a banker. Some marriages encountered problems that involved litigation. One woman complained to the authorities that in fifteen years of married life, not only had her husband never given her gifts, jewelry, or clothes, but he also distressed and beat her.[15]

Husbands possessed a cruel and powerful weapon with which to terrorize their spouses. They could, and sometimes did, threaten to run off to some foreign part without divorcing their wives, thus leaving them in a perpetual state of marital limbo, neither divorced nor living with a husband. Two tragic cases involve the husband's failure to perform his sexual obligations to his wife. In one of these cases, the girl declares that she is still a virgin and that whenever her husband attempts to consummate the marriage he terrifies her by collapsing in a convulsive fit. Another records the plight of a wife who modestly describes herself as "a thirsty woman," denied any drink for nine months: "I am a thirsty woman; the man is useless. Let him separate; let's annul the marriage."[16]

Other family troubles were, happily, of the more ordinary variety. A husband on a business trip to India writes to his wife about how much he yearns for her. He is particularly sad that he cannot provide her "rights on every sabbath and festival," traditional times for sex. An itinerant cantor, away from home making a living by officiating at sabbath and wedding services, has obviously offended his wife in some way and tries to make it up to her by opening his letter to her in an especially warm and complimentary fashion.[17] For her part, one wife was appalled by her husband's absence from home and the news that he might be contemplating a trip to Turkey. Writing on behalf of the whole family, both male and female, she lectured him in no uncertain terms about the damage that would be done to their reputation if he stayed away and how such behavior would adversely affect the marriage prospects of their single daughter.[18]

There were some Jewish mothers who opted to spend their money on the promotion of their children's Jewish education and communal involvement. One shrewd matriarch took the trouble to send a festival gift to her grandchild's private tutor. Two other female family members made efforts to involve themselves in synagogal matters. A mother and grandmother made a generous donation to the community on condition that their son/grandson would be invited to undertake the public reading of the Esther scroll on the feast of Purim and, for fear of objection by the boy's father, drew up a legal document to that effect.[19]

As far as boys were concerned, educational activity at home was soon complemented by attendance at school, and behavior was not always perfect. A scribbled note from a rather cross teacher informed the father of little Abu al-Hassan that his son had at first been most conscientious, but that one of the class, egged on by the others, had soon put to a stop to this by breaking the newcomer's writing board. Two little boys who came late to school brought a note explaining that the elder had been delayed by studying Arabic at home, and the younger, who could not make his own way, had had to wait for his brother. The teacher is politely asked to refrain from spanking either for the tardiness of their arrival. Education was admired and teachers were generally held in high regard. There was competition for pupils, and this inevitably helped to keep the standard of teaching high, but it is clear from the Genizah documents that some teachers suffered from the late payment of fees.[20]

It comes as no surprise to find many references to outstanding rabbis and to their advice being sought in matters of Jewish law and ritual by communities many hundreds of miles away. There is information about an Iraqi scholar traveling to Greece, as well as a French rabbi serving as a Jewish judge in Alexandria. It was not, however, usual for 'Western' rabbis to hold positions in the Egyptian communities, since a kind of discrimination was operated against them by the 'Orientals.' They were sometimes ridiculed and even insulted for their lack of Arabic and their allegedly primitive approach to study.

Travel was generally the exception rather than the rule for scholars and for the many craftsmen and artisans—represented in as many as 250 different trades—then living in the Egyptian Jewish community. Businessmen, on the other hand, had to travel across the Mediterranean and undertook voyages in the Indian Ocean. Such trips not only involved painful separations for months or years; they also carried all the dangers associated with any form of contemporary travel. The most dreaded outcome was capture by an enemy, or by pirates, who knew that Jewish communities everywhere would always be willing to pay generous ransoms to release fellow Jews. At one stage this cruel business became so profitable that the Jewish religious leaders had to cite Talmudic law and forbid communities to pay more than the 'going rate,' for fear of encouraging the taking of additional hostages.[21]

There were some travelers who built new lives in and around the communities that they visited on business. Abraham Ben Yiju, who had family in Egypt, North Africa, and Sicily, was a scholar, traveler, and adventurer whose commercial activities in the twelfth century ranged from the Mediterranean Sea to the Indian Ocean. Ben Yiju freed and converted a female Indian slave and took her into his household as wife or mistress. She bore the name Ashu and belonged to the matrilineal Nair caste on the Malabar coast.[22]

Wide varieties of goods—ranging from bales of cloth, through animal hides and articles of clothing, to items of food and drink—were imported and exported by the Jewish merchants of Fustat/Cairo (sometimes women as well as men). Their primary concern was not with particular commodities, but with anything that could keep their capital working for them. There was always the danger of price fluctuation. Merchants continually complain of this ("Prices are in God's hands; they follow no principle"),[23] although most of the documents indicate a reasonable degree of stability in prices. Jews and Muslims who were partners arranged for profits made on the Jewish sabbath to be directed only to the latter. When David ben Solomon wished to move a huge amount of capital from Fustat/Cairo to Qayrawan in 967, he asked his friend Isaac ben Abraham to take the money as a loan from him in Egypt and repay it to him later in the Tunisian city.[24] Payment by check rather than cash was also an accepted procedure. You deposited your cash with a banker or broker, and you made your payment by writing on a piece of paper the sum in Coptic numerals and words that the banker was to pay the specified bearer, together with the date, and a biblical verse intended to ward off any attempt at fraud! To ask for an overdue payment was even regarded as something of an impudence, and 'final demands' had consequently to be couched in the most delicate of terms. Abu Ishaq Abraham ben Burayk's device with one of his debtors was to get a mutual friend to write and say that he—Abu Ishaq—urgently wanted to travel to Spain but could not do so until he received settlement of that account. Not everyone maintained the highest standards of honesty. A case referred to Maimonides for a ruling dealt with the matter of a broker's son who had run off with Jewish and Muslim property.

Where there is business, there is always a government ready to demand taxes and customs dues. And so there are tales about the problems and harassment faced by Jewish merchants some nine centuries ago. The police of the day apparently kept a particularly close watch on the boats sailing up and down the Nile, and one unlucky dealer from Tunisia had no sooner boarded one of these when he found himself in the custody of five officers of the law. He obtained his freedom only after satisfying the authorities in the matter of some excise duty.

Poverty being what it then was, many Jews were terrified when special poll tax payments (demanded of Jews and Christians) became due, since they knew that they had to carry with them a receipt indicating that they had paid or face a fine, a beating, imprisonment, or even possibly death in custody from starvation. Among the greatest acts of Jewish charity was therefore the payment of this tax for the poor, and the community sometimes had to arrange this. One letter written by Moses Maimonides himself introduces two friends of his to colleagues in another city and requests the community there to pay their poll taxes for them. A man who had known better times complains bitterly of the communal leader's lack of response to his appeal and stresses the gravity of his plight. He is most anxious to include wine and meat in his diet but is forced to restrict himself to bread and onions.[25]

The Jews of Egypt practiced many trades, and they passed on their skills to the next generation by a system of apprenticeship. Formal arrangements for such vocational training were usually made orally, but there are occasional Genizah items that shed light on specific cases. In one text we are informed that a silversmith had to serve an apprenticeship of two years, while another suggests that a weaver could learn his trade in two months.[26]

The synagogal affairs referred to in the manuscripts from medieval Egypt have a familiar ring to them. The Babylonian and Palestinian congregations in Fustat vied with each other for new members, the former boasting of the honors they gave to visitors and the fine cantors they engaged, while the latter parried with claims that they had more attractive Bibles and Torah scrolls (as well as beautiful carpets), that their services were shorter, and that young boys were permitted to take part in the services. At times, the tensions about who had the greater authority over the whole community grew so great that representations were made to the Muslim caliphate requesting a ruling. Apparently, such rivalries and other differences of opinion in the synagogue setting were not always of a friendly type, and the sources indicate just how seriously people took such matters. A letter from Ramla in 1052 reports a fracas on Yom Kippur between Jews from Tyre and others from Tiberias that had to be broken up by the police.[27] One cantor asked Maimonides for permission to abandon the recitation of some liturgical poems introduced in a small Egyptian village where he officiated. Although he received a response that was sympathetic to his disapproval of the novel poetry, he was advised, for the sake of communal harmony, to continue to recite it.[28] A direct descendant of the same outstanding sage took a community to task for the preacher they engaged. He was an ignoramus who repeated, like a parrot, speeches on the mysteries of religion that he did not himself understand.[29]

With regard to broader culture elements, there are illuminations, diagrams, and pictorial representations, generally of course without human faces, that are in use for illustrative and educational purposes. Verses and comments on verses may attract such artistic attention, and there is one remarkable example, from among the later Genizah material, that is attached to the Arabic story of the lioness and her cub. Favorite targets for illustration were the beginnings of biblical books, Passover haggadot, marriage documents, and children's alphabet primers. There is also a colored block print, probably dating from the late fourteenth century, that contains the verse "Blessed are you in your coming in, and blessed are you in your going out" (Deuteronomy 28:6) for use in a synagogue, in a classroom, or perhaps in a sukkah during the festival of Tabernacles. The musical notes recorded by the proselyte Obadiah Ha-Ger (formerly John Oppidans) have become one of the Genizah's most famous items.

Illness and its treatment were of major concern to the public and to the doctors who represented one of the most important professions. Their training was based on the famous textbooks of the ancient Greeks, translated into Arabic and updated to take account of the latest expertise. Jews cooperated widely with their Muslim colleagues and were even granted special certificates to enable them to practice in both communities. Some distinguished specialists worked at the royal court or with other public figures and could command large fees, but most made their living from less grand clients. Their day-to-day activities kept them busy and were remarkably varied. They might be called upon to provide certificates of ill health for those applying for financial assistance from the community. Sometimes they were summoned to court to give specialist evidence. The direct treatment of disease took up most of their time. Many patients came to their offices and they had to diagnose the problem, often by an examination of the patient's urine, and suggest the necessary treatment. Part of their training involved an understanding of how to make and use drugs, derived from many different kinds of plants, each with its own special effect. The most common complaints related to the eyes, and they were fortunately able, even at that period, to perform operations to remove growths and obstructions. Headaches also troubled many folk and, in those cases, in addition to drugs, they were able to offer such external treatment as cold compresses. Large numbers were troubled by sexually related matters. Men came to see doctors about impotence and fertility and were anxious to locate the best aphrodisiacs. Women asked about period pains and loss of blood, and about pregnancy and abortion. The medical experts did their best, but some admitted to their patients that true healing was in the hands of heaven.[30]

There is no doubt that 'alternative medicine' also played a central role in the lives of many of the community in Genizah times. The origins of some of their mystical ideas are to be sought in ancient Mesopotamia, although the immediate background appears to have been Palestinian, rather than Babylonian. When faced by a health problem, a romantic entanglement, or a personal disaster, many individuals sought solace and guidance in the use of herbal remedies, the wearing of amulets, the recitation of incantations, and the interpretation of dreams. Although biblical and rabbinic literature was used and cited, and references were made to divine power, combinations of letters and numbers played a part, and there were special roles for angels and other heavenly bodies.[31]

Religious Groups and Leading Lights

Contrary to what is sometimes thought, it is now clear that Muslims, Christians, and Jews in medieval Egypt did not live intellectually ghettoized lives. They were aware of each other's religious texts and traditions, sometimes recording these in their own languages and literatures and at other times subjecting them to criticism and even derision. In a religious debate with Rabbanites and Karaites conducted at the end of the tenth century, the Fatimid vizier, Ya'qub ibn Kilis, a convert from Judaism to Islam, cited the content of the prayer book of Sa'adya ben Joseph in order to heap ridicule on the Jewish liturgy. Religious thinkers took account of what was being said and written by the theological opposition, so much so that it is at times possible to reconstruct that opposition by way of the views of such thinkers.

Although there was the occasional romantic tryst between a man and woman of different religious allegiance, intermarriage was not a phenomenon of the time. Conversion, however, certainly was. Just as in Christian Europe, there were Jews who were so anxious to climb the social and political ladder that they felt constrained to convert to the dominant faith. Some of them made life difficult for their former coreligionists, while others retained a certain sympathy for them, even engaging them in religious dialogues. But the movement was not always in one direction, and there are accounts of Muslim and Christian anger at conversions to Judaism. The records of rabbinical courts make reference to approaches made by non-Jews wishing to convert. As was the Talmudic custom, they were initially rebuffed, but there were a number, some of them women, who were determined enough to repeat their applications until they were finally accepted and even married into the Jewish community. One convert missed only one thing from his former life—the Jews could not make bread like the non-Jews!

Even if they enjoyed fewer privileges than their Muslim counterparts, the Jews of medieval Cairo were generally permitted to live where they wished and to engage in most of the professions and trades of the day. They socialized with their non-Jewish neighbors (sometimes even sharing buildings with them) and exchanged formal greetings with them, especially on festive occasions. There are numerous examples of Jews working in partnership with Muslims and Christians. This was of special benefit to the Jews, who could use such business relationships to overcome the problem of making profit on the sabbath. The arrangement was that in a joint venture, profits from Friday would accrue to the Jew and those from Saturday to the Muslim. In areas such as medicine and pharmacology there was a high degree of integration between the religious communities, and there are numerous instances, relating to a variety of professions, in which members of such communities expressed favorable opinions about the expertise of those belonging to one of the other groups. Although 'mixed marriages' were a rare phenomenon, they were not unknown, as documented by the case of the eleventh-century businesswoman Wuhsha, daughter of Ammar, who scandalized her Jewish coreligionists by her formal liaison with a Muslim. Not only was there an awareness on the part of the Jews of the religious ideology and practice of Muslims and Christians; they also sometimes came under the influence of such non-Jewish teachings. The best-known example is that of Abraham, the son of Moses Maimonides, who, early in the thirteenth century, after the death of his father, became highly attracted to the ideas of the Muslim Sufis and promoted a form of mystical Judaism that had much in common with their religious notions.

The Karaites, who championed a non-rabbinic Judaism that was closely based on the Hebrew Bible and its literal interpretation, were no minor sect that broke away from the rabbinic norm and soon declined. Far from it. Many Genizah texts testify to the considerable success of their religious philosophy, practice, and communal life. Starting with Schechter's discovery of the eighth-century law book of Anan ben David, the earliest proponent of the movement, a century of Genizah research has demonstrated the major role played by the Karaites in the social, economic, cultural, and religious development of the Jewish communities of the Near East from the eighth to the twelfth centuries. First, it is clear that they had a number of doctrines, traditions, and linguistic terms that match those recorded in the literature uncovered in the Dead Sea Scrolls. It therefore seems unlikely that their religious commitments were totally novel and revolutionary. Their early existence in the first few centuries of the Christian era appears to have been in small groups with theologically divergent views and interpretations. What they had in common was that they were not part of, or at least not central to, the rabbinic movement. In the post-Talmudic period, however, they seem to have given themselves additional communal strength and achieved more of a theological impact by joining forces. This ultimately led to a blossoming of Karaite culture from the tenth to the twelfth centuries, precisely the period best represented in the Genizah texts. Such texts testify to close social relations and even intermarriage, as well as religious differences, between Karaites and Rabbanites. The Karaites had important representatives at the Muslim court, and such contacts were widely used by all the Jews to promote their interests.

Karaite communities were especially strong in Egypt and Palestine. Commercial successes led to the emergence of powerful and influential families. Such families founded and supported communal institutions and synagogues, where the stress was on the use of verses from the Hebrew Bible, particularly from the Psalms. Devotion to Zion and a love of the Hebrew language became the characteristic features of many adherents to the faith, and large settlements were built up in the Palestinian cities of Jerusalem and Ramla. Groups of such settlers followed the custom of bewailing the loss of the Temple, the Holy City, and the homeland, referring to themselves as 'the mourners for Zion.' The 'holy tongue' and the 'holy books' were of course their alternatives to the Aramaic language and the Talmudic texts beloved of the rabbis, and they emerged as champions of both biblical study and Hebrew grammar. They moved from Aramaic to Arabic and from Arabic to Hebrew as they strove to establish a linguistic and literary identity, and in the process they made a major contribution to the Jewish interpretation of Scripture. One of their most outstanding leaders, Daniel al-Qumisi (ninth to tenth centuries), was a prolific Bible commentator who rationally explained away the existence of angels and contemptuously dismissed the views and criticized the activities of both Karaite and Rabbanite predecessors. The rabbinic leadership was ultimately shamed into demonstrating that they too had a love for Zion, Hebrew, and the Hebrew Bible. One of the results was an increase in the quantity and an improvement in the quality of biblical exegesis. Even in the area of religious law, the Karaite concern for fixing their own calendar, kosher food, ritual impurity, avoiding marriages between relatives, and maintaining a fire-free sabbath were strong enough to leave an impact on rabbinic behavior. Sometimes the Talmudic Jews felt under pressure to intensify their own strictness, while at other times they positively flaunted their own interpretations.

Two of medieval eastern Jewry's most famous personalities functioned in the area of Fustat/Cairo, one in the final period of his life and the other for almost forty years. The poet and philosopher from Muslim Spain Judah Ha-Levi (born about 1075) spent time in Egypt toward the end of his life. It was always well known that he set out from his native Andalusia on a pilgrimage to the Holy Land, where he expected to spend his last days, but it has now become clear that he stopped off in Egypt for a few months early in 1141 and enjoyed a remarkable period of local acclaim and poetic productivity. He was the guest of honor at many soirées, and he penned a number of lyrical compositions in honor of his patrons. Judah Ha-Levi was enjoying himself so much that there were those who believed he would never fulfill his intention of leaving for 'Eretz Yisra'el. Indeed, the difficulties of undertaking the trip by land, and the winter storms that were making the sea journey impossible, kept him in Egypt, and the Genizah material uncovered in the first half of this century about his experiences there seemed to confirm this failure to undertake his final religious pilgrimage. Despite the longstanding tradition that told of his death under the hooves of a galloping horse as he recited his poems before the walls of Jerusalem, it appeared more likely that he never actually reached his sacred destination. Might he perhaps have ended his days in Egypt in a dizzy spell of parties and paeans? Thanks to the Genizah discoveries, the story is now known to have a more romantic ending. In a small fragment of a few lines that he found in Cambridge in 1975, S.D. Goitein was able to decipher the name of the famous poet and the information that he set sail eastward from Alexandria on 14 May 1141, presumably arriving in Palestine within ten days. That would have given him a month to visit the holy sites before his death in July, a pilgrimage that is hinted at, if not clearly spelled out, in another Genizah text.

Known to the Muslims as Abu 'Imran Musa ben Maymun ibn 'Abd Allah, to the Christians as Maimonides, and to the Jews as Rambam, Moses ben Maimon of Cordova ('the Sefaradi,' as he called himself) settled in Fustat in the 1160s and from then until his death in 1204 built himself a reputation as one of Jewish history's greatest figures. That such a reputation was well deserved has become clearer as some sixty fragments in his own handwriting and others closely relating to him have surfaced among the Genizah treasures. Folios from draft copies of his three most famous works on the Mishnah, rabbinic law, and Jewish philosophy show him at work and reveal some of his thought patterns, particularly concerning the order in which he presented his material, the degree to which he justified his views, and the terminology that he employed. He found time not only for composing three of Judaism's major textbooks but also, as is convincingly demonstrated by the fragments from the Ben Ezra synagogue, for so much else besides. As a medical expert who, as well as teaching medicine, ran clinics in the Islamic court of what was then new Cairo, he was much in demand for specialist opinion, consultations, and prescriptions, and there are even a few survivors from his medical library. When asked by one of the Ayyubid rulers to write on sexual matters, Maimonides prepared a draft text in Judaeo-Arabic before forwarding his definitive text in Arabic.

The majority of inquiries addressed to him were of course on matters of Jewish law. They opened with a welter of epithets that referred at some length to his distinguished learning, his outstanding leadership, and his unique reputation before finally coming to the controversial point. Rushed off his feet with professional, literary, and communal commitments, Maimonides could rarely do more than append a brief decision to the foot of the inquiry, but the survival of hundreds of such 'responsa' indicate that he dealt efficiently with many of the questions addressed to him. Other letters and documents relate even more closely to Maimonides the man. It had always been a puzzle how an immigrant to Fustat in the middle of the twelfth century could so quickly make himself indispensable to the community and win their recognition as a leader. Now it turns out that it was his success in mounting a major fund-raising campaign that played an important part in his rise to fame. On 3 November 1168, the crusader king of Jerusalem, Amalric, captured the town of Bilbays and took many of its inhabitants, including a large number of Jews, as prisoners. As was the custom of the Christian knights, he sought ransoms for these unfortunate individuals from their coreligionists, but at the enormous rate of one hundred gold pieces for every three Jews. Intensive efforts were required to raise the money, and it was Maimonides who enlisted the support of many communal leaders, cajoled the public to associate themselves with the appeal, and undertook the administration of the finances.

Although we do have correspondence between Maimonides and his sister, Miriam, who had remained in the Maghreb when he emigrated east, it is the detail of his relationship with his brother, David, and how it ended tragically, that makes for the most moving reading. Moses had warned his younger brother about the dangers of trips across the desert and voyages by sea, and David's last and fatal trip was indeed beset with unfortunate incidents, but he optimistically thought that these were over when he reached the Sudanese port of 'Aydhab in the spring of 1169. Unaware that this would prove to be the last communication he would have with his brother, David addressed him affectionately and longingly and reported his plan to set sail for India, together with a number of his companions, where he hoped to find the business that had until that time eluded him. Sadly, of course, he went down with his ship in the Indian Ocean, and Maimonides felt truly bereft for years afterward.

Biblical Study

What kind of biblical texts did the Jews of Fustat/Cairo use a thousand years ago, and how do they slot into the overall history of Jewish engagement with the Hebrew Bible? Although there are some textual variants to be found in the Genizah remnants of scrolls and codices (themselves significant for the history of scribal techniques), the consonantal text was substantially as it is today. It is rather in the area of Hebrew pointing that major discoveries have been made. It emerges that there were three major systems, two emanating from the Holy Land and one from Babylon, that were in vogue in the classical Genizah period. The tenth-century Tiberian system of Ben Asher that later came to be regarded as the standard way of pointing Hebrew texts (when pointing was thought to be required) took some two or three centuries to establish its dominance in the field. Whether inspired by the Syriac Christian example, by Muslim concern for the accuracy of the Qur'an, or by an internal feud with the Karaite Jews, who preferred the biblical to the rabbinic tradition and who had a particularly strong, learned, and successful community in Egypt, such attention to the accurate recording of the vocalized text left its mark on exegesis. The schools of Masoretes (literally, 'transmitters,' or perhaps 'counters') flourished mainly among the Jews living in the Syro-Palestinian area. They surrounded the text with vowel points, cantillation signs, and explanatory notes, inevitably recording pari passu their own understanding of its meaning or the understanding that they had inherited from generations of readers. Their methodical approach also encouraged the development of those Hebrew philological studies that provided the basis for the literal interpretation of the Hebrew Bible in later medieval and modern times. Jewish scholars in the world of medieval Islam compared the three Semitic languages that they knew and used—namely, Arabic, Hebrew, and Aramaic—and thus, in at least a primitive sense, became the first students of comparative Semitic grammar and syntax.

The interest in making sense of the Hebrew text was of course primarily inspired by its regular recitation in the synagogue. The material from the Cairo Genizah confirms that there existed annual Babylonian and triennial Palestinian reading cycles for both Pentateuchal and prophetic readings. They did, however, exist in such variety that it is impossible to identify any one order that can be traced back to the early Christian centuries. Both these cycles were used in Fustat/Cairo in the Fatimid period before the Palestinian version disappeared. In addition, Palestinian Syriac versions of the Christian scriptures have also been discovered. The range of biblical translations found in the Genizah testifies to the wide variety of languages in use when that archive was first built up. In the pre-Islamic centuries, the dominant language of the diaspora Jews was Greek, so it is hardly surprising to find sixth- and seventh-century fragments of translations first prepared for them by Aquila some five hundred years earlier. Was it Jews or Christians who were using such versions in the sixth century, and how did they come to be consigned to the Genizah? The medieval texts from Jewish Cairo also add considerably to our knowledge of the development of that popular genre of Aramaic translation known as targum. Various compilations of targumic material, some hitherto unknown, have been identified among the Genizah texts. They include lengthy elaborations of the biblical text, poetic versions of the narratives, and even interpretations of verses that run counter to what is found in the Talmudic sources.

Because of its ancient nature, the custom of translating the Hebrew Bible into Aramaic was not abandoned when Arabic replaced Aramaic and Greek as the Jewish vernacular. Rather, it was incorporated into a trilingual version in which Arabic appeared side by side with Hebrew and Aramaic. The Arabic rendering, written in Hebrew characters and recording the popular dialect of that Semitic language used in the Jewish communities, originally existed in a variety of forms. These gradually gave way to the version created by the tenth-century rabbinic authority in Babylonia, Sa'adya ben Joseph, which became the standard. It was Sa'adya who championed the rabbinic traditions against their Karaite opponents, who rejected all the traditions emanating from the Talmudic authorities and sources. For their part, the Karaites also made a polemical point by means of linguistic usage. At one point in their history, they demonstrated their independent religious identity by recording the text of the Hebrew Bible in Arabic and not Hebrew characters.

Fresh understanding of the development of the Jewish exegesis of Scripture, known as midrash, throughout the millennium following the destruction of the Second Temple, also owes much to Genizah research. Hitherto, the earliest manuscripts were from the initial period of Ashkenazi Jewry in the West. Now, documented in the Cairo Genizah, there are hundreds of fragments written in the East at a much earlier date and representing older textual traditions. What is more, new midrashic anthologies and commentaries have been discovered, some relevant to religious law and others to what could justifiably be called lore, and a new picture has been drawn of the colorful and heterogeneous Jewish interpretation of the Hebrew Bible in the early Middle Ages. Such a variegated approach gave way to the more linguistic and philological commentaries of the tenth to the twelfth centuries, and the written evidence from the Genizah records one of the factors that precipitated such a change: it was effected by the centralized and centralizing powers of the Babylonian rabbinic authorities in an effort to thwart Karaite efforts to discredit rabbinic interpretation as lacking a serious and literal dimension.

There are also some intriguing questions concerning the link between the biblical and quasi-biblical texts that occur both amid the literature of the Dead Sea sect and in the Genizah corpora. It is sometimes forgotten that the first and fullest text of one of the sect's major religious tracts, the Damascus Document (or Zadokite Fragments), came to light among the Genizah finds fifty years before the contents of the Qumran caves made their sensational impact on Jewish and Christian history. Nor, indeed, would it have been possible for the long-lost Hebrew text of the Wisdom of Ben Sira, written in the second pre-Christian century, to have been reconstructed without extensive input from the fragments found in the Ben Ezra Synagogue.[32] But in which context did these two works, as well as some similar literary items, continue to circulate in the intervening centuries, and who copied them—and for what purpose—in Fatimid Cairo? On the one hand, it is not perhaps so remarkable to find versions of Toledot Yeshu, recording early Jewish folklore about Jesus, among the fragments. On the other hand, no wholly satisfactory reason can be offered for the existence in the Cairo Jewish community of parts of a Nestorian Syriac hymn book. Perhaps these thirteenth- or fourteenth-century texts belonging to a feast of the Virgin Mary were sold as scrap when Cairo's Nestorian community faded out of existence at that time or shortly afterwards. Perhaps one may go further and suggest that the major Muslim, Christian, and Jewish groups were neither unaware of each other's religious works nor totally averse to attempting to refute them, nor even, at times, uninfluenced by their content.[33]

Rabbinic Learning

The rabbinic texts emanating from medieval Fustat/Cairo are no less remarkable than the other genres of Jewish literary material from that source. Their existence in that center indicates a lively and productive activity in the fields they represent. It is not rare to find Talmudic passages that were later, and/or elsewhere, lost or removed, or to discover that post-Genizah texts have attracted spurious accretions. An unusual linguistic usage, a word of Greek or Persian origin, the exchange of one letter for another, a forgotten place name, or an unexpected abbreviation—such phenomena often led to corruptions in the text, and Genizah versions often uncover the authentic readings. Fragments of incunabula (prints until 1500) and early editions of Talmudic texts, some of them on vellum/parchment, and many of them from Spain and Portugal, are of great interest to the history of printing.

Genizah versions also contribute to a better understanding of linguistic developments. A clearer distinction between the Western Aramaic of Palestinian texts and the Eastern Aramaic of their Babylonian counterparts has become possible, with the result that the relevant dictionaries and grammars have been improved or, indeed, created from scratch. Early and reliable glosses on the text have sometimes helped to restore long-lost meanings, while the use in some manuscripts of vowel points has enabled experts in Hebrew linguistics to explain how different communities pronounced the Hebrew of their rabbinic texts.

Two other developments, which are certainly reflected in the Genizah evidence, were the creation of supplements to the Talmudic text, in the form of brief, additional tractates in the premedieval period, and the compilation of commentaries at a later date. Themes that are briefly treated in the standard tractates of the Talmudic and immediate post-Talmudic periods, or are dealt with there in scattered statements attached to various contexts, are expanded upon in the so-called 'minor tractates.' If these tractates constitute the first stage of the process of commentary, the second stage is to be located in the statements made by various premedieval authorities about the meaning of individual Talmudic passages and preserved in their responsa (responses to questions in religious law). The third stage is that of the compilation of running commentaries, such as that which appears to have been undertaken in the Babylonian center of Pumbedita by Hai Gaon in the tenth and eleventh centuries (most of which has been lost) and that of his later contemporary, Hananel ben Hushiel, in Qayrawan, one of the most important Jewish communities in North Africa. Investigative Genizah scholarship has made nothing short of a massive contribution to the recovery of the later work of Nissim ben Jacob ibn Shahin in eleventh-century Qayrawan. In one of his most important treatises, he assisted the student of the vast Talmudic literature by providing sources and parallels for many statements, as well as explanations of many recurrent themes.

The Genizah texts have also clarified the early expansion of guidance in Jewish religious law (halakhah). The earlier distinctions between the Babylonian Talmudic traditions and their equivalents in 'Eretz Yisra'el also found later expression in the formulation of their respective laws and customs. As the Babylonian teachers and institutions between and around the Tigris and the Euphrates began to grow in stature and influence, so it became necessary for the Palestinian communities to put on record those instances (ma'asim in Hebrew) in which they differed. A body of literature thus came into being, perhaps early in the seventh century, the purpose of which was to clarify, recall, and maintain these differences. Refugees from the Crusades subsequently brought evidence of these to Egypt.

The later Genizah material includes hundreds of fragments of the halakhic digest of the Babylonian Talmud that Isaac Alfasi prepared in the eleventh century. The first fully comprehensive code of Jewish law, the *Mishneh Torah of Maimonides*, completed in Cairo in 1180, is also, not surprisingly, well represented among the medieval fragments from the Ben Ezra Synagogue. Equally unsurprising is the fact that many of these fragments cover such themes as ritual slaughter and marital matters, both of which were clearly issues of major concern to the daily lives of the Egyptian community. In the case of the latter, there are important remnants of Palestinian religious practice that demonstrate that, in matters of personal status, the émigrés from the Holy Land succeeded in maintaining their halakhic individuality for some time. Via the Genizah, hundreds or maybe even thousands of authentic and original halakhic responses have now been recovered. The original groups of decisions sent by the authority by way of guidance to a number of questioners have surfaced. It should not be forgotten that there are also Genizah responsa that date from the twelfth and thirteenth centuries, many of them emanating from Moses Maimonides himself or his son Abraham, occasionally in their own hands.

As far as Sa'adya Gaon's practical guide to Jewish rules on testimonies and deeds (*Sefer Ha-Shetarot*) is concerned, fifty Genizah fragments (forty of them in Cambridge) have produced some two hundred folios, amounting to over 90 percent of the original work. Sa'adya (d. 942) was an Egyptian Jew who became the head of a leading rabbinical academy in Babylonia. Since the first scientific edition of Sa'adya's prayer book was published, almost sixty years ago, many more fragments of the work have been located. Some of Sa'adya's successors in the Babylonian academies followed his example and produced their own halakhic monographs. Hai ben Sherira Gaon and Samuel ben Hofni of Sura were among these, and the latter, together with Sa'adya himself and the later scholar Tanhum ben Joseph Yerushalmi, also wrote commentaries on the Hebrew Bible that demonstrated how one could remain faithful to the source and at the same time provide rational and philosophical responses to the problems raised by the texts.

In the field of rabbinic liturgy, the discoveries have been legion and have included novel or otherwise unknown benedictions that were subsequently forgotten or rejected; unknown texts of the major prayers and unusual epithets for sabbaths and festivals; indications of a more extensive usage of the Hebrew Bible, of novel ceremonials inside and outside the synagogue, and of the honorific mention of living personalities; the inclusion of the Ten Commandments, the Song at the Sea, and various mystical and messianic expansions as integral parts of the liturgy; the mutual and wider influence of what were clearly the two major rites, that is, those of Palestine and Babylon, and the special success of the latter; the use of Hebrew, Aramaic, and Judeo-Arabic not only in prayers and liturgical poems that had traditionally been expressed in one or other of these particular languages, but also in other contexts; and the wide dissemination, acceptance, and influence achieved by liturgical poetry.

As far as special prayers for individuals are concerned, one invoked God's blessing on the twelfth-century Imam al-Amir bi-ahkam Allah and read as follows:

> *And we pray for the life of our distinguished sovereign lord and Muslim leader . . . commander of the faithful, and for the royal princes and for all the royal family, and for those who devotedly assist the king and for those who do battle for him against his foes. May Almighty God come to their assistance and to ours, subdue those who arise against us and against them, and inspire them to deal kindly with us and with all his people, the house of Israel, and let us say Amen.*

Where they once had some forty thousand compositions available to them, enthusiasts for medieval Hebrew poetry now have, thanks to the Genizah source, 150 percent more material to contend with. Earlier texts—some on papyrus, perhaps dating from as early as the eighth century—are now available, authorship is better established, and whole new schools of poets have been added to the history of Hebrew verse. It is clear that the whole literary genre blossomed in post-Talmudic Palestine and may have represented the primary Jewish entertainment of the time. It is possible to uncover the emergence of a Sa'adyanic school in Babylon and to identify the linguistic and structural innovations that it daringly made. Comparisons can be made between the style and content of such poems and those composed in places as far away as Byzantium, Italy, North Africa, and Spain. One of the most exciting of recent finds relates to a married couple: none other than the famous tenth-century linguist and poet Dunash ibn Labrat and his wife. When he left Spain soon after the birth of their son, his wife wrote him a poem expressing her sadness and questioning his loyalty. His lyrical reply assured her of his faithfulness.

There is also a whole range of mystical material in the Genizah, called hekhalot literature because it purports to describe what is supposedly transpiring in the celestial palaces. The difficulty here is in dating the origins of these traditions, establishing the precise context in which they were used, and defining how they related to what are regarded as more standard rabbinic works. It is by no means clear whether what is found in the Genizah is a mere remnant of a religious expression that was once much more powerful and influential, or a move toward the more mystical and spiritual in reaction to the growing centrality of the halakhic voice. Some have argued that these texts represent the devotions of pious individuals and small mystical groups, while others prefer to give them a greater communal relevance within the rabbinic practice of the early medieval period. What also remains to be clarified is whether what we are seeing is evidence of borrowings by one set of traditions from another or overlaps within a rabbinic Judaism that was broader than is sometimes credited.[34]

Conclusion

The Dead Sea Scrolls have undoubtedly attracted wide attention because they are so closely linked in location and chronology with the world of Jesus and the emergence of early Christianity. The Genizah texts from Fustat/Cairo, in contrast, cover a wider variety of literary genres and historical events in the Islamic world and represent a unique source of illumination for the early medieval period. Without them, we would have little idea of the significant—even exciting—contributions made by the religious communities of Egypt to major cultural developments in eastern Mediterranean areas of the tenth to the thirteenth centuries. Thanks to the research done on them in the 110 years since their discovery and their earliest decipherment and analysis, it has become clear that the Jews of medieval Cairo played a significant part not only in the development of Jewish life and lore, but also in the overall history of the Eastern Mediterranean.

THE CHRISTIAN HERITAGE OF OLD CAIRO

Gertrud J.M. van Loon

THE CHURCHES OF OLD CAIRO

Introduction

Enclosed within the relatively small area of the Fortress of Babylon are no fewer than six churches and a convent. Atop the southern gate of the old fortress is the Church of the Holy Virgin, also called 'the Hanging' or 'the Suspended' (*al- Mu'allaqa*) Church because of its location. Occupying the northern tower of the fortress, another prominent location, is the Greek Orthodox Church of St. George. Hidden within the precinct are the Church of Sts. Sergius and Bacchus (*Abu Sarga*), the Church of St. Barbara, the Church of St. George (*Mari Girgis*), the Church of the Virgin of the Pot of Basil (*al- 'Adra Qasriyat al-Rihan*), and the Convent of St. George. The Church of St. Michael was sold to the Jewish community and turned into a synagogue in the ninth century (see the chapter "The Jewish Heritage of Old Cairo").[1]

In the immediate vicinity of the fortress are two clusters of churches. To the northwest is the Monastery of St. Mercurius (*Dayr Abu Sayfayn*), with the Churches of St. Mercurius (*Abu Sayfayn*), St. Shenute (*Anba Shenuda*), and the Virgin 'al-Damshiriya' (*al-'Adra al-Damshiriya*), as well as the Convent of St. Mercurius. To the south of the fortress are situated the Church of the Virgin of Babylon (*al-'Adra*) al-Darag and a small walled precinct called the Monastery of St. Theodore (*Dayr al-Amir Tadros*), enclosing the Churches of St. Theodore the Oriental (*al-Amir Tadros*) and Sts. Cyrus and John (*Abu Qir wa Yuhanna*). Farther south lies the Church of the Archangel Michael al-Qibli.

Historical Works and Travelers

The historical sources that provide the most knowledge about the churches in and around Old Cairo are *The History of the Patriarchs* and *The History of the Churches and Monasteries in Egypt*. Such contemporary Islamic historians and geographers as Yahya ibn Sa'id (d. 1027), al-Maqrizi (d. 1442), al-Kindi (d. 961), and Ibn Duqmaq (d. 1407) also wrote about the location of the churches and Christian matters.

The History of the Patriarchs is a chronicle of the history of the Coptic Church covering the period from the first to the thirteenth centuries. It is organized in the form of biographies of the successive patriarchs. The earliest compilers wrote in Coptic, but in the eleventh century the authors switched to Arabic. For a long time, it was attributed to Sawirus ibn al-Muqaffa, bishop of al-Ashmunayn (tenth century). Recent scholarship, however, has identified the Alexandrian deacon and notable Mawhub ibn Mansur ibn Mufarrig (ca. 1025–1100) as the principal compiler and translator of the work, as well as the author of the biographies of the contemporary patriarchs. From the twelfth century, various authors took over the task, sometimes elaborating the earlier text with their own observations. The period from the fourteenth to the early twentieth century is recorded very briefly.[2]

The History of the Churches and Monasteries in Egypt was traditionally ascribed to Abu Salih al-Armani, but it is now generally attributed to the Coptic priest Abu al-Makarim. This three-volume topographical handbook is a mine of information about churches, monasteries, pilgrimages, and the customs of the time. Several authors, Abu al-Makarim possibly among them, compiled the basic text around 1160–87, and information was added from the late twelfth to the fourteenth century.[3]

The works of Islamic scholars supplement the picture drawn by these two key sources. Geographers included the location of important Christian monuments in their descriptions of cities, and historians reported on events in which Christians played a role or devoted parts of their work to the history of the Christians. Al-Maqrizi, for example, wrote a study on Coptic history in which he not only listed monasteries and churches, but also added short descriptive notes about them. These notes provide valuable documentation that helps to trace the existence and status of specific monasteries and churches in the early fifteenth century.[4]

Medieval Western travelers in Egypt almost invariably visited the churches in this area: they were places of pilgrimage because of their connection with the Flight into Egypt of the Holy Family. The reports such pilgrims made of their visits and experiences are another valuable—albeit sometimes confusing—source.[5]

For the seventeenth century, our main resource is the Dominican monk Johann Michael Wansleben (d. 1679), who is better known as Vansleb (the Gallic form of his name). In 1664 and again in 1672–73, he traveled widely in Egypt, where he paid special attention to Christian antiquities.[6] He lists the churches of Old Cairo in his 1671 book.[7] Clearly he confused some dedications, and his report of his second visit in 1672 is more extensive and apposite.[8]

In the late nineteenth century, two authors stand out. The first of them is Father Michel Marie Jullien S.J. (d. 1911), founder of the College de la Sainte Famille, a boys' school in Cairo. He traveled all over Egypt, and detailed reports of his visits to churches and monasteries were initially published in the Jesuit journal *Les missions catholiques* and later collected in several volumes.[9] He was one of the first to take photographs to illustrate his stories.[10]

The second author is Alfred Joshua Butler (d. 1936), private tutor to Prince Tawfik in 1880–81, who carried out fieldwork in Coptic churches and focused particularly on those in Cairo. His publication *The Ancient Coptic Churches of Egypt* (1884), illustrated with woodcuts, is an extremely important document that describes his visits to the churches of Old Cairo in great detail, meticulously noting their architecture and most interesting features. These descriptions are interesting in their own right, but also because Butler recorded the state of these churches immediately before the launch of a large-scale project to restore them.

Prince Johann Georg, Duke of Saxony (d. 1938), is a good example of a traveler with a scholarly interest in Christian antiquities in Egypt. He published three books on his journeys in Egypt.[11] Prince Johann Georg was also an enthusiastic photographer and he has extensively documented all monasteries and churches he visited.

Christianity in Babylon

Our knowledge about early Christianity in and around the Fortress of Babylon is very incomplete. Cyrus, bishop of Babylon, attended the Second Council of Ephesus in 449,[12] but where Bishop Cyrus actually resided is not known. At that time, the designation Babylon was not confined to the fortress itself but extended to the surrounding area, and it is here we should look for Cyrus's church. Before the fortress fell to the Arabs in the seventh century, it served a solely military function and the building of churches inside the walled precinct or on the fortifications would have been unthinkable. Apart from the plausibility of a chapel for the military personnel (which has not been located), church building inside the Fortress of Babylon must have begun only after the Arab conquest of Egypt.[13] It was at this time that the city of Fustat began to take shape on the site of the former military camp around the fortress; later, this settlement came to be called Misr and the name 'Babylon' was restricted more and more to the fortress alone.

Theodore, metropolitan bishop of Misr (Fustat), was present at the election of Patriarch Michael I in the Church of St. Shenute in the Monastery of St. Mercurius (743).[14] *The History of the Churches and Monasteries in Egypt* states that the Church of St. Mercurius (situated next to the Church of St. Shenute) "had been the episcopal church until the death of Anba Philotheus, bishop of Cairo; but Christodulus transformed it into a patriarchal church."[15] Patriarch Christodoulos (1047–68 CE) definitively transferred the seat of the Patriarchate from Alexandria to Cairo. However, the Church of St. Mercurius and the Hanging Church both served as the patriarch's place of residence during the eleventh and twelfth centuries, and it is difficult to establish which patriarch lived where and when.[16]

It might be possible that the Church of St. Mercurius initially served as the bishop's church: the original fabric of the present church is dated to the sixth century,[17] and no older church in the neighborhood of the Fortress has been found so far. On the other hand, the *History of the Patriarchs* mentions that the Church of Sts. Sergius and Bacchus was the bishop's church at the time of the patriarchate of Abraham (975–78).[18]

Architecture, Art, Restoration, and Renovation

After the siege by 'Amr ibn al-'As (640–41), the Fortress of Babylon was transformed into a residential quarter. The people who had lived scattered outside the defenses fled inside during the siege and never left. The new settlement of Fustat Misr grew up near the fortress, with the mosque of 'Amr ibn al-'As as its focus.[19] To allow better access to the new city, the new governmental and administrative center, the northern wall of the fortress was demolished and the former canal filled in to make a street. The old road system inside the fortress was maintained and a number of Roman buildings continued to be reused until a relatively late date (possibly the tenth or eleventh century). Archaeological evidence shows that the northwestern part of the fortress was originally occupied by sophisticated urban structures. The rest of the area inside the defense walls developed into a predominantly Christian quarter, characterized by a relatively large number of churches.[20] Since the ground plans of residential houses seldom reveal the religious affiliation of their owners, it is possible that the northwestern area was also part of the Christian neighborhood.

The earliest churches to have been established inside the fortress—the Church of Sts. Cyrus and John, later known as the Church of St. Barbara, and the Church of St. George or the Church of St. Sergius (pp. 96–113)—were probably founded by Athanasius, scribe *(katib)*[21] to 'Abd al-'Aziz ibn Marwan, governor of Egypt from 685 to 705. Other churches inside or beyond the fortress walls cannot be dated as precisely.

It is likely that most of the churches in and around the fortress were originally built on a basilican plan: a nave and side aisles (which might have a return aisle at the western end, a typical Egyptian element) plus an apse and side chambers, the whole structure covered by a wooden roof. Although later renovations have added or changed elements, this ground plan is still the layout of the churches of St. Barbara and of Sts. Sergius and Bacchus, as well as those of St. Mercurius and St. Shenute.[22] Those churches that were completely rebuilt in the eighteenth or nineteenth century either retained the traditional plan (for example, the Church of the Virgin 'al-Damshiriya') or were built according to a later style of Egyptian church-building, based on a centralized four-pillar structure that transforms the nave and side aisles into similar dome-covered bays (for example, the Church of the Virgin of the Pot of Basil and the Church of St. Theodore the Oriental). The number of bays varies; there are usually three domed altar rooms or *haykals*.[23]

Waves of renovation and reconstruction have constantly characterized the architectural history of the churches in and around the fortress. *The History of the Patriarchs* describes a general rebuilding of the churches of Fustat under Patriarch Mark II (799–819), after they had been destroyed during the time of his predecessor John.[24] Archaeological evidence has revealed that some of the churches within the fortress were extensively rebuilt between the end of the ninth and the middle of the eleventh century.[25] Literary confirmation for this rebuilding exists for the Hanging Church (see pp. 80–95) and the Church of St. Mercurius (see pp. 182–95), and for the churches of Sts. Sergius and Bacchus, and, perhaps, St. Barbara (see pp. 114–25). The burning of Fustat in 1168 and the subsequent abandonment of the area were said to have been carried out to prevent the crusaders from attacking the walled city of al-Qahira, the administrative and governmental center founded by the Fatimids in 969. A series of natural disasters (earthquakes, low Nile levels, plague, and famine) in the second half of the eleventh century—upheavals which led to social turmoil and chaos—also contributed to the abandonment of Fustat.[26] It is generally acknowledged that the fire did not reach the former Fortress of Babylon, and consequently the churches would have remained relatively unharmed.[27] The Church of St. Mercurius did, however, suffer badly in the general unrest and was renovated and solemnly reopened in 1175 (see pp. 182–95).

Today the interiors of the churches retain only a few elements of their ancient decoration, of which the main medium was wall painting. Remnants are still visible on the columns and in the southern haykal of the Church of Sts. Sergius and Bacchus (see pp. 96–113), on some columns in the Hanging Church in the Chapel of Takla Haymanot (see p. 93), in the Church of St. Mercurius, and in the Church of St. Shenute (see pp. 196–207). Alfred Butler saw paintings in the Church of St. Barbara, which disappeared shortly after his visit (see pp. 114–25). The Coptic Museum preserves a fifth-century wooden altar from the Church of Sts. Sergius and Bacchus, the unique fourth- to fifth-century wooden doors found in the Church of St. Barbara (both obviously reused elements), and a magnificent eleventh-century wooden altar screen from the Church of St. Barbara.[28] The Church of St. Mercurius still has two eleventh- to twelfth-century screens in the ground-floor chapels.[29]

After Fustat was abandoned, the area around the Fortress of Babylon deteriorated into a wasteland and rubbish dump. The ruins became quarries for extracting building material and provided a refuge for the poor.[30] Nineteenth- and early twentieth-century woodcuts and plans still depict the area as lying vacant; along the road into the city were (from south to north) the churches of the Archangel Michael, the Monastery of St. Theodore, Babylon al-Darag, the fortress, the Mosque of 'Amr ibn al-'As, and the Monastery of St. Mercurius.[31]

Peter Sheehan suggests extensive thirteenth-century building activity in the churches of the fortress.[32] However, in the light of the ongoing discussion about such matters as the dates of the wall paintings and architecture in the Church of Sts. Sergius and Bacchus, the large hall of the Convent of St. George, and the Church of St. Barbara, this can be neither confirmed or denied.

A period that has been noted for its general open-mindedness ended with the foundation of the Ayyubid dynasty in 1250. In subsequent centuries, the construction of new churches was expressly forbidden, and any restoration or renovation was bound by strict rules and limitations.[33] Nevertheless, Egyptian Christian culture flourished in other fields, such as literature and the copying of manuscripts. Before his election as patriarch, Gabriel III (1268–71) had been a priest at the Hanging Church and had developed a fine reputation as a scribe and copyist.[34] This was also the era of the great encyclopedias of Coptic religious knowledge and traditions, among them *The Book of the Lamp of Darkness* by Ibn Kabar (d. 1324), who was also a priest at the Hanging Church, and *The Book of the Precious Pearl* by Ibn Saba.[35] In this period, Old Cairo also became a popular destination for Western pilgrims. We owe quite some knowledge about the fortress churches to the details these pilgrims noted down in their journals.[36]

Between the thirteenth and fifteenth centuries, the church interiors were enriched with marble *ambons* (St. Barbara, the Hanging Church), the marble *opus sectile* work of the *synthronon* of the apses (Sts. Sergius and Bacchus, the Hanging

Church, St. Barbara),[37] finely carved wooden altar screens (Sts. Sergius and Bacchus, the Hanging Church), and ciboria, wooden canopies raised over the altar, for example in the Hanging Church).[38] Restoration projects have brought to light a small corpus of icons painted from the thirteenth century to about 1500, the majority of them in the Hanging Church and the churches of St. Mercurius and St. Barbara. At first glance, the gilded background and Byzantine vestments in these icons give the impression that they are Byzantine work. Closer study, however, reveals the use of local wood for the panel and typical Egyptian compositions, saints, iconography, and inscriptions in Coptic/Greek and Arabic. The superficial resemblance is probably the result of the training in Byzantine styles received by local painters. Influences from Palestine, Syria, Cyprus, and Western Europe have all left their mark.[39] This so-called crusader art is characterized by a mixture in the choice of themes, composition, and style from Europe generally and from the other countries in which the crusaders created their strongholds: the crusader kingdoms.[40]

One remarkable element recurring in the ecclesiastical structures within the Fortress of Babylon is the high-ceilinged hall (qa'a), examples of which include the large, richly decorated hall in the Convent of St. George and what is known as the Wedding Hall near the Coptic Orthodox Church of St. George (see pp. 126–32 and 148–51).[41] This type of hall, used for receptions and to entertain guests, is a remnant of Fatimid and Mamluk domestic architecture (eleventh to fourteenth century) and was usually elaborately decorated with stucco, painting, and carved woodwork. Since both the halls in the fortress are located in the northwestern section, Sheehan suggests that this quarter had had a residential function before the buildings were taken over for religious purposes.[42] An eleventh-century narrative in which a donor expresses a wish to build a church dedicated to St. Barbara near his home (see pp. 114–25) supports Sheehan's interpretation.[43] It goes without saying that this high Coptic official, a vizier who had the money to be able to finance the building of a church, would have owned a large house. The story offers clues to the existence of substantial domestic architecture in Old Cairo. Moreover, at the qa'a in the Convent of St. George, recent archaeological research has revealed a large house, built of brick and dating to the ninth or tenth century, below the present hall. The ground plan of the earlier structure deviated from the one above it, suggesting that the house had been demolished before the construction of the present building.[44]

In 1903, on the exterior of the eastern wall of the Church of St. Mercurius, members of the Comite de conservation des monuments de l'art arabe (hereafter, Comite) discovered the complete stucco decoration of a western wall of a large hall. No further research was carried out at that time and the function of the hall, located inside the Monastery of St. Mercurius, is not known. The decoration was removed to the Musee arabe, now the Museum of Islamic Art, with permission of Patriarch Cyril V.[45] The report of the Comite dates the ensemble to no later than the time of Sultan Qaytbay (fifteenth century).[46] The location of such a lofty hall adjacent to the Church of St. Mercurius gives rise to some intriguing speculations. The Monastery of St. Mercurius, which contained the churches of St. Mercurius, St. Shenute, and the Virgin 'al-Damshiriya,' was surrounded by a high wall, probably built in the last quarter of the twelfth century. At that time, until 1300 in fact, the Church of St. Mercurius was the residence of the patriarch. Few historical sources from the fourteenth or fifteenth century shed any light on the function of the church.[47] The home of a wealthy family at this location seems out of the question; was it once part of the patriarch's residence? Unfortunately, it has proved impossible to find a detailed description or study of this wall and decoration.

In the second half of the seventeenth century (Ottoman period), when the political climate was more tolerant, a wave of restoration and reconstruction of often long-neglected churches and monasteries began. This turned into a veritable boom in the eighteenth century. Wealthy, influential Christians, often high government officials, used their contacts to obtain permission for building and restoration from the Muslim authorities. The renovation/rebuilding of the Church of the Virgin 'al-Damshiriya,' for example, was financed by a prominent Copt from Damshir in the Delta, hence its name. The Church of the Virgin of the Pot of Basil was rebuilt in the late eighteenth century, when the Hanging Church was restored. It was not only the churches in and around the Fortress of Babylon that benefited from this ardor, but indeed the whole country. The activities of the brothers Ibrahim and Girgis al-Guhari, who were later buried in Old Cairo, close to the Church of St. George, are particularly famous.[48] They were involved in the building of new churches, and the restoration and refurbishing of existing churches and monasteries all over Egypt.

Apart from restoration and building, icons and manuscripts were commissioned to be either dedicated and donated to churches and monasteries or kept for personal use.[49] Some sixteenth- and seventeenth-century icons have been preserved and can be seen in the churches of the Monastery of St. Mercurius and the Church of St. Barbara,[50] but the grand corpus of surviving icons dates from the eighteenth and nineteenth centuries. By this time, the painting of icons was no longer confined to wooden panels; canvas or even paper were now also used.

The most famous icon painters of the eighteenth century were Yuhanna al-Armani and Ibrahim al-Nasikh (John the Armenian and Abraham the Scribe). They worked individually, but also frequently signed their work together. Ibrahim— scribe, calligrapher, and painter—was a Copt; Yuhanna's name reveals his ancestry. The iconography and style of their work reflect a fusion of local tradition, influences from religious painting in Western Europe and from various Middle

Eastern communities, and Islamic art. These artists did not restrict their talents to painting icons and wall panels; they also decorated ciboria, reliquaries, chalice thrones,[51] and even produced wall paintings.[52] Wall painting, which had been the main medium of church decoration until around 1400, became rare in later centuries. A new fashion was to fix wooden panels, painted with designs originally executed directly on the walls, onto the walls of a *haykal*. Well-preserved examples can be seen in the central *haykal* and first-floor chapel of the Church of Mari Mina in Fumm al-Khalig (eighteenth century, restored in the nineteenth century).[53] The wall panels were painted using icon-painting techniques and reflect all the characteristics of contemporary icon painting in Egypt. This method continued to be used in the nineteenth century, as can be seen in the central haykal of the Church of St. Mercurius (see pp. 182–95) and the Church of the Virgin of Babylon al-Darag (see pp. 230–33). Prince Johann Georg of Saxony visited the Church of St. Mercurius in 1910 and again in 1912. He noticed that the paintings on the wooden panels repeated the older subjects painted on the walls, which were still visible at that time.[54] The most important painter of this period was A[na]stasi al-Qudsi al-Rumi (Anastasius the Greek from Jerusalem), together with his workshop, which was active from 1832 to 1871.[55]

Butler, who documented the churches of Old Cairo in 1880–81 and 1884, repeatedly drew attention to the neglect, ignorance, and greed that were gnawing away at the most ancient church buildings in Cairo, causing them to deteriorate rapidly.[56] In his wake, the British architect Somers Clarke pointed to the deplorable state of repair of these churches. He stressed the need to preserve and protect them, not least from well-intentioned wealthy patrons who could do what they liked. One example of such over-lavish attention was the Hanging Church, which he described as having been "'restored' to death," while other ancient churches in Cairo had been demolished and "replaced by some new structure." Ancient Egyptian monuments fell under the aegis of the Department of Antiquities, and the Comité took care of Islamic monuments, which left a yawning gap in the middle. "The continuity of history seems to have been forgotten," Somers Clarke complained. "Interest ends with hieroglyphics only to reawaken over Saracenic art."[57]

The Comité was established in 1881 as part of the Ministry of Awqaf (Charitable Endowments) for the purpose of recording and restoring Islamic monuments, for which the ministry would set aside an annual sum. This committee was dominated by European architects and scholars.[58] Seeking publicity to redress the neglect of Cairo's Christian heritage, Somers Clarke wrote to a newspaper in 1895. Although the Comité did take the trouble to inspect the churches of Old Cairo, Somers Clarke had to admit that in view of its mandate, this body could not be expected to take charge of Christian monuments.[59] Alarmed by the restoration of the Hanging Church, however, the Comité had also inspected the Fortress of Babylon and expressed the wish to register the Roman remains as a monument.[60]

Butler and Somers Clarke were not the only people who championed the need to protect and restore Christian monuments and artifacts; their passion was a sign of times. In 1889, the Cairo–Helwan Light Railway was opened, connecting the old fortress, then still isolated among the rubbish dumps of Fustat, to the city. Following in Butler's footsteps, European tourists and antiquarians began to visit the ancient churches and the Roman fortress, looking for the roots of Christianity as well as pilgrimage sites.[61]

The situation changed in 1897, when 10 percent of the money allotted to the Comité was set aside for Coptic monuments on condition that the Coptic patriarchate would contribute a significant proportion to the expenses of restoration. At the request of Patriarch Cyril V (1874–1927), the Comité compiled a report about the state of the churches in and around the Fortress of Babylon and drew up an estimate of costs for the proposed restoration.[62] This list of monuments was the start of a large-scale and lengthy restoration project that encompassed all the churches in the area.

Church buildings were officially included in the list of registered monuments for the first time in 1910.[63] Apart from the Churches of the Virgin of the Pot of Basil and the Archangel Michael al-Qibli (where only the wooden screens were registered), all the churches in the fortress appear on this list, including the Chapel of St. George (the *qa'a*, or hall) in the Convent of St. George and the *Qa'at al-'Irsan*, the Wedding Hall, near the Church of St. George. The Churches of St. Mercurius and St. Shenute in the Monastery of St. Mercurius were registered, as were the Church of the Virgin of Babylon al-Darag and the Church of Sts. Cyrus and John in the Monastery of St. Theodore, located to the south of the fortress.

The bulk of the activities of the Comité consisted of the documentation and preservation of monuments so as to prevent further dilapidation and to stabilize and consolidate the fabric of the building. Usually, the limited financial resources permitted nothing more. Only when restoration was necessary for the functional use of the building, larger programs were initiated. The building was studied in order to determine the original state, which was the starting point for restoration. Consequently, the additions of later eras were often removed. The architect played a key role in this interventionist philosophy: his study, ideas, and ability determined the outcome. Preservation and restoration of monuments was a heavily debated topic in late-nineteenth-century Europe, ranging from pure conservation to a complete recreation of monuments according to the ideas of restoration architects. The policy of the Comité represented a moderate position in this discussion.[64]

Before restoration commenced, photographs were taken and plans and elevations were drawn to record the existing situation and study the building. In the case of such large projects as the restoration of the Church of St. Barbara (1918–22), progress was carefully documented in both photographs and a written study.[65] Valuable objects were often transferred to the newly founded Coptic Museum.

At that time, Old Cairo was a densely populated, run-down residential quarter.[66] The church buildings, hidden among the houses and shops, were part of an inextricable tangle of everyday and religious life. One of the concerns of the Comité was to remove the domestic and administrative arrangements that had developed in the western part and in the galleries of the churches, including the Church of St. Shenute, the Church of St. Barbara, and the Church of Sts. Sergius and Bacchus (see pp. 96–113)—and to free the churches of the accretions that were now huddled around them. This isolated the buildings from their surroundings; they were thus transformed into monuments rather than being woven into the social fabric.[67] Fire hazard was an anxiety expressed repeatedly by both the patriarch and the Comité: the narrow, cluttered streets prevented any quick response from the fire brigade if fire broke out.[68] Ironically, when the Greek Orthodox Church and surrounding buildings burned down in 1904, part of the area was cleared—in line with the goals of the Comité.[69] Since the turn of the twentieth century, Old Cairo has slowly lost its residential function and is now essentially a historic and tourist quarter.

The densely packed buildings and intensive use of the area have meant that, from an archaeological point of view, most of Old Cairo was inaccessible for a long time. The Old Cairo Archaeological Monitoring Project (OCAM Project, 2000–2006), directed by Peter Sheehan of the American Research Center in Egypt (ARCE), was part of a broader USAID project to lower the groundwater levels in the area. The high groundwater levels, due in part to a leaking sewage system, had caused flooding in parts of Old Cairo and threatened the integrity of the buildings.[70] The crypt of the Church of Sts. Sergius and Bacchus, for example, has been inaccessible for years as a result. During the project, Sheehan's team studied the archaeological remains and was able to collect vital information, vastly enriching our knowledge of the (architectural) history of the Fortress of Babylon and its churches. In his book, *Babylon of Egypt* (2010), the history of the fortress is told on the basis of these recent finds.

Old Cairo is a popular destination for an increasing number of tourists, and the Copts' growing consciousness about their religious past has aroused new interest and attracted more donors. A visit to Old Cairo on a Sunday means meeting large numbers of Egyptians, Christian and Muslim alike, who go to the churches and the convents for prayer and a blessing, but also simply to socialize in the tea gardens of St. George and St. Barbara. This popularity has boosted the area and inspired new projects in and around the fortress.

Sheehan also describes the restorations/renovations from the 1980s to the present. The picture is not positive: the motives, aims, and methods of the various parties involved in restoration and heritage management have become the subject of conflict; contractors are more concerned about getting projects off the ground than achieving results; there is a shortage of skilled conservation architects and artisans familiar with traditional techniques; tons of concrete are hidden under cosmetic layers of traditional finish. In contrast to the restorations undertaken by the Comité, documentation of the work is often neglected and there is no overall plan to protect and conserve the area.[71]

The most recent restorations of church interiors reveal a fondness for red brick: layers of plaster have been removed from walls, domes, and pillars, for instance in the Church of St. Shenute in the Monastery of St. Mercurius and the Church of St. Theodore in the Monastery of St. Theodore. It must be said that, flooded with soft light from ceramic lamp holders, the newly flushed brickwork of these church interiors gives a pleasant, peaceful ambience. Nonetheless, three main dangers threaten the current restorations: uniformity, following the trend of current taste, and the risk of disregarding the history of the building.

Sheehan ends his book on an optimistic note: notwithstanding the mistakes and problems of recent times, there is still hope for an all-encompassing conservation program. This important publication has given a new impetus to the study of ancient Babylon and the subsequent phases of its history. Sheehan advocates that archaeology be the basis for all research. This is no doubt a sound principle, but his book also makes clear that, as far as churches are concerned, it is not enough: archaeologists, historians, architects, and art historians must work together to counter the vicissitudes suffered by these venerable buildings, their interiors, and their surroundings. There are still mountains to be moved. For example, Magdi Guirguis has shown that archival sources for the seventeenth and eighteenth centuries are an extremely rich but as yet almost unexploited source for the study of church building and decoration.[72]

Through the ravages of time and the twists and turns of history, the churches in and around the Fortress of Babylon have undergone repairs, rebuilding, and modernization. Political conditions and a lack of funds have led to periods of neglect and decay, counteracted by phases when Christian society in Egypt benefited from tolerance and stability and had access to financial resources. In their present state, the church buildings are often less ancient than might be thought. Nevertheless, they are places of worship venerated as holy for centuries and they symbolize the resilient faith of the Coptic community in Egypt, past and present.

The Hanging Church. In the nave, to the left, are the stairs going down in the Roman structure. The outline of the gate tower on which the 'Little Church' or Chapel of Takla Haymanot was built, is clearly visible. Courtesy Dr. Peter Grossmann.

To the left of the entrance portal, water was provided for the thirsty traveler or passerby. The text above reads: "Everyone that drinketh of this water shall thirst again: but whosoever drinketh of the water that I shall give him shall never thirst (John 4:13–14). Provided by Nakhla Bey Yusuf, the Nazir: Year 1899." To the right of this public water dispensary is a door that once led to a school; above the door is the inscription "The Coptic Orthodox School, established in 1614 AM/1898 CE."[83]

OPPOSITE:
The entrance portal on Mari Girgis Street (end of the nineteenth century).

THE HANGING CHURCH
(al-Mu'allaqa)

THE CHURCH OF THE HOLY VIRGIN is more commonly known as 'the Hanging' or 'the Suspended' *(al-Mu'allaqa)* Church: It was built on top of the remains of the southern gate of the Roman fortress. Its location makes clear that it must have been built after the fortress was no longer in use as a military structure.[73]

The date of the church's construction is unknown, but it was certainly standing by the ninth century: *The History of the Patriarchs* records its demolition and subsequent rebuilding.[74] References to this church are also found in the medieval accounts of Western pilgrims, where it is called "the Church of the Steps" (after the stairway to the entrance) or "the Church of the Column." The latter name alludes to the miracle of the moving of Muqattam Mountain. The vizier of the caliph (either al-Mu'izz, 953–75 or al-'Aziz bi-Illah, 975–78) wanted the patriarch to prove that faith could move a mountain (Matthew 17:20; Mark 11:23). Prior to the test, Patriarch Abraham (d. 978) fasted for three days and nights in the Hanging Church. On the third day the Virgin appeared to him—near a column, according to some sources—and told him to go out into the great market. He would find a one-eyed man carrying a water jar on his shoulder: the saintly Simeon the Tanner, who distributed water among those too poor to buy it from the water carrier. Simeon told Abraham what to do, and the mountain moved. As a reward, the caliph allowed Patriarch Abraham to restore the Hanging Church, which was by then extremely dilapidated: "a great part of its walls had fallen down and part of them was in a state of decay."[75]

Originally, the church seems to have been built on a basilican plan: a nave and aisles with galleries, a central apse with side chambers. A small church, which was connected to the main church by a colonnade, was constructed on the southeastern gate tower. Around 1100 an upper floor, which served as a cell for the Patriarch, was added to this smaller church.

The Hanging Church was the residence of patriarch Abraham, and it served as the patriarchal residence until about 1300, alternating with churches in the Delta or other churches in the city.[76] From the eleventh to the fourteenth century, it played an important role in ecclesiastical life: patriarchs were elected, consecrated, and buried in the church, synods were convened, and, occasionally, the Holy Chrism was consecrated here.[77]

At various times throughout the turbulent thirteenth and fourteenth centuries, the church was pillaged, attacked, looted, and closed for short periods of time. Nevertheless, according to historical sources it was always restored.[78] The Dominican monk Father Vansleb praised it as the most beautiful church in Egypt.[79] At the end of the seventeenth century, however, the church underwent yet another restoration, this time financed by Mu'allim Girgis Abu Mansur al-Tukhi, a high-ranking government official.[80]

In 1880–81 Butler reported ongoing restoration.[81] Shortly thereafter, a large renovation financed by Nakhla Bey Yusuf, nazir of the church (the man responsible for financial and administrative affairs),[82] completely altered the church building. The British architect Somers Clarke described the works that were carried out in 1892–93: The western end of the church was reconstructed and a small courtyard added. The galleries disappeared and a four-aisled church emerged. The wooden screens that had partitioned the space into sections for men and women were removed. The interior was plastered and painted with an all-over decorative pattern, similar to the decoration of the Ben Ezra Synagogue. The colonnade connecting the church to the small church was closed in. The small church was converted into a side chapel

Contemporary mosaics in the courtyard of the Hanging Church.

ABOVE:
The miracle of the moving of Muqattam Mountain.

FAR LEFT:
St. Anthony, Star of the Desert and Father of all monks, depicted with images of monasteries on his garment to become a personification of monastic life, with novices gathering at its gate.

LEFT:
The angel warning Joseph to take the Mother and Child and flee to Egypt (Matthew 2:13).

OPPOSITE:
The courtyard of the church with a flight of steps leading up to the entrance. On the left, the wall is decorated with modern mosaics.

LEFT:
The entrance portal to the church proper (end of the nineteenth century).

The eastern part of the church
without pews and carpets. In front of
the central altar room is the ambon.
At the right, in the southern side
aisle, is the entrance to the Chapel
of Takla Haymanot. The decorative
paintings on the arches are late
nineteenth century.

The platform of the ambon *probably
dates to the fourteenth century, while
the staircase incorporates sixth- to
seventh-century marble plaques.*

A hidden passage in the nave of the church going down to a lower floor in the Roman structure.

The church as it appears today, showing the center altar, dedicated to the Virgin Mary. The altar to the right is dedicated to St. John the Baptist, the left altar to St. George. The splendid screen adorning the central altar room features rosette designs, inlaid with ebony, ivory, and an unidentified species of red wood. It dates from the fourteenth–fifteenth century.

and dedicated to the thirteenth-century Ethiopian saint Takla Haymanot; it continued to be used as the baptistery. Preparations were made and construction was begun for the large flight of stairs, the courtyard, and the entrance on Mari Girgis Street. Part of the curtain wall of the fortress was pulled down to make way for the gate and enclosing wall.[84]

The renovation evoked mixed feelings. Somers Clarke showed some understanding for these efforts ("with the best motive, the work has been thoroughly and utterly overdone. . . . The reaction from so sad a state of neglect is likely to result in doing too much.") but deeply regretted the destruction of the fortress walls.[85] Father Jullien was pleasantly surprised to find a clean, orderly church free of the screened-off partitions.[86] Prince Johann Georg of Saxony thought it successful. Apart from mentioning the church, the prince also described his 1912 visit to "the small Coptic Museum," a storeroom for endangered artifacts provisionally housed in a side-room of the church.[87]

The Comité deplored the transformation of the church: it was impossible to determine how much of the old fabric still remained. In subsequent years, some structural repairs to the church and side chapel were executed; windows were opened in the walls to let in more light, and the Comité decided to transfer one of the most valuable pieces to the Coptic Museum: an eighth-century wooden lintel depicting the Entry of Christ into Jerusalem.[88] Among the treasures still present in the church are wooden altar screens of outstanding quality, the magnificent fifteenth-century ciboria covering the three altars in the main church, and a marble *ambon*. The church also houses more than sixty icons painted by the eighteenth- century artists Yuhanna al-Armani and Ibrahim al-Nasikh. Although the majority of them were specifically commissioned, inscriptions on some of them show that they were originally intended for personal devotion and were donated to the church at a later date.[89]

In the course of the restoration activities in the 1980s,[90] a wall painting of the Nativity (thirteenth century) was discovered in the Chapel of Takla Haymanot. It is situated to the right of the apse, which is decorated with a painting of the Virgin and the twenty-four elders of the Apocalypse. The damage caused by the earthquake of 1992 ushered in a new phase of restoration carried out jointly by the church and the Coptic Museum.[91] Even more paintings came to light in the Chapel of Takla Haymanot: an archangel and fragments of the Presentation in the Temple (Luke 2:22–39), as well as fragments of a row of apostles or saints. Although the latter paintings clearly belong to different phases of decoration, it is unfortunately no longer possible to distinguish the older and newer layers of plaster on which they were painted. On the basis of style, they probably date to the end of the twelfth or the thirteenth century.

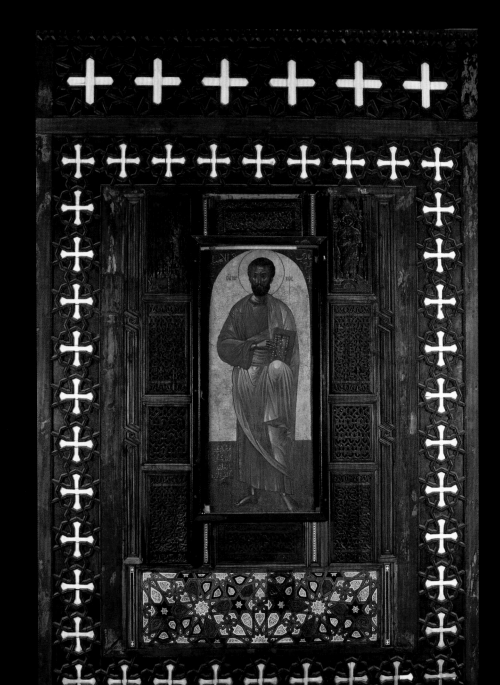

Icon of St. Mark the Evangelist (fourteenth century). The frame is assembled of twelfth to fourteenth-century pieces of woodwork. According to tradition, St. Mark is the founder of the Coptic Church.

The interiors of the domes of the ciboria crowning the altars of the church (fifteenth century?). Angels are carrying a circular composition of Christ Pantokrator.

The top of the central screen is adorned with a series of eighteenth century icons. The enthroned Christ is in the center; to His right are the Virgin Mary, the Archangel Gabriel, and St. Peter. To His left, John the Baptist, the Archangel Michael, and St. Paul.

A little-noticed decorative ceiling panel to the left of the entrance. In mirror image, two angels flank the crucified Christ.

OPPOSITE:

A majestic image of the Virgin Mary with the Christ Child on her lap and St. John the Baptist leaning against her knee. John is dressed as a desert ascetic. According to apocryphal stories, he lived in the desert from early childhood. This nineteenth-century icon on canvas shows western influence and might have been painted by an Armenian artist.

Built over the eastern tower
of the fortress' south gateway,
the Chapel of Takla Haymanot,
named after a thirteenth century
Ethiopian saint, is part of the
oldest section of al-Mu'allaqa.
The chapel houses a baptistery
with, at the left, the font. Mosaics
of marble and mother-of-pearl and
strips of marble decorate the walls
and the arches of the niches.

Recently discovered fragments of wall paintings in the Chapel of Takla Haymanot are shown here. Toward the top is a layer with fragments of a series of apostles or saints. Lower down are an archangel, and the aged Simeon and the prophetess Hannah of a representation of the Presentation in the Temple (Luke 2:22–39).

Thirteenth-century wall painting in the Chapel of Takla Haymanot of the Nativity.

Nineteenth-century icon of the
Virgin and Child in the so-called
Akhmim style.

Patriarch Abraham, St. Simeon the
Tanner, and, in the upper right-hand
corner, the Virgin appearing near a
column in the Hanging Church. Icon
painted by Ibrahim al-Nasikh (1750).

Eighteenth-century icon (painted by Yuhanna al-Armani and Ibrahim el-Nasikh) of the Virgin Mary and Child, surrounded by

Plan of the Church of St. Sergius showing various building phases. Courtesy Dr. Peter Grossmann.

The present entrance to Sts. Sergius and Bacchus opens into the northern side-aisle.

OPPOSITE:
The south door of the western entrance of the church. Above the doorway, the lower part of a cross with the abbreviation YC ΘC has been preserved. A late-nineteenth- century engraving shows the complete cross, with the abbreviation IC XC in the upper quarters. Together, they stand for 'Jesus Christ, Son of God, Savior'. Below the vertical cross arm was an Omega. At the time, the accompanying Alpha had already disappeared.[100]

LEFT TO RIGHT:
Entrance to Sts. Sergius and Bacchus, circa 1800s; late 1900s–2000; as of 2009. The alley entrance leads to the western doors of the church.

THE CHURCH OF STS. SERGIUS AND BACCHUS

(Abu Sarga)

ATHANASIUS, A SYRIAN FROM EDESSA, was scribe (katib) to 'Abd al-'Aziz ibn Marwan, governor of Egypt from 685 to 705. He might have been the founder of the Church of Sts. Sergius and Bacchus in the late seventh century.[92] The army officers and friends Sergius and Bacchus both suffered martyrdom in Edessa. They are commemorated on 4 and 10 Babeh / 1 and 7 October.[93]

The annals of Eutychius, Melchite patriarch of Alexandria (also known as Sa'id ibn Batriq, 877–940), mention the foundation of two churches by Athanasius, scribe to 'Abd al-'Aziz, dedicated to St. George and St. Cyrus. The dedication is consistent in the majority of manuscripts containing this text, although some refer to the Church of Sts. Sergius and Bacchus instead of St. George. The Ethiopic Synaxarion explicitly mentions churches dedicated to Sts. Sergius and Bacchus and Sts. Cyrus and John, but names the scribe "Andrew."[94]

Whether or not it was Athanasius who founded a church in honor of these saints, it is certainly possible that it might have existed in the seventh century: Patriarch Isaac is said to have been elected in this church (689).[95] The first explicit references to the Church of Abu Sarga date to the eighth century, when two priests of the church figure in the biography of Patriarch Michael I.[96] By the twelfth century, a number of patriarchs had been elected in this church. And although sound evidence is lacking, it is probable that patriarchs were also consecrated here.[97] In the time of Patriarch Abraham (975–78), it was the bishop's church,[98] also mentioned as such in the eleventh and twelfth centuries.[99]

The present basilican church with a nave and side aisles, a western return aisle, an apse with two side chambers, and galleries above the side aisles is the result of centuries of rebuilding and restoration. The recent archaeological work carried out beneath the floor by the ARCE OCAM Project has yielded important new information on the building history of the church. At least two main construction phases have been discovered that predate the present church building, which probably dates to the tenth or eleventh century. The remains of the first phase cannot be identified with certainty; the second-phase remains, about 1.85 meters beneath the floor, indicate a basilican structure with colonnades to separate the nave and aisles. This might be the late-seventh-century church.[101] The eleventh- century date for the origin of the existing

Postcards from the late 1800s showing
interiors of the church. Above: the southern
side aisle; below: the nave with view of the
altar screen.

Interior (ca. 2009) of the
church looking northeast.
The marble ambon to the
left of the altar is a modern
copy of that in the Church
of St. Barbara.

98

building might be supported by a later narrative, which recounts the construction of the churches of St. Barbara and St. Sergius (see "The Church of St. Barbara").[102]

According to tradition, the crypt of the church, below the central *haykal*, is one of the places where the Holy Family stopped either on their journey to Upper Egypt or on their way back to Palestine. The oldest sources mentioning this resting place date to the twelfth or thirteenth century.[103] In the thirteenth and fourteenth centuries, Western pilgrims reported having visited this locus sanctus. For them, the dwelling place of the Holy Family was the chief attraction and the church is habitually called 'the Church of the Cave.'

The research carried out by the OCAM Project indicates the construction of a crypt as well as vaulted burial chambers beneath the naos during the building period in the tenth- or eleventh-century church. The tombs were probably destined for ecclesiastical dignitaries.[104] At a later period, possibly the second half of the twelfth century, the sanctuaries were shifted eastward, and the whole church underwent extensive reconstruction work. The paintings discovered in the southern side-room date to this period.[105] The northern side-room was rebuilt in the fourteenth to fifteenth century.[106] The beautiful marble incrustation of the synthronon in the central haykal probably also dates to this period.[107]

From the fourteenth to the eighteenth century, Franciscan friars (who ran a hospice near the Church of Sts. Sergius and Bacchus[108]) had the privilege of celebrating the liturgy and baptizing in the crypt.[109] The present layout of colonnades and a baptismal font existed in the seventeenth century, although it is not clear when these elements were put into place.[110] In the eighteenth and nineteenth centuries, the southern part of the church was incorporated into the housing arrangement of the priest of the church. Alfred Butler and Father Jullien documented these modifications, as well as the partitioning of the nave using screens to separate men and women.[111]

This situation changed when the Comité de conservation des monuments de l'art arabe (hereafter the Comité) commenced renovations after its investigation of the churches in and around the fortress in 1897. From 1908 to 1919, the domestic furnishings were removed and the interior of the eastern part rearranged, the partitions in the nave were taken out, buildings adjacent to the church were demolished, and the fabric of the building was repaired.[112] Large-scale restorations followed from 1987 to 1992 as part of the battle to control the rising groundwater—which had already made its presence felt—and secure the stability of the building. The flooded crypt was one of the main targets of the most recent restoration (completed in 2005). Unfortunately, it has not yet yielded the desired result.[113]

Through the centuries, the church has been enriched and embellished with paintings, delicate woodwork, icons, manuscripts, and textiles,[114] befitting one of the most sacred sites of the fortress. One famous piece of furniture, a fifth-century wooden altar, is now in the Coptic Museum.[115] The collection of icons mainly dates to the eighteenth and nineteenth centuries. The ciborium covering the central altar is considered to be an exceptional work of Yuhanna al-Armani, painted in an Italian-Flemish style.[116]

OPPOSITE AND ABOVE:
Wooden panels showing the Last Supper (the fish is a traditional early Christian component of dinner scenes), an equestrian saint—thought to be St. Theodore—a geometric floral, and the Nativity. These fourteenth-century panels are now part of the modern altar screens flanking the fourteenth- fifteenth century screen in front of the central haykal.

View through the nave to the return aisle (the western part of the church) from the doors of the central haykal. In the corner to the right is the baptistery.

OPPOSITE:
Three recently restored ancient columns with Corinthian capitals. On the shafts are remnants of life-size paintings depicting military saints.

The synthronon *of inlaid marble in the central* haykal.

RIGHT:
Details of the synthronon.

OPPOSITE:
Interior of the ciborium, painted by Yuhanna al-Armani (eighteenth century) in an Italian-Flemish style. Christ enthroned is surrounded by the Four Living Creatures and the heavenly hosts.

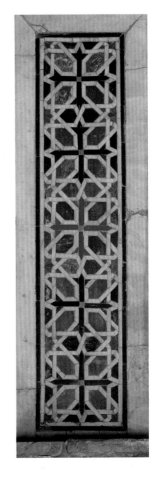

The entrance to the crypt is in the northern (left) side room of the altar. Visitors can be seen through the screen separating the main altar room and the side room as they look down the stairs to the crypt below.

RIGHT:
The crypt with the stairs leading up to the side room beside the haykal.

Directly below the central haykal is the crypt of the church, which is divided into three bays. Tradition says that the crypt was a resting place of the Holy Family on their journey through Egypt. Over the last decades throughout Old Cairo, the water table rose significantly, covering the crypt floor for years in several feet of water. In a drainage project and subsequent restoration, the earlier stone floor with Roman stonework is now covered with marble.

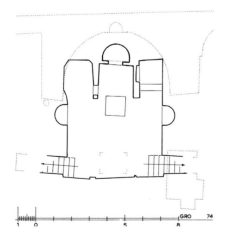

Crypt floor plan.
Courtesy Dr. Peter
Grossmann.

A cross carved into a niche.

The crypt just after the draining of ground water.

A nineteenth-century postcard, showing the interior of the crypt.

Icon of the Archangel Michael. He is viewed as the field commander of the Army of God. The scales in his left hand refer to his role in the Last Judgment where he will weigh the souls.

Icon of the Harrowing of Hell. Apocryphal sources tell that Christ descended into hell after his death. He conquered Satan and freed the souls of the Old Testament patriarchs, prophets, and forefathers.

Nineteenth-century icon of the Flight of the Holy Family to Egypt (Matthew 2:13). According to apocryphal sources, Salomé, cousin of the Virgin, accompanied the family.

The Chapel of the Patriarchs Abraham, Isaac, and Jacob and of the holy monk Bashnounah in the southern gallery. Human remains found during church renovations in 1991 were identified as the relics of St. Bashnuna. From the Anba Maqar Monastery in Wadi al-Natrun Natroun, he was murdered in Cairo during the patriarchate of John V (1147–67) because he refused to convert to Islam. He was buried in the Church of St. Sergius.

The wooden altar screen of the northern gallery chapel.

Wooden openwork screens partition the gallery (left) and serve as a barrier between gallery and nave (below). The gallery columns with Corinthian capitals are ancient spolia.

THE CHURCH OF ST. BARBARA

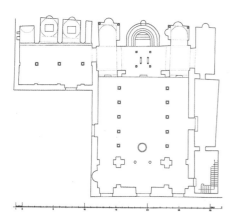

Plan of the Church of St. Barbara. In the upper left corner is the small Church of Sts. Cyrus and John. Courtesy Dr. Peter Grossmann.

OPPOSITE:
A modern image of St. Barbara on the façade of the church.

ATHANASIUS OF EDESSA, scribe (katib) to Amir 'Abd al-'Aziz ibn Marwan (685–705), traditionally founded a church in Old Cairo dedicated to St. Cyrus (Abu Qir/Apa Kir) and St. John, martyrs. From the seventh to the ninth century, their shrine at Menouthis (near Alexandria) had been famed as a center of healing and pilgrimage.[117] In the tenth century, their relics were transferred to Old Cairo, to the church dedicated to their memory. The historian Yahya ibn Sa'id (d. 1027) records the destruction of the Church of Sts. Cyrus and John by an angry mob in 960.[118]

A seventeenth-century manuscript relates the history of the building of the churches of St. Barbara and Sts. Sergius and Bacchus in the eleventh century: A Christian vizier had obtained the caliph's permission to build a church near his home. Instead, he built two churches—the most beautiful in the city: one dedicated to Sts. Sergius and Bacchus, the other to St. Barbara, who was the daughter of a nobleman who wanted to keep her in seclusion. St. Barbara lived in a tower with two windows. She had a third window added to honor the Holy Trinity. When her father discovered that she had become a Christian, he handed her over to the magistrate. She suffered martyrdom in the company of St. Juliana, who was tortured and killed because she had wept when she saw St. Barbara's sufferings. St. Barbara is commemorated on 8 Khihak/4 December.[119] The relics of St. Barbara originally rested in the Hanging Church.

Nobody dared to object, but when the caliph heard about two churches being built, he ordered that one of churches be demolished; he left to the vizier the agonizing choice of which church to destroy. Pacing between one and the other, the vizier could not bring himself to choose between his two churches. Then, halfway between the two, he collapsed and died. To honor his memory, the caliph decided to leave both churches unharmed, and the vizier was buried in the Church of St. Barbara.[120] This story explains the similar architecture of the two church buildings, which are often called 'twin churches' or 'sister churches.' They are both built on a basilican plan with a tripartite sanctuary and upper-floor galleries. In the story, the vizier's wife says that the church will be dedicated to St. Barbara and that her body will rest there.[121] Nevertheless, an actual transfer of St. Barbara's relics is not recorded.

It might be that this story brings together the restoration of the old church, ruined after the attack in 960, and the transfer of the relics. Both names can still be found in thirteenth–fifteenth century manuscripts: relics of Saint Barbara resting in the Church of Abu Qir.[122] Medieval Western pilgrims frequently mention the church[123] and it quickly became one of the important churches in the fortress.

The exterior of the church.

The interior of the church with pews and carpets. To the left is the marble ambon of similar design to that in the Hanging Church (end of thirteenth century).

OPPOSITE:
The interior of the church is shown without pews and carpet. The basin in the floor (laqqan) was used for the ceremony of foot washing on Maundy Thursday and on the Feast of St. Peter and St. Paul. The eighteenth-century icons above the altar screen depict Christ (center) with the Virgin and St. John the Baptist, archangels, and the four evangelists.

Over the centuries, the building was pillaged and closed, then rebuilt and restored. The eastern wall, and probably also the southern outer wall still belong to the original structure.[124] According to Alfred Butler (1884), "the church obviously has suffered a good deal, and is still undergoing a mischievous restoration." The priest had annexed the western part as a reception room, while the gallery served as part of the domestic quarters for his family. Butler noted several layers of wall painting on the southern gallery as well as a remarkable altar screen.[125] Apparently the murals contained dates corresponding to the first half of the twelfth century.[126] The paintings have since disappeared, but the eleventh-century altar screen is one of the major exhibits in the Coptic Museum.[127]

In 1912 Prince Johann Georg, Duke of Saxony, dryly noted that the church was an interesting building, although unfortunately roofless.[128] The Comité initiated a full-scale restoration, which was carried out between 1918 and 1922. The interior was cleared of the domestic arrangements; outside, the clutter of buildings adjoining the walls, which had served various functions, was removed. The structure was consolidated, old windows were reopened, and the former floor level was restored. Building phases of the eleventh and thirteenth century were identified, supporting a similar building history for the churches of St. Barbara and Sts. Sergius and Bacchus. While unblocking the original three entrances in the western wall, a unique set of richly sculpted wooden doors was found (fourth–fifth century) and immediately transported to the Coptic Museum.[129] The doors were adapted to the proportions of the entrance and had no doubt once been part of an older building, almost certainly situated outside the fortress, judging from the Christian themes carved on the doors. In 1927, Prince Johann Georg noted with pleasure that the church had been largely renovated, although it still lacked a roof.[130] The Comité continued making repairs until the early 1950s.[131]

The Church of St. Barbara is also rich in icons. The large eighteenth-century beam icon of the khurus screen, which once spanned the width of the nave, is now displayed in four parts on the south wall of the church. The icons above the altar screen also date to the eighteenth century. The most famous icon, however, is a magnificent thirteenth-century image of the Virgin enthroned holding her Son. Although the painter was Byzantine-trained, the sycamore wood panel was made locally. This icon is an example of 'crusader art,' reflecting Byzantine, Italian, and local influences.[132]

A small church at the northeastern end of the Church of St. Barbara is still dedicated to Sts. Cyrus and John. The present building is a modern addition that has replaced an older structure on the same spot.[133]

The Annunciation

The Nativity

The Presentation in the Temple

The Baptism of Christ

The Wedding at Cana

The Transfiguration

*The eighteenth-century beam icon
of sixteen feasts, originally placed
on top of the former khurus screen.*

The Raising of Lazarus

The Entry into Jerusalem

The Last Supper

The Crucifixion

The Descent from the Cross

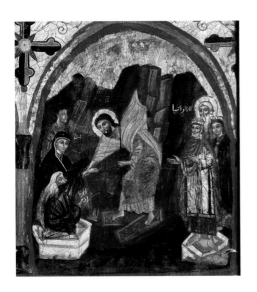

The Harrowing of Hell

Christ meeting one of the women in the garden ("Noli me tangere")

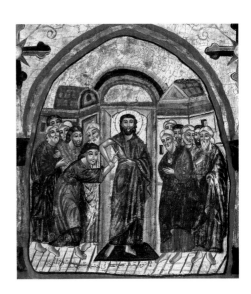

Doubting Thomas

The Ascension

Pentecost

119

ABOVE AND OPPOSITE:
The fourteenth–fifteenth century altar screen in front of the central haykal. *The geometric motifs are inlaid with ebony and small, delicately carved ivory or bone panels. Behind the altar is the* synthronon, *decorated with marble panels.*

Details of the door frame of the central altar screen inlaid in ivory. Above, exquisite renderings of the Virgin Mary with Child and, at right, angels and flowers.

The northeastern part of the interior, with the marble ambon (end of thirteenth century). At the beginning of the twentieth century, it was reassembled and restored to its former position; fortunately, although it had been taken apart, all its elements were still present.[134] At the back (northern side aisle) is the thirteenth-century icon of the enthroned Virgin and Child.

The thirteenth-century icon of the
Virgin Mary and Child is one of the
greatest treasures of the church.

The former northern side-room, now a shrine with several reliquaries of martyrs and saints. To the left of this room is the small Church of Sts. Cyrus and John.

OPPOSITE:
The Church of Sts. Cyrus and John.

THE COPTIC ORTHODOX CHURCH OF ST. GEORGE (Mari Girgis) AND THE WEDDING HALL (Qa'at al-'Irsan)

Entrance to the Coptic Orthodox Church of St. George.

THE CHURCH OF ST. GEORGE was possibly built in the late seventh century by Athanasius, scribe *(katib)* to 'Abd al-'Aziz ibn Marwan, whose name is also connected with the churches of Abu Sarga and Sts. Cyrus and John (now the church of St. Barbara).[135] Ibn Duqmaq and al-Maqrizi (fourteenth to fifteenth century) both mention a church dedicated to St. George, but neither the appearance of this church building nor its subsequent history is known.

The equestrian St. George is one of the best-loved saints in Egypt. The stories of his life and passions are numerous. According to the Coptic tradition, St. George was a native of Cappadocia. He served as an officer and suffered martyrdom no fewer than three times: after grueling tortures and death, he was brought to life again by an archangel. Each time this happened, many people were converted and subsequently martyred. Eventually he was awarded the crown of martyrdom. In Egypt his cult has been attested to since the eighth century; the Coptic Synaxarion commemorates him on 23 Barmuda / 18 April.[136]

In the middle of the nineteenth century, the Church of St. George burned down. Afterward, a new church was built on a cross-in-square plan, covered by domes. It had been assumed that nothing of the earlier structure survived, but during the rebuilding of the nineteenth-century church carried out over the past ten years, the Old Cairo Archaeological Monitoring Project discovered that the eastern end, the altar rooms, must have survived the fire. The oldest brick structure probably dates to the tenth or eleventh century and incorporates Roman remains.[137] This ancient part is now integrated into the new church, although it is indistinguishable from the new construction.[138]

In the late nineteenth century, the church could only be reached by crossing a large hall, according to Alfred Butler "a magnificent piece of work" which retained "tracery and carvings of great beauty" but at that time "a neglected ruin."[139] This so-called Wedding Hall (Qa'at al-'Irsan) is a remnant of a thirteenth- to fourteenth-century Mamluk palace or mansion. The name derives from the wedding ceremonies that used to take place there. The large hall *(qa'a)* consisted of a central hall *(durqa'a)* with a reception area *(iwan)* to its north and south. Small, vaulted utility rooms and a first-floor gallery opening onto the hall, with screened compartments for women and minstrels' galleries, once ran along the eastern and western sides.[140] It is not known when this hall was incorporated into the ecclesiastical complex of St. George and given over to weddings.

The Comite was interested exclusively in the hall. Plans and elevations were made and restorations were carried out in the first half of the twentieth century.[141] The present entrances (north and south) are not part of the original design. Presumably, the entrance used to be at the northern end. Inside, the rich stucco decoration of the southern *iwan* is remarkable. The stucco and the painted decoration of the ceiling most likely date from the fourteenth century, while the other paintings (naturalistic floral motifs) adorning the woodwork of the hall date from a much later period.[142]

Outside, on the street, a gate to the right of the hall and an adjoining utility building gives access to the church premises, which also contain a pretty tea garden. Adjacent to the church is the tomb of the brothers Ibrahim and Girgis al-Guhari, prominent eighteenth-century Coptic notables who initiated and financed the restoration of churches and monasteries all over Egypt.[143]

127

According to the Vision of Isaiah (6:2–4) seraphim have six wings. These heavenly beings grace each corner of the ciborium.

LEFT:
The central altar. At the back, mosaics of the twenty-four elders of the Apocalypse.

Interior view of the Coptic Orthodox Church of St. George, looking northeast.

The interior of the ciborium, with Christ enthroned surrounded by angels, seraphim, and cherubim (third quarter nineteenth century). Cherubim and seraphim, angelic beings with four or six wings, are part of the heavenly host around the throne of God (for example in Isaiah 6:2–4 and Ezekiel 11:22). They also figure in Coptic literature, where they accompany Christ when he is present during the celebration of Holy Liturgy. While taking photographs for this volume, photographer Sherif Sonbol discovered this old ciborium hidden in a newer structure.

Detail of the heavenly host: angels and a cherub.

The domes of the three altar rooms of the Coptic Orthodox Church of St. George.

THE WEDDING HALL
(Qa'at al-Irsan)

Directly across from the main doors of the Coptic Orthodox Church of St. George is the unassuming entrance of the Wedding Hall, which opens surprisingly into a richly decorated central hall.

RIGHT:
The southern iwan (central hall), decorated with stucco and painted geometrical and floral motifs. The ceiling decoration and the stucco probably date to the fourteenth century.

132

The upper-level gallery with the open-work screens which give a private view of the central hall.

OPPOSITE:
The west wall with stairway to the gallery and the doorway leading to the street. The open-work screens allow observers to be present without being seen.

THE TOMB OF IBRAHIM AND GIRGIS AL-GUHARI

Carolyn Ludwig

THE TOMB OF IBRAHIM AND GIRGIS AL-GUHARI, recently renovated by the Supreme Council of Antiquities under the direction of Dr. Zahi Hawass, is adjacent to the Coptic Church of St. George in Old Cairo. Ibrahim al-Guhari (d. 1795) is one of the most significant Coptic personalities in Coptic history. He was born to a poor family; his father was a cotton weaver. As a child, Ibrahim excelled in writing and arithmetic and studied the Bible, acquiring the lasting qualities of love, peace, and justice. Later, as a young adult, he transcribed religious books and donated them to churches at his own expense. After coming to the attention of Pope John XVIII, Ibrahim was appointed as head scribe of Mo'alem Rizk, another prominent Copt of the time.

Mamluk Ibrahim Bey, who did not care what a person's religious affiliation was, as long as they had the ability to do the job with confidence, appointed Ibrahim chief scribe of Egypt, a position that was the equivalent of finance minister. Using his financial and political influence in the Egyptian state, he succeeded in restoring many monasteries and churches. Building new churches was important because Copts were not allowed to repair old churches or build new ones without official government approval, which was rarely granted. Ibrahim, through his position, was able to obtain the permission needed. As documented in the Coptic Orthodox Patriarchate, Ibrahim al-Guhari was a great benefactor to the Coptic Church, giving both money and land for construction.

Girgis al-Guhari (d. 1810), Ibrahim's brother, also an influential Coptic official, was appointed dean of Copts and, following in his brother's footsteps, served as director of the Egyptian administration of taxes and finances under both Napoleon Bonaparte and Muhammad 'Ali. Girgis, who was witness to the birth of modern Egypt, served the Coptic Church and continued the mission of his brother Ibrahim. Without the al-Guhari brothers, it is possible that the churches of Old Cairo as we know them would not exist.

The superstructure of the tomb is roofed over with decorative timbering and contains a beautiful *mashrabiya*. The attractive lectern is adorned with geometric designs. There is a tombstone beneath the *mashrabiya*, decorated on the top with a Coptic cross and inscribed below with the names of Ibrahim and Girgis al-Guhari and the dates of their deaths. The inscription, in Coptic and Arabic, reads: "The righteous shall be in everlasting remembrance."

Portrait of Girgis al-Guhari by Michele Rigo. This is one of six paintings executed during the Egyptian expedition of Napoleon. It is now at Rueil-Malmaison, Musée National des Chateaux de Malmaison et de Bois Préau in France.

Tomb of Girgis and Ibrahim al-Guhari. Steps lead to the chapel behind the mashrabiya above the tombs.

Light filters through the mashrabiya into the interior of the small chapel over the tombs of Girgis and Ibrahim al-Guhari.

137

THE CHURCH OF THE VIRGIN OF THE POT OF BASIL

(Qasriyat al-Rihan)

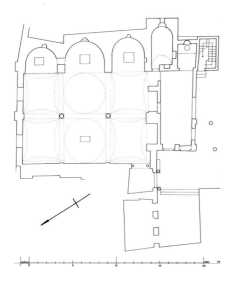

Plan of the Church of the Virgin. To the right of the church runs the long gallery leading to the baptistery. Courtesy Dr. Peter Grossmann.

The old bell tower.

THERE IS STILL NO CONVINCING EXPLANATION of the name 'Pot of Basil.' Possibly the epithet dates to the time when the church was Greek Orthodox (eleventh century): basil is used in the Greek Orthodox Church in the Blessing of Water, and so pots of basil for this purpose might have been cultivated here.[144] It has also been suggested that 'pot of basil' is a metaphor for the Virgin.[145]

According to the *History of the Patriarchs*, this church "of the Lady, the Mistress" served as a temporary residence of Patriarch Michael III (880–907).[146] It is certainly one of the oldest church foundations in Cairo: the original floor level was, like those of the churches of Sts. Sergius and Bacchus (*Abu Sarga*) and St. Barbara, a few meters below the present one. Little is known about the history of the building. Father Vansleb visited it in 1672, but says no more than that it was a small, dark church.[147] It was completely burned down on 15 October 1777, after which it was rebuilt and refurbished at the expense of the administrator of the church, Mu'allim Salib 'Abd al-Masih. Yuhanna al-Armani painted at least twenty-one icons for the new church.[148]

The rebuilt church was almost square—a centralized type with domed bays and three *haykal*s with semi-domes. Each haykal had a square altar; the altar of the central haykal was placed under a ciborium. The dome in front of the central *haykal* rested on *muqarnas* squinches. In his description of the church interior, Raouf Habib noted the numerous icons and the wall paintings of the central altar room and described the eighteenth-century altar screens.[149] Ancient columns flanked the church entrances. To the right of the main entrance was a doorway to a gallery that ran the whole length of the southern side of the building and ended in a baptistery, in line with the *haykal*s, at the eastern end. The doorframe was extensively decorated with geometrically patterned sculptures, similar to the decorated entrances in eighteenth-century domestic architecture.

The Comite registered the wooden altar screens of the church in the 1897 list and noted that the dome construction was unusual for the churches within the fortress. Its bad state of repair required the restoration and consolidation of the structure. The low situation of the church combined with the humidity of the soil required constant monitoring. Minor repairs and problems with groundwater were recorded until the early 1950s.[150]

A devastating fire completely destroyed the eighteenth-century building in March 1979. Fortunately, some of its treasures, among them a fifteenth-century silver gospel casket, were already part of the collection of the Coptic Museum.[151] The ruins were cleared in 2000 to make way for the construction of a new church—still not completed—built according to the eighteenth-century plan.[152] The old entrance to the church premises, with its beautiful *mashrabiya* window and elegant bell tower, a well-known landmark of Old Cairo, was recently demolished.

OPPOSITE:
A new church following the eighteenth-century outline and design is being built on the site of the burned original.

ABOVE AND LEFT:
Domes of the new church. All domes are built along the old designs. The bridging element between the square space and the round dome, the squinch, has various designs.

After the fire of 1979, only this small piece of a haykal *screen curtain, embroidered with a picture of the Virgin Mary and Child, was saved.*

Standing saints painted on wooden panels
and fixed to the curved wall of the central
haykal (destroyed in the fire of 1979).
Photograph courtesy of Mr. Ramsy Nagib.

OPPOSITE:
The interior of the Church of the Virgin of the
Pot of Basil before the fire 1979. The altar
screens date from the eighteenth-century
rebuilding of the church. Photograph
courtesy of Mr. Ramsy Nagib.

The courtyard of the Qasriyat al-Rihan complex. To the left is the new church under construction; at the far right is the entrance to the wooden Church of the Virgin.

FOLLOWING PAGES:
The interior of the wooden church dedicated to the Virgin of the Pot of Basil.

THE CONVENT OF ST. GEORGE
(Mari Girgis)

THE CONVENT OF ST. GEORGE is located in the northwestern part of the Fortress of Babylon and is centered around a high, lofty hall, a *qa'a*, which was once part of a palace or mansion. The southwestern reception area (*iwan*) of the *qa'a* is used as the Chapel of St. George, where chains in which he is said to have been held captive are preserved. According to tradition, the chains are imbued with healing power because they were once drenched in the martyr's blood.[153] The chapel has magnificent wooden doors about seven meters high with intricately sculpted panels, dating to the eleventh century.[154]

There is no consensus regarding the building date: the hall might date to the time of the doors; the ground plan corresponds to the early Fatimid *qa'a* designs (ninth to eleventh century). Decorative motifs on part of the ceiling point to the Mamluk period; they could be part of a later restoration. A second possibility is the rebuilding of the hall along the original plan in the thirteenth or fourteenth century (the date of the ceiling), when Fustat was rebuilt and repopulated after the destruction caused by the fire of 1168. In such a situation, the high doors could be reused building elements.[155] Recent archaeological research by the Old Cairo Archaeological Monitoring Project has revealed the ground plan of a large domestic building, built in brick and dating to the ninth or tenth century, beneath the present hall. This building had a different layout and was demolished so that the present building could be constructed.[156]

Regardless of the original foundation, it is clear that as long as the *qa'a* was part of a domestic structure, there could never have been a convent here; the Mamluk ceiling decoration indicates a secular use until at least the fourteenth century. Historical sources only mention the Convent of St. George quite late: the Dominican Father Jean Michel Vansleb was the first to record a visit to the Convent of the Daughters (*Dayr al-Banat*) in 1672.[157] He does not say anything about the location or the layout of the convent, and there is some doubt about whether the *qa'a* was already in use as a chapel.

Alfred Butler does not make any reference to the convent, but Father Jullien mentions the hall with the relics of St. George in 1887. The hall was not used for services; the mother superior told Father Jullien that the nuns attended mass in their chapel, but there is no explanation of where this chapel was located.[158] Sheehan suggests that, before its mid-nineteenth-century destruction by fire, the Coptic Church of St. George might have served as the convent church.[159] So far, I have not found any corroboration for this idea.[160]

The *qa'a* was a main focus of interest of the Comite de conservation des monuments de l'art arabe. In 1900, the plans and report testify to cells for the nuns on either side of the hall on a *mi-etage* (half-story) especially constructed for this purpose and provided with a gallery and staircases.[161] From 1900 to 1907, the hall, chapel, and doors were cleaned and restored; structural accretions from later periods were removed.[162] Around that time, the old convent buildings were demolished; new domestic and administrative buildings and the Old Church of St. George were erected on either side of the hall. The present arched entrance corridor to the *qa'a* also dates to this period.[163] The latest restoration of the hall, part of the USAID-funded project to lower the groundwater level, has not yet been completed.

At present, the convent has three churches. Apart from the Old Church, there is a new Church of St. George, and there is a Church of the Virgin. The Old Church contains a well, in fact a cistern, which probably goes back to the Fatimid building phase.[164] The water of St. George's well is said to have miraculous power.

The most recent collection of buildings (1980s) has been erected around a garden. The nuns run an atelier for making stained-glass windows (established in 1990).[165] They attend to the numerous visitors and pilgrims, of all denominations, seeking spiritual guidance, blessing, and healing from the miracle-working chains of St. George.

The Chapel of St. George. A nun holds "the chains of the saint," which are believed to heal and to exorcise evil spirits. The eleventh-century wooden folding doors at the right are about seven meters high.

The Chapel of St. George in the southwestern part of the ancient qa'a.

The corridor giving entrance to the qa'a, which contains the Chapel of St. George. The mosaic of St. George battling the dragon at the back was put in place in 1988.

THE GREEK ORTHODOX CHURCH OF ST. GEORGE (*Mari Girgis*) AND THE SLEEPING MARY GREEK ORTHODOX CHURCH

(Church of the Dormition of the Virgin Mary)

Small embossed silver icon of St. George depicted slaying a dragon. (Captions on pages 154–77 are by Carolyn Ludwig and Morris Jackson.)

AT THE BEGINNING OF THE NINETEENTH CENTURY, Edmé François Jomard wrote that the Church of St. George, built on a mound of the same name, could be seen from afar.[166] The mountain is the northern tower of the Fortress of Babylon; the church still towers above street level, although the view is now obstructed by residential quarters.

Fifteenth-century historians and travelers are our earliest source for a Greek Orthodox church and nuns' convent built on and around the tower, which contained a Nilometer.[167] It seems that in the early fifteenth century, the church passed temporarily into the hands of the Copts.[168] Various seventeenth-century travelers visited the church and convent.[169] Father Vansleb saw both the convent and church in 1672 and recorded a holy image of the saint that was claimed to cure people suffering from mental disorders.[170] Other travelers speak of a relic: the arm of St. George.[171] Old traditions relate this spot directly to the saint: he was said to have been kept prisoner and martyred here. The founding of a church dedicated to his memory, which might have existed at the time of the Arab invasion in the seventh century, is attributed to soldiers.[172] Through the centuries, the complex housed not only a convent but also a school, a hospital, a home for elderly people, a hospice, and an orphanage. It also served as a place of refuge for the persecuted.[173]

The Reverend Greville Chester (1872) noted a "large and richly decorated Church of St. George, of which the walls are partly lined with superb Arabian and Persian or Rhodian tiles."[174] Alfred Butler says that the church was plundered by a rampaging mob in 1882. He was very interested in the construction of the Roman tower, of which he gives a detailed description.[175] In 1887 Father Jullien mentioned nothing about the plundering, but did note that the church was almost hidden between the adjacent buildings, which housed the priest and his family. Until the eighteenth century, there had been a convent of nuns near the church, but a new building on that spot now housed a hostelry or hotel. The arm of St. George, a relic imbued with the powers of healing, especially for people afflicted by mental problems, was kept in the church. The patient was chained to the wall in front of it for a period of twenty-four hours. He or she was provided with a wooden seat and some bread and water. After twenty-four hours, the patient was declared cured.[176] Father Jullien had no faith in the method: he was certain that the enormous chain and collar did not inspire fond devotion!

According to Somers Clarke's 1896 report, the church had by then been thoroughly "done up," and around the church, buildings were renewed or added.[177] Unfortunately, there are hardly any plans or descriptions of the building.[178] A destructive fire on 4 August 1904 left the building a smoldering ruin, from which the icon and the relics of St. George were miraculously saved. Before the church was rebuilt, the Roman tower was carefully repaired according to the exacting standards of the Comité.[179]

In 1909 Patriarch Photius I consecrated the new church, designed by Fabricius, architect of the khedivial palaces. The circular ground plan seems to have been the patriarch's personal idea.[180] The church was built on a concrete platform, constructed on top of the tower, supported by a colonnade. In the early 1940s, these columns were replaced by walls. The ground plan of the church on the platform reveals a double circle: the exterior walls and the interior colonnade, which supports the dome.[181] A staircase connects the church with chapels on the floor below. A bell tower stands at the northwestern corner.

The 1940s were also a time of excavation and renovations. The hostelry/hotel was demolished, and north of the church a new building was erected to serve ecclesiastical and monastic functions.[182] To the northeast lies a cemetery (mentioned in historical sources since the sixteenth century) enclosing the Sleeping Mary Greek Orthodox Church, or the Church of the Dormition of the Virgin Mary. It contains an underground room where the Holy Family is said to have rested, with a well containing holy water.[183]

The impressive entrance to the Church of St. George. A large relief of St. George battling with the dragon is placed at the top of the stairs.

FOLLOWING PAGES:

The Greek Orthodox Church of St. George iconostasis with icons of Christ and the Holy Virgin.

Under Constantine the Great (d. 337), the Edict of Milan (313) granted freedom of religion to Christians. Christianity became the state religion at the end of the fourth century, under Emperor Theodosius I. Constantine launched a large building programme in the Holy Land, founding churches in holy places. His mother Helena (d. 330) devoted herself to good works, and, according to legend, found the Holy Cross on which Christ was crucified as well as the three nails.

Icon of, from left to right, St. Therapion, St. Sozon, and St. Panteleimon. St. Panteleimon was educated as a physician, and he dedicated his life to the suffering, the sick, the unfortunate, and the needy.

Η ΑΓΙΑ ΜΑΤΡΩΝΑ.

1930

Ἐν Χίω, Σκήτη Ἁγ. Μάρκου

Icon of St. Matrona of Chios. She is an
excellent example of a devoted Christian
who tried in every sense of the word to be
closer to her Lord, and guide and help her
fellow man. She continues to perform
many miracles for the worthy faithful.

Icon of Photios I of Constantinople. Photios (c. 810 – c. 893) was
a well-educated man from a noble family. He is regarded as one of
the important intellectuals of his time and the most powerful and
influential Patriarch of Constantinople after John Chrysostom.
He played an important role in both the conversion of the Slavs to
Christianity and the estrangement of the Eastern Orthodox
Church from the Roman Catholic Church.

FOLLOWING PAGES:
Chapel directly beneath the sanctuary. The iconostasis shows the
Virgin Mary to the left of the altar, Christ to the right of the altar,
and John the Baptist to the right of Christ. In the foreground is
the bishop's chair.

Views of the undercroft beneath the main staircase of the church (left) leading to the balcony (above) overlooking the archaeological remains of the Roman barracks. Note the 'Owl of Athena' motif used in the decoration of the large column capital (all 1940s construction).

163

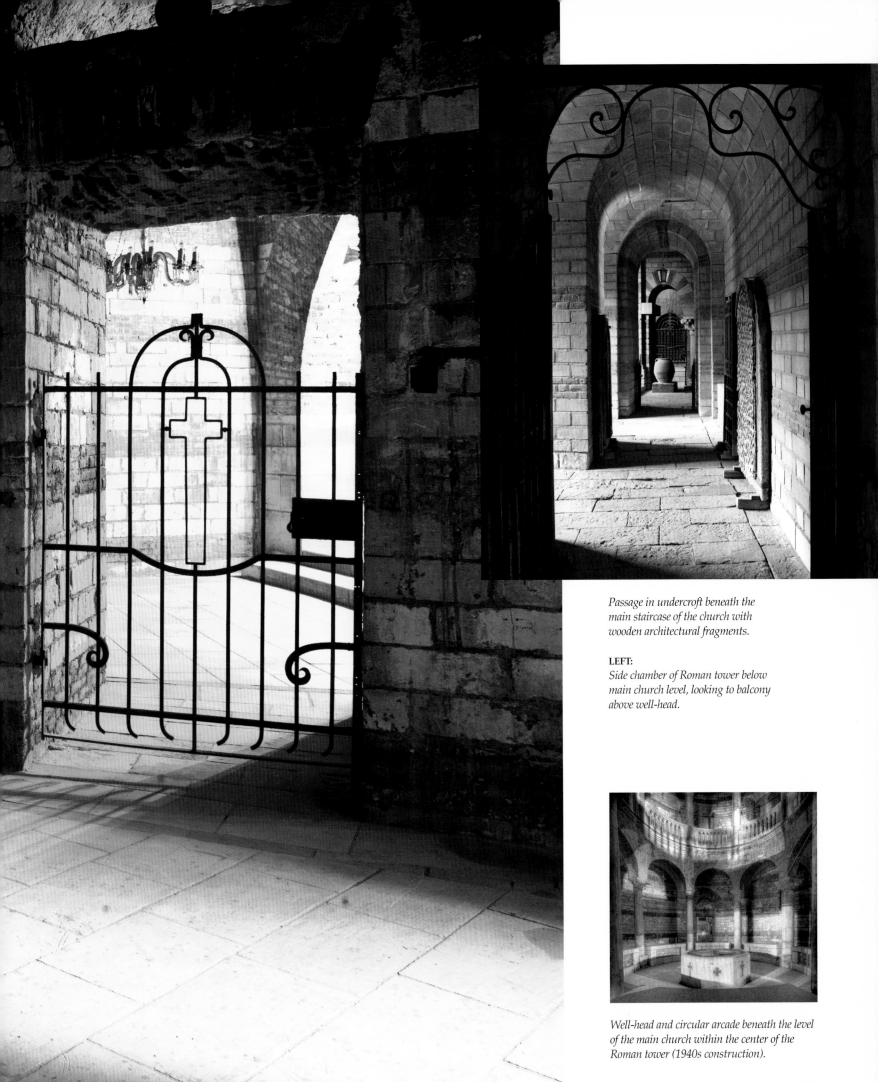

Passage in undercroft beneath the
main staircase of the church with
wooden architectural fragments.

LEFT:
Side chamber of Roman tower below
main church level, looking to balcony
above well-head.

Well-head and circular arcade beneath the level
of the main church within the center of the
Roman tower (1940s construction).

165

ABOVE:
Corridor leading to the prison cell where it is believed that St. George was held.

RIGHT:
The Chapel of St. George just outside the entrance to his prison.

Icon of St. Theodore (19th century)

RIGHT:
Side chamber of Roman tower at the level of the well-head beneath the main church, with re-used wooden door frame.

View of the Greek Orthodox Church of St. George from the passageway leaving the Greek Orthodox cemetery.

North of the Church of St. George, tombs and monuments in the Greek Orthodox cemetery line the path to the Sleeping Mary Greek Orthodox Church.

171

Contemporary crypts and tombs in the Greek Orthodox Church cemetery.

OPPOSITE:
Adorning the front of the Sleeping Mary Greek Orthodox Church are four Orthodox-style crosses. The church itself is surrounded by the Greek Orthodox Church cemetery.

Interior of the Sleeping Mary Greek Orthodox Church or the Church of the Dormition of the Virgin Mary. Through the iconostasis one has a glimpse of an icon of the Holy Family entering Egypt. The doorway on the left leads to the well and the Holy Family cave below.

Cave with shrine where it is
believed the Holy Family
stayed while on their journey
back to Jerusalem.

OPPOSITE:

Well believed to be a source of
miraculous or healing water.
Tradition says that when the
Virgin Mary was thirsty,
Jesus would raise a well in
the name of his Mother,
saying that "whosoever shall
believe and partake of this
water will be healed."

Icon of the Dormition of
Mary. Christ, watched by
two angels, receives the soul
of his mother which is
depicted as a small figure,
in his arms.

THE MONASTERY OF ST. MERCURIUS

(Dayr Abu Sayfayn)

The alley with, immediately to the right, the façade of the Church of St. Shenute and, farther along, the Church of St. Mercurius.

NORTHWEST OF THE FORTRESS OF BABYLON stands a cluster of three churches and a convent which is known as the Monastery of St. Mercurius (*Dayr Abu Sayfayn*). Away from the busy tourist area, situated in a street opposite the Mosque of 'Amr ibn al-'As, these churches are a well-kept secret. The once impressive walls are now partly hidden below the present street level. Visitors enter a gate on the right-hand side of the street and go down a flight of steps to a narrow alley. On their right are two churches, the Church of St. Shenute (*Anba Shenuda*) and the Church of St. Mercurius (*Abu Sayfayn*). It is necessary to descend yet another flight of stairs to enter these churches. To the left of the alley, a street leads to the Church of the Virgin 'al-Damshiriya.' Continuing along this street, one reaches the new nuns' convent of St. Mercurius, formerly situated near the Church of St. Mercurius.

Abu Sayfayn (*St. Mercurius*), 'Father with the Two Swords,' was a commander in the army of the Emperor Decius (249–51). On the eve of an important battle an angel gave him the second sword from which his name derives, and the next day he destroyed the enemy. Despite his victory, when he refused to sacrifice to pagan gods, he was tortured and beheaded. In answer to the prayers of St. Basil of Caesarea (d. 379), he miraculously appeared on the battlefield to slay Emperor Julian the Apostate (d. 363). He is one of the most beloved military saints in Egypt, and he is usually depicted on horseback in the act of killing the emperor. He is commemorated on 25 Hathor/21 November.[184]

In the tenth century, the Church of St. Mercurius was still situated on the bank of the Nile. Since then, the river has gradually receded.[185] Historical sources mention the building of a wall, probably around the complete set of buildings, at the end of the twelfth century.[186] In the eleventh century, the patriarchal see was transferred from Alexandria to Old Cairo, to the Church of St. Mercurius. Although it was moved again in 1300, nearly all the seventeenth- and eighteenth-century patriarchs are buried here.[187] Father Vansleb visited the Monastery of St. Mercurius in 1664. He calls the alley along the churches "the Street of the Patriarch" and adds that, according to his information, the patriarch lived here.[188] In his second book, he calls the monastery "the Quarter of the Patriarch," "a suburb of itself." It is enclosed by a high wall.[189]

Nineteenth-century woodcuts of the area show an imposing complex surrounded by high walls in fairly empty countryside.[190] Father Jullien wrote that the entrance was concealed. There were three churches, a nuns' convent, apartments for priests, charity dwellings for the poor, and a cemetery whose use had been forbidden since the cholera epidemic of 1883.[191] Standing on the roof of the Church of St. Shenute, Alfred Butler described the view as "exceedingly fine; to the east one sees long ranges of low rubbish hills backed by the white Mukattam mountains which trend away toward the lofty mosque and minarets of the citadel of Cairo: to the west one looks across what seems a forest of tamarisks and palms, between which now and then tall white sails are moving, while boats and river alike unseen: and beyond the Nile rise the Pyramids of Gizah in that distant blue aerial mist of excessive brightness, which is the charm of an Egyptian landscape."[192]

To the left, the entrance gate to the Monastery of St. Mercurius topped by a small dome. To the right, behind a residential building, the Church of St. Shenute.

THE CHURCH OF ST. MERCURIUS

(Abu Sayfayn)

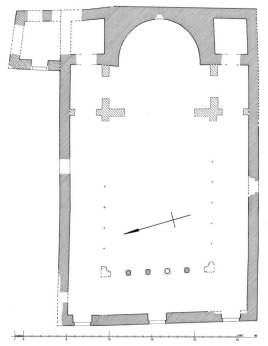

Plan showing the Church of Saint Mercurius before the rebuilding of Patriarch Abraham (d. 978). The basic outline is still extant in the present building. Courtesy Dr. Peter Grossmann.

The interior of the main haykal. At the back is the marble synthronon. Wooden panels fixed to the walls are painted with the twelve apostles (Anastasi al-Rumi, nineteenth century), with Christ enthroned (Ibrahim al-Nasikh, eighteenth century) in the center. The mural painting at the top, Christ borne up by two angels, is also by Anastasi al-Rumi.

THE CHURCH OF ST. MERCURIUS is the largest church in the monastery complex. It was probably built in the sixth century, which makes it the oldest church in the area of Old Cairo. At that time, the Fortress of Babylon still retained its military function. The church was originally built as a basilica, with a return aisle, a large apse, side chambers, and possibly galleries. A *khurus* was built at a later date (see plan). By the tenth century the church had become dilapidated, and it is said that "nothing was left to mark it except the walls, which were also in a state of decay; and it had been turned into a storehouse for sugarcanes."[193]

Patriarch Abraham (d. 978) received permission to rebuild the church after showing the caliph that faith can literally move a mountain (for the miracle of Muqattam Mountain, see "The Hanging Church" (*al-Mu'allaqa*). When Patriarch Abraham restored the church, pillars replaced the columns of the nave, and galleries were rebuilt or added. During the riots and fire in Fustat in 1168, the church was pillaged and largely burned down. The restoration started shortly afterward, and the church was solemnly reopened in 1175. At this stage were built the dome above the present *haykal* and the half-domes in the nave. The half-domes reduced the width of nave and thereby also the width of the wooden roof. Abu al-Makarim reported that private donors from wealthy Coptic families donated money for the construction and furnishings of the church. Three chapels to the north of the main building, accessible via a small courtyard, were also rebuilt at that time.[194] The gallery chapels still preserve wall paintings from these phases of restoration.[195]

A small crypt in the north aisle is dedicated to St. Barsuma the Naked. After the death of his parents, an uncle claimed his inheritance. Barsuma did not protest but went to live in a crypt in the Church of St. Mercurius, with only a dangerous serpent for company. He was arrested by the authorities (it was forbidden to live in churches) and sent to a monastery near Helwan, where he died in 1317. He is commemorated on 5 Nasi/28 August.

There are few historical sources for the early period of this church. According to al-Maqrizi, the historian al-Kindi (d. 961) mentioned a church dedicated to the martyr Mercurius; Patriarch Abraham's story is recorded in *History of the Patriarchs*.[196] The church has, however, played an important role in the history of the Egyptian church. According to Abu al-Makarim, it was the episcopal church of the city until Christodoulos (1047–77) definitively moved the patriarchate from Alexandria to Old Cairo.[197] From the eleventh century until about 1300, the patriarchs resided alternately, sometimes even simultaneously, in the Hanging Church and the Church of St. Mercurius.[198] Patriarchs were consecrated, synods convened, and once, in 1299, it was

The ciborium of the main altar room, painted by Yuhanna al-Armani (eighteenth century). In the domed structure, Christ is surrounded by the sun, the moon, and the Four Living Creatures. The composition is borne by angels. The exterior is painted with scenes from the Old Testament. Visible are the Purification of Isaiah's Lips (Is. 6:1–7) and the Sacrifice by Abraham (Gen. 22:1–19).

The marble tank formerly used for the service of the Blessing of the Waters on the Feast of the Epiphany.

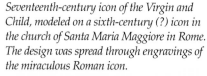

Seventeenth-century icon of the Virgin and Child, modeled on a sixth-century (?) icon in the church of Santa Maria Maggiore in Rome. The design was spread through engravings of the miraculous Roman icon.

the venue for the preparation of the chrism—sacramental oil used for anointing (at that time, this ceremony normally took place in the Monastery of St. Macarius in the Wadi al-Natrun).[199] Two thirteenth-century patriarchs and almost all the seventeenth- and eighteenth-century patriarchs are buried here.[200] A mundane aspect in the history of the church was its use to house Frankish prisoners who were working on the construction of the citadel of Roda Island (1239–44).[201]

During his second visit to Egypt from 1672 to 1673, Father Vansleb witnessed the ceremony of the Blessing of the Waters on the Feast of the Epiphany, which took place around the tank in the western end of the church; this part of the church must have been partitioned off when Vansleb was there, because he describes "a Chamber near the Church."[202]

The church was renovated in the mid-eighteenth century. New icons were commissioned, and the older icons and woodwork in the church were restored. Manuscripts were also restored and copied. This work was carried out by Yuhanna al-Armani and Ibrahim al-Nasikh. This church also houses almost one hundred icons by these artists, representing all phases of their careers.[203]

The Comité examined the church in 1897. A plan was drawn up to repair the fabric of the building by removing walls that had been built in later, stripping layers of plaster, and cleaning the woodwork. With some interruptions, these restorations were completed in 1909.[204] A second restoration was carried out in the 1930s and 1940s.[205] The Church of St. Mercurius served as the church of the nuns' convent in the monastery complex until 1962. A number of the icons in the valuable icon collection (dating from the thirteenth century until the present) were restored between 1991 and 1996.[206] The most recent renovations, including extensive renewal of brick pillars and the interior gallery walls, have not yet been completed.

Icon of St. Mercurius with scenes from his life. This large icon was painted by a Byzantine-trained master, probably in the thirteenth century. The central part, the portrait of the saint on horseback slaying Julian the Apostate, was repainted by an unknown artist around 1700.

Three nineteenth-century icons, painted by Anastasi al-Rumi, set in an ornate contemporary reliquary. In the center, St. Dimiana and her forty virgins are depicted. Pious believers have put notes with petitions, prayers or expressions of gratitude in the lower left corner (see detail).

Icon of St. Mercurius with the two swords, by Yuhanna al-Armani (1772). It is still in its original setting, a reliquary.

Icon of the physician saints Cosmas and Damian with their mother Theodota and their brothers Anthimus, Leontius, and Euprepius, by Ibrahim al-Nasikh. The family suffered martyrdom during the persecution of Emperor Diocletian.

OPPOSITE:
The entrance to the crypt dedicated to St. Barsuma the Naked.

Detail of the former khurus *screen:*
two holy monks.

Standing saints. Detail of the former khurus *screen*
of the Chapel of St. George.

ABOVE: *in the lintel above the doorway of the former* haykal *screen, two sphinxes are depicted.* **BELOW:** *details of both*
screens: crosses, antelopes, birds and foliage.

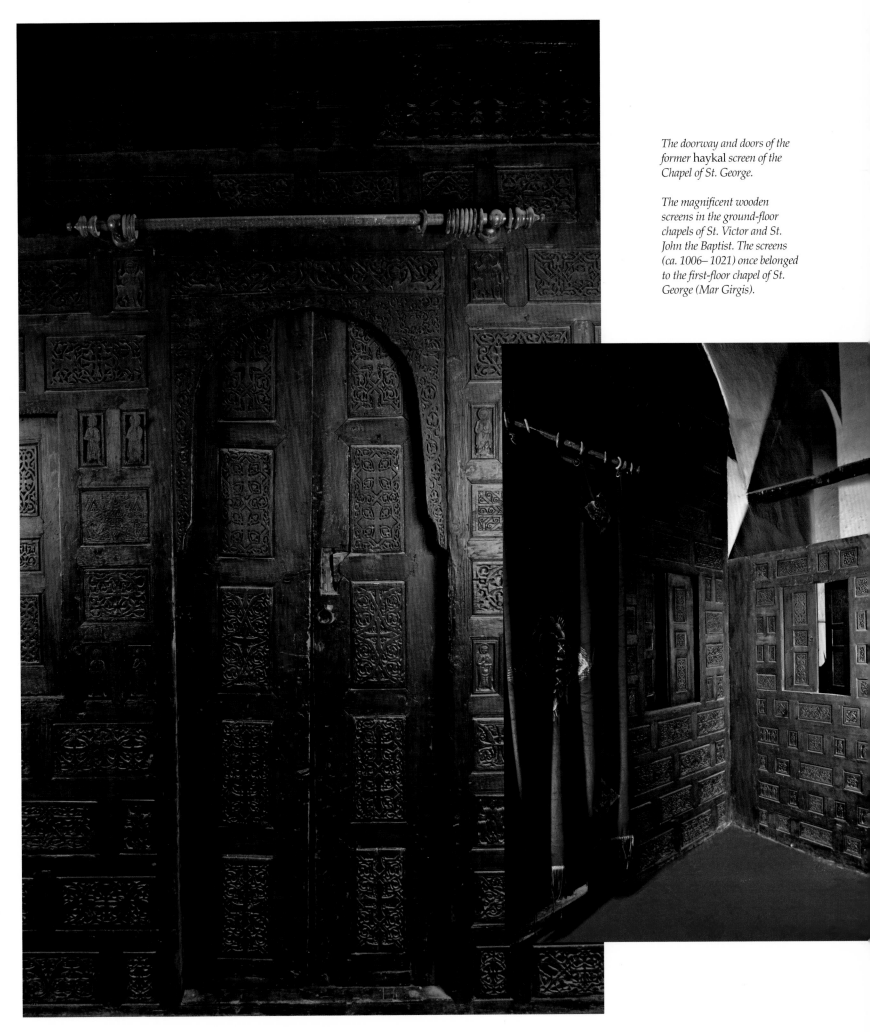

The doorway and doors of the former haykal screen of the Chapel of St. George.

The magnificent wooden screens in the ground-floor chapels of St. Victor and St. John the Baptist. The screens (ca. 1006–1021) once belonged to the first-floor chapel of St. George (Mar Girgis).

The Chapel of Mar Girgis on the first floor. Christ enthroned with the Virgin and two archangels below (probably 1168–75).

In the northern niche in the east wall (probably 1168–75), a painting of the Transfiguration (Matthew 17:1–8; Mark 9:2–9; Luke 9:28–36).

The Chapel of the Virgin (al-'Adra) on the first floor. There are three niches in the eastern wall, containing paintings. They probably date to the restoration after the fire of 1168. The central niche shows a double composition of Christ enthroned and the Ascension.

The Chapel of al-'Adra on the first floor.

In the southern niche in the east wall, a painting of the Presentation in the Temple: the aged Simeon holding the Christ Child (Luke 2:22–39).

View of the screen shielding the central haykal. *All icons belong to the eighteenth-century refurbishing of the church by Yuhanna al-Armani and Ibrahim al-Nasikh.*

THE CHURCH OF ST. SHENUTE
(*Anba Shenuda*)

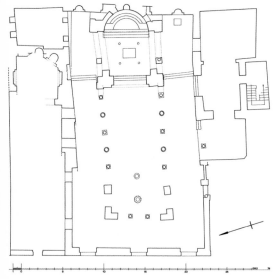

*Plan of the Church of St. Shenute
Courtesy Dr. Peter Grossmann.*

*From present street level, a flight of stairs goes
down to the entrance to the Church of St.
Shenute (detail of photograph on pp. 180–81).*

THE CHURCH IS DEDICATED TO ST. SHENUTE (*Anba Shenuda*) of Atripe (d. ca. 465), abbot of
the monastery near Sohag that bears his name (also called the White Monastery). St. Shenute (commemorated
in the Synaxarion on 7 Abib / 14 July) was one of the fathers of Egyptian monasticism. He was the founder of a
monastic federation, which included various cenobitic monasteries for men and women, in which the Pachomian
rules of shared work and prayer were interpreted strictly. He is also remembered as the first prolific writer in
Coptic, which was at that time the language of the common man.[207]

In 743 Patriarch Michael I was elected in this church.[208] Earlier references to the existence of this house
of worship have so far not been found. The building was destroyed and completely rebuilt in the tenth
century; it was pillaged in the early eleventh century. [209] At that time, as said by al-Maqrizi (d. 1442),
Muslims were called to prayer in the Church of St. Shenuda.[210] According to Peter Grossmann, the building
shows no signs of being used as a mosque. On the other hand, he discovered remains of a small mosque
constructed between the churches of St. Mercurius and St. Shenute, which are only a few meters apart.[211]
Another major renovation took place under Patriarch Benjamin II in the fourteenth century,
commemorated on a plaque in the church.[212]

The church has a basilican plan with nave, side aisles, and a western return aisle with three doors.
The large apse with dome is not original. Marble columns, partly ancient, support a wooden architrave;
the lower part of the wall above is pierced with small arches. The roof is covered with a wooden barrel
vault. In the southeastern corner is a doorway to the baptistery. Some columns preserve paintings of saints.
On the upper floor are chapels dedicated to the Archangel Michael and the Virgin.

The interior of the present building is the result of a huge early-twentieth-century restoration project.
In his 1884 book, Alfred Butler described a much smaller church area: the western half of the nave and
side aisles was taken up by several (store) rooms, a well with pulley, and staircases leading to the upper
floor, which had additional chapels. Occupying the western part of this upper story was the apartment
for the priest and his family.[213]

The Comité wanted to restore the church to its former ground plan. This restoration was realized in several
phases from 1909 to 1935, often hindered by lack of financial resources and bureaucratic difficulties. The western
part of the nave was cleared and the colonnade reconstructed. Research and excavations were undertaken to
determine the original outline of the church. The fabric of the building was repaired, and the three doors at the
western end were opened again. The restoration provided an opportunity to introduce measures to protect the
church.[214] A second large restoration project, which included the upper chapels,[215] has just been completed. In
1994, during this restoration, human bones were discovered below floor level in the return aisle. A monk of Dayr
Abu Mina (*Maryut*) (Monastery of St. Menas) was informed in a vision that they belonged to St. Julius of Aqfahs,
an officer in the Roman army, who assisted martyrs, secured their relics, and recorded their sufferings. At the
end of the Diocletian persecutions he publicly declared
himself a Christian, for which he was tortured and killed.
The relics are in a reliquary placed in the western part of
the church, adorned by a copy of the icon of St. Julius by
Ibrahim al-Nasikh (1757) from the Church of St. Mercurius
(*Abu Sayfayn*).[216]

OPPOSITE:
*Interior of the church. The basin in the floor
(laqqan) was used for the ceremony of foot
washing on Maundy Thursday and on the
Feast Day of Sts. Peter and Paul.*

The interior of the
Church of St. Shenute
(Anba Shenuda). *Most
of the antique columns
have Corinthian capitals;
some columns have been
placed upside down. To
the left of the central*
haykal *is a wooden*
ambon *(inset detail).*

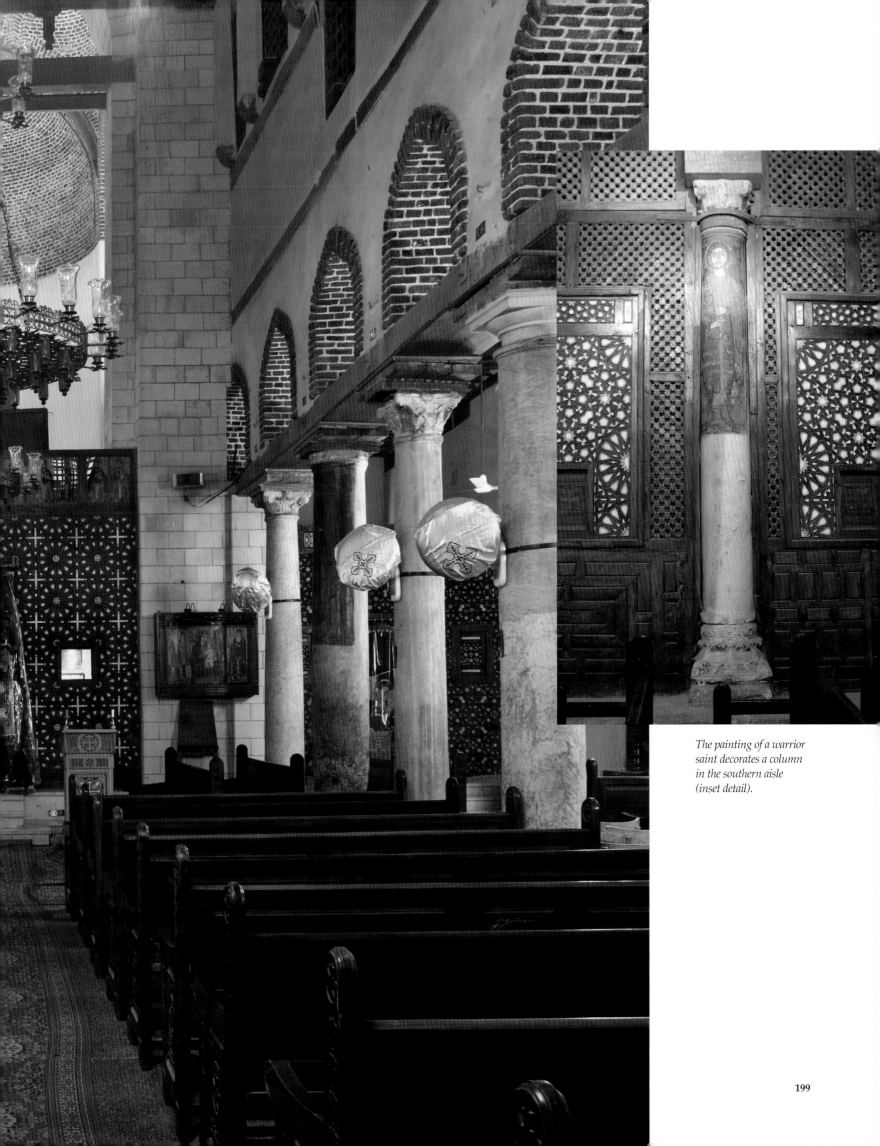

The painting of a warrior
saint decorates a column
in the southern aisle
(inset detail).

A column, hidden for many centuries in the wall, was discovered in the last restoration.

The southern side-aisle. A painting of a patriarch graces the left-hand column.

The south entrance to the baptistery.

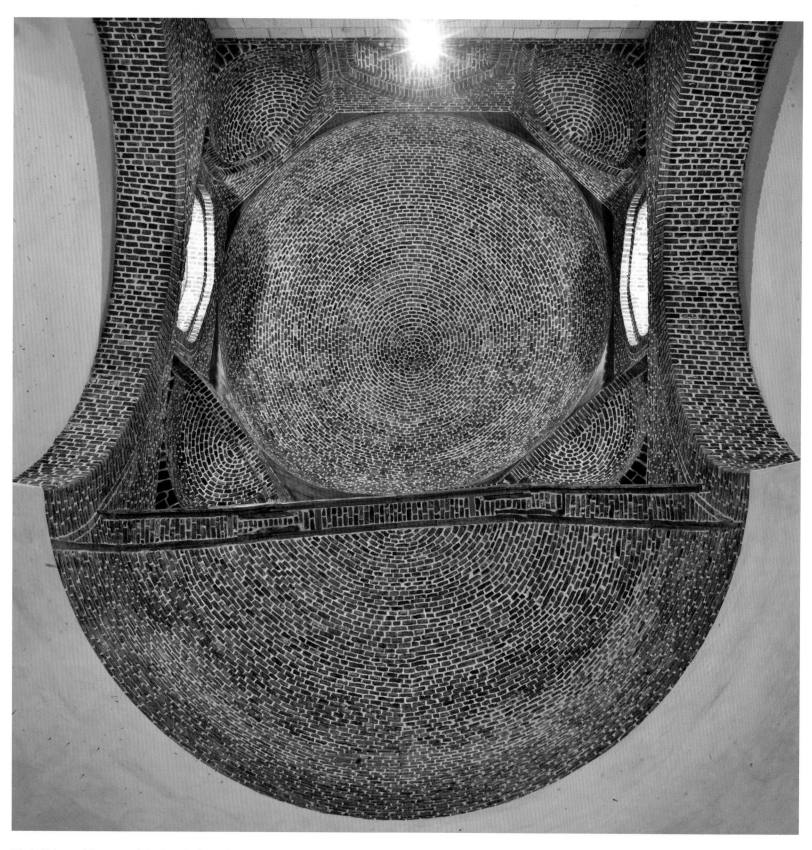

The half-dome of the apse and the dome in front of the apse. During the most recent restoration, the earlier plaster layers were removed to reveal the brickwork of the dome construction.

OPPOSITE:

The niche in the apse, with a panel painting of Christ enthroned, by Anastasi al-Rumi (nineteenth century).

Detail of the screen of the upper-floor chapel dedicated to the Virgin Mary.

OPPOSITE:
The chapel in the northern gallery of the church, dedicated to the Virgin Mary.

Detail of the screen of the Chapel of St. Michael.

OPPOSITE:
The chapel in the southern gallery is dedicated to the Archangel Michael.

THE CHURCH OF THE VIRGIN 'AL-DAMSHIRIYA'

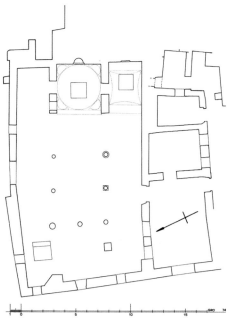

Plan of the Church of the Virgin al-Damshiriya. Courtesy Dr. Peter Grossmann.

THE EARLY HISTORY OF THIS CHURCH is vague. According to historians writing in Arabic in the tenth and the fifteenth centuries, the church must have existed as early as the eighth century: it was demolished in 785–86 and rebuilt soon after.[217] Hardly anything is known about it until the mid-eighteenth century. At that time, the church was in ruins. The rubble was cleared and a completely new church built, financed by a prominent Copt from Damshir—hence its name, al-Damshiriya.[218] Since the new building is located at a much higher level than the churches of St. Mercurius and St. Shenute, the street level of the area must already have risen considerably by that time.

The ground plan of the church follows the conventional layout of nave, side aisles with a western return aisle, and three altar rooms. The central altar room is covered by a dome, and the rest of the church has a wooden roof that is barrel-vaulted above the nave and flat above the aisles. At present, the northern altar room is used as a shrine to the Virgin Mary. The columns with Corinthian capitals, which separate the nave and aisles, differ in material and size: they are *spolia*, reused building elements.

The new church was consecrated in 1752. In subsequent years, the famous icon painters Yuhanna al-Armani and Ibrahim al-Nasikh painted at least nine (but possibly eighteen) icons for the church,[219] some of which are now preserved in the Coptic Museum.[220] The ciborium covering the altar in the central *haykal* is the work of the nineteenth-century painter Anastasi al-Rumi.[221]

The Comité registered the church in the late nineteenth century.[222] Alfred Butler remarks that at the time he was writing, it had only just been renovated.[223] Additional repairs were carried out in the first half of the twentieth century.[224] Recently, the church has been completely restored.

The gate to the corridor leading to the church is decorated with a reproduction of the icon of the Virgin al-Damshiriya.

OPPOSITE:
The Church of the Virgin is hidden in a cluster of utility buildings. This passageway leads to the church entrance.

FOLLOWING PAGES:
The entrance to the church. Icons of equestrian saints by Ibrahim al-Nasikh are displayed in the glass case to the right.[208]

A nineteenth-century Ethiopian icon of the nursing Virgin.

The interior of the Church of the Virgin, looking east. The columns with Corinthian capitals are reused building elements.

The Resurrection of Christ, by Anastasi al-Rumi (nineteenth century).

Icon of St. Michael the Archangel and the rich man, who had "laid up treasure for himself, and is not rich toward God," dying in his bed (Luke 12:16–21), one of the works painted by Yuhanna al-Armani. The soul of the dying man is escaping through his mouth, depicted as a small figure wrapped in white, looking almost like a mummy. The scales are a reference to the Day of Judgment at the end of time.

St. George and the Dragon, by Ibrahim al-Nasikh (second half of eighteenth century).

The Virgin 'al-Damshiriya.' This is the
most important icon of the Virgin and
Child in the church (nineteenth century).

Reliquary in the western part of the church. In the center is the icon of the Virgin al-Damshiriya (nineteenth century) surrounded by equestrian saints painted by Ibrahim al-Nasikh (eighteenth century).

THE CONVENT OF ST. MERCURIUS
(Abu Sayfayn)

The courtyard in front of the entrance to the Convent of St. Mercurius. The gate to the right gives access to the street.

A garden of the convent with a portrait of Tamav Irene. At the rear, the Church of the Virgin Mary.

THE CONVENT OF ST. MERCURIUS *(Abu Sayfayn)*, also called the Convent of the Maidens *(Dayr al-Banat)*, is now situated to the west of the Church of the Virgin 'al-Damshiriya.' In 1912–13, Patriarch Cyril V (1874–1927) had the present building constructed for the nuns. The old buildings were on the verge of collapse, so a stretch of the convent garden was used to build a fortress-like complex.[225] Alfred Butler described the old convent near the Church of St. Mercurius as hidden behind the churches and shaded by ancient trees.[226] The Church of St. Mercurius was originally used as the convent church, and it was directly linked to the old convent building. A shrine dedicated to St. Mercurius was installed in the new convent, but the nuns continued to use the Church of St. Mercurius for mass. It was, however, far away, making it difficult for elderly nuns to attend. Thus in 1962 the shrine of St. Mercurius was transformed into a church. This change occurred during the term of office of Tamav Irene, mother superior of the convent from 1962 until her death in October 2006. Tamav (Coptic for 'mother') Irene reformed monastic life along cenobitic communal rules, installed workshops, and raised the nuns' level of education.[227] Her reforms attracted large numbers of novices, in light of which Tamav Irene initiated the renovation, rebuilding, and expansion of the convent. At present there are four churches. Apart from the Church of St. Mercurius, the convent contains the Church of St. Dimiana (a female virgin saint, martyred with forty other virgins and deeply venerated in the Coptic Church), the Church of St. Michael the Archangel, and the Church of the Virgin Mary.[228]

Two more convents were added to the community: at Krair (north coast, west of Alexandria) and at al-Qanatir al-Khayriya (near Shatanuf, in al-Munufiya Governorate). In both these convents, the nuns run a dairy and a poultry farm. Fruit and vegetables are cultivated at Krair, while at al-Qanatir there is an apiary and a houseplant nursery.[229] These economic ventures were unprecedented for a nuns' convent. Desert communities at that time were male; women's convents were always located in or near the inhabited world.

Tamav Irene contributed significantly to changing the character of female monasticism: pious retreats for widows and elderly maidens developed into contemplative establishments for often highly educated women.[230] Inside their convent walls, they pursue a life of spirituality and serve the Coptic community. Since her death, Tamav Irene's shrine in the Convent of St. Mercurius has become a place of pilgrimage.

ABOVE AND LEFT:
The Church of St. Mercurius, the oldest church of the convent. To the right above is an icon of St. Mercurius with the two swords, set in a reliquary.

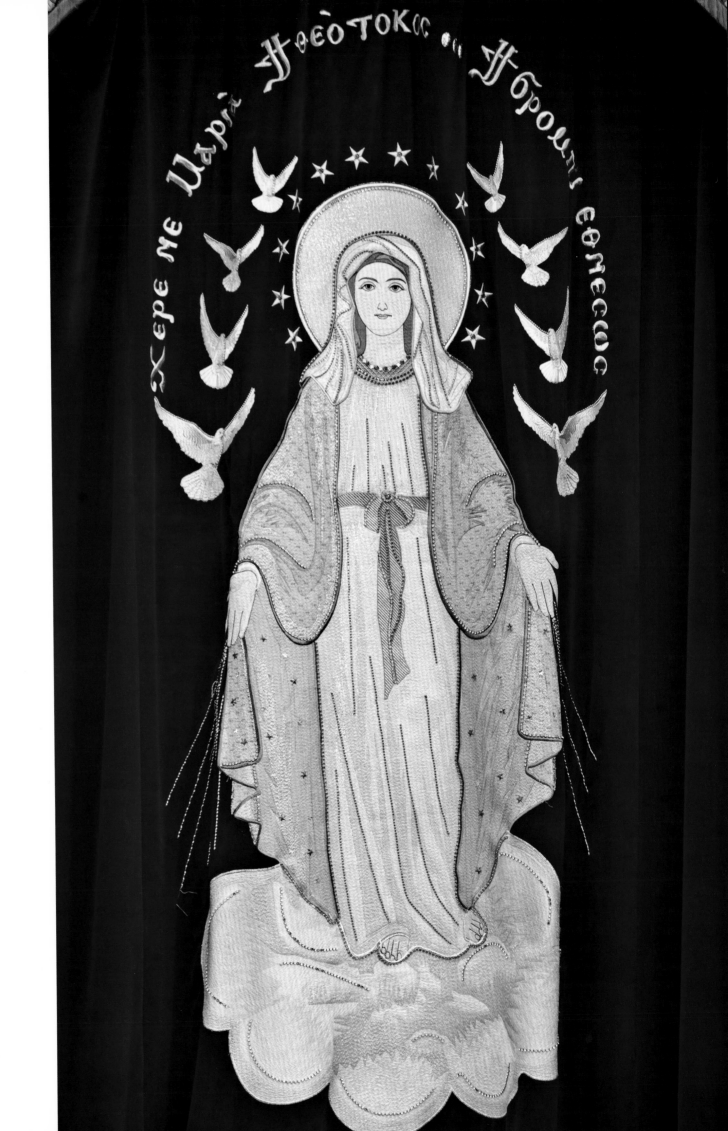

OPPOSITE:

The Church of the Virgin Mary. Interior view toward the east. The church is not yet finished: the roundels above the colonnades are still empty frames for icons.

An image of the Virgin Mary is embroidered on the curtain covering the doorway to the altar.

Stained-glass windows in Church of the Virgin Mary were designed by the nuns. Left to right: Nativity, Flight into Egypt, Presentation in the Temple, Ascension, Pentecost. In the Pentecost window the Virgin Mary and—unusually—two other women are present among the Apostles, highlighting the female contribution to the church and monastic life.

riptych of the Entry into rusalem. In the crowd (left) e a number of women; to e right are the Apostles.

Icon of the Deliverance of Matthias, the apostle who took the place of Judas (Acts 1:26). According to tradition, he was delivered from prison by the Virgin.

Icon of the Miracle of the Moving of the Moqattam Mountain. Saint Simeon the Tanner and Patriarch Abraham are depicted in the center.

Modern icon of St. Mercurius Abu Sayfayn, "the Father with the two swords," shows the saint on the battlefield and an angel giving him the second sword. St. Basil of Caesarea points to the two swords which would kill Emperor Julian the Apostate.

Icon of Abba Tegi, better known as Anba Ruways (d. 1404). The saint was born as Ishaq Furayg. He worked on his father's farm and transported salt on his camel Ruways, "little head." Later, when he became a wandering ascetic, he took the name of his friendly camel. He was known for his piety, his gift of healing, and his help to fellow men. He is buried in the crypt of the Church of Anba Ruways in the Papal compound in Abbasiya.

OPPOSITE:
Icon of the Archangel Michael depicted in his two major roles: battling evil (the slaying of a dragon) and the weighing of souls in the Last Judgment.

The shrine of Tamav Irene with portraits of the Reverend Mother on the walls. Since her death, the shrine in the Convent of St. Mercurius has become a place of pilgrimage.

CHURCHES TO THE SOUTH OF THE FORTRESS

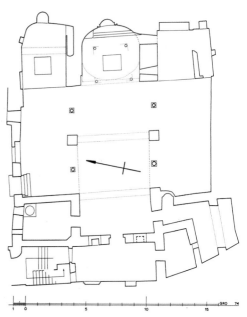

Plan of the Church of the Virgin of Babylon of
the Steps. Courtesy Dr. Peter Grossmann.

The new enclosure with the entrance to and modern bell
tower of the Church of the Virgin of Babylon al-Darag.

Nowadays, the Church of the Virgin of Babylon al-Darag and the
Monastery of St. Theodore *(Dayr al-Amir Tadrus)* are situated in a busy residential quarter. For centuries, however,
this was wasteland, and the churches were small buildings scattered among "mounds of rubbish," as described
by Alfred Butler in 1880–81.[231]

The Church of the Virgin is surrounded by a high wall; the nearby Monastery of St. Theodore has its own
perimeter wall. Nineteenth-century visitors all comment on the isolation, silence, and gloom of these churches.
Some old women lived around the Church of the Virgin, but the complex of St. Theodore was uninhabited. The
priest of the Monastery of St. Mercurius (Dayr Abu Sayfayn) used to ride over on his donkey on Saturday evening
for Vespers. After spending the night in the Church of St. Theodore and saying Matins on Sunday morning, he
returned to his own church.[232]

Little is known about their architectural history and their relationship to the churches in the fortress. They
all had their share of the eighteenth-century renovations and refurbishment. In 1887, the Comité suggested
classifying the churches, and some repairs were subsequently carried out.[233] Over the past thirty years, the
complexes have undergone major renovations and rebuilding.

The Church of the Virgin *(Babylon al-Darag)*

The official name of the church is "The Church of the Virgin of Babylon of the Steps." It is clear
that 'Babylon' refers to the fortress, situated just north of the church. 'The Steps,' however, is a
puzzling allusion. Certainly at present the church is below street level with flights of steps
leading down to the entrance. But 'the Steps' is not a modern epithet. It also appears in the
History of the Patriarchs: in 1031–32 Patriarch Zacharias was buried in "the Church of the
Mistress at Banî Wâyil, known as the Church of the Steps."[234] So far, no accepted
explanation has been found.[235]

In the eleventh century, this church was also mentioned as one of the places in which the
Holy Family had sojourned during their flight into Egypt,[236] an assertion confirmed by various
pilgrims from the fourteenth and fifteenth centuries.[237]

The Dominican Father Jean Michel Vansleb visited the Church of the Virgin during his first
trip to Egypt in 1664. He reported that Babylon was a very old church below ground level that
had been founded by the apostles; the Copts told him several stories, he said, that needed to be
examined in more detail. He also wrote that the Copts believed this was the church mentioned
by St. Peter in his first letter: "The church that is at Babylon, elected together with you, saluteth
you" (1 Peter 5:13).[238] After his second visit to the area in 1672, he added that this was the first
church built in Cairo after the advent of Christ, and that St. Mark had prayed here.[239]

The church building is a basilica type, forming a virtual square. There are three altar rooms,
and piers and columns separate the nave from the side aisles and, originally, the western return

OPPOSITE:
*The entrance to the courtyard. Above the doorway are the Virgin and Child, flanked by images of
Pope Cyril VI and Saint Menas.*

The entrance to the church in the northwestern part. View on the steps: from the church to a small courtyard, and from the courtyard to street level.

Interior of the church. The ancient columns and Corinthian capitals are spolia, reused building material, and they all differ in size, material, and ornamentation.

aisle. At present, the western part contains a baptistery. In the former narthex, which seems to be the oldest part of the building, are two more baptismal fonts. The nave is covered with a barrel vault.

The original date of construction is not known; like a number of other ancient churches, the height of the street level in relation to the church is certainly a sign of the latter's antiquity. The first reference to the church was made in the context of the burial of Patriarch Zacharias in 1031–32. Over the centuries, the building has been altered, restored, and renewed, and hardly anything of the original fabric or ancient furnishings still remains. In 1721, a restoration was begun after some of the church walls collapsed—part of the large-scale movement to restore and renovate monasteries and churches.[240]

In the nineteenth century, the icon painter Anastasi al-Qudsi al-Rumi and his workshop painted the ciborium of the central altar room. They also painted the images of apostles on wooden panels, which were later fixed to the walls of the altar room; in the central niche was an icon of Christ enthroned.[241]

The most recent works were undertaken in the early 1990s.[242] During this restoration, human remains were discovered below the floor of the church. They are believed to be the relics of the tenth-century saint Simeon the Tanner, the man who was able to help Patriarch Abraham move Muqattam Mountain through his faith in God (see "The Hanging Church"). On the orders of Patriarch Shenuda III, his relics were divided between this church, the Hanging Church (*al-Mu'allaqa*), and the Church of St. Simeon the Tanner in Muqattam.[243]

233

The solid ancient door of the monastery, set in a new frame.

The Monastery of St. Theodore
(Dayr al-Amir Tadrus)

The small enclosure of the Monastery of St. Theodore *(Dayr al-Amir Tadrus)* contains two churches: the southern church dedicated to St. Theodore and the northern to Sts. Cyrus and John *(Abu Qir wa Yuhanna)*. Each is situated in its own small courtyard.

There are a number of auxiliary rooms around each church that might once have served as cells. At present, the surrounding wall and the main entrance, with its massive, ancient wooden door, are being renovated.

The Church of St. Theodore the Oriental

While today this church is consistently called 'St. Theodore the Oriental,' historical sources (eleventh and fourteenth century) and nineteenth- and early-twentieth-century travelers and scholars give it a variety of different names: St. Theodore, St. Theodore the Martyr, or St. Theodore the General.[244] St. Theodore Stratelates (the General, feast day 20 Abib/14 July) battled with a dragon and is one of the most popular saints in Egypt. His namesake, St. Theodore the Oriental (feast day 12 Tubeh/7 January), was also an army officer. The stories of their lives overlap, and it is often difficult to distinguish between the two saints.[245]

Little is known about the building history of this church. The first record dates from the eleventh century (1061) and mentions a miracle: a number of pictures (whether these were icons or wall paintings is not clear) sweated, "so that their sweat flowed like water, and lo, its trace and its course remain until today upon its walls."[246]

The present church, which probably dates to the eighteenth century, preserves some old elements: part of the west wall and the two western pillars. The nave and side aisles and bays of the centralized structure are surmounted by six domes, which rest on the western pillars and twin columns in front of the altar room. The western part has been turned into a narthex. The columns are reused late-antique building elements with Corinthian capitals. The dome in front of the central altar room is higher and rests on stalactite squinches. The northern altar room is no longer used.[247] Recently, the church has been completely restored.

Bird's-eye view of the Monastery of St. Theodore (Dayr al-Amir Tadrus). In front are the domes of the Church of St. Theodore. In the background, the new bell tower of the Church of the Virgin of Babylon al-Darag is visible.

View of the interior, looking east, showing the twin columns and the stalactite squinches of the dome. On the screen of the central altar room, dedicated to St. Theodore, are icons of the twelve apostles surrounding the Virgin and Child. Above, the Last Supper and the Crucifixion. In glass cases on the left and right, icons of the Annunciation and the Baptism of Christ are displayed.

FOLLOWING PAGES:
View of the interior, looking north. St. Theodore is depicted on the curtain covering the altar door.

The Church of Sts. Cyrus and John
(*Abu Qir wa Yuhanna*)

In the second courtyard is the church dedicated to St. Cyrus (*Abu Qir/Apa Kir*) and St. John (commemoration of their martyrdom 6 Amshir / 31 January). A shrine dedicated to the pair (at Menouthis, near Alexandria) was a well-known center of healing.[248] In the tenth century, their relics were moved to Old Cairo, to the Church of St. Barbara, which was then dedicated to these two saints. While some of their relics remain in the small church of Sts. Cyrus and John in the Church of St. Barbara, they are venerated with those now kept in this church in the Monastery of St. Theodore.[249] The dedication to the holy brothers is known to have existed since the fourteenth century.[250]

Remodeling and rebuilding over the centuries have resulted in a small, irregular church whose original plan is difficult to discern. There are three altar rooms, closed off by a continuous screen. Two vast pillars indicate the former khurus, a transverse space in front of the altar rooms introduced into Egyptian church architecture in the seventh century. The ancient columns and their newer counterparts separating the nave and side aisles are different in height, color, and form, needing some adjustment to make them fit. One of the columns is encased in glass: according to believers, the grayish, shadowy pattern represents the Virgin Mary and Child. Notes with petitions, prayers, and expressions of gratitude testify to the deep belief in the holiness of the image.

In the southeastern corner of the church is a shrine with relics of saints (among them St. Cyrus, St. John, and St. George) enclosed in cabinets, as well as nineteenth-century icons representing the Virgin Mary, saints, and biblical subjects. The woodwork and icons were cleaned and restored in 1999.

A ceramic vessel discovered near this church is believed to be the container that St. Simeon the Tanner—whose relics were discovered in the Church of the Virgin of Babylon al-Darag—used to carry water. The pot is now kept in the Church of St. Simeon at Muqattam Mountain.[251]

Courtyard entrance to the Church of Sts. Cyrus and John.

Plan of the Church of Sts. Cyrus and John. Courtesy Dr. Peter Grossmann.

View of the central **haykal.** *Over the altar screen are icons of the Virgin and Child and the twelve apostles; a Crucifixion scene is mounted on top.*

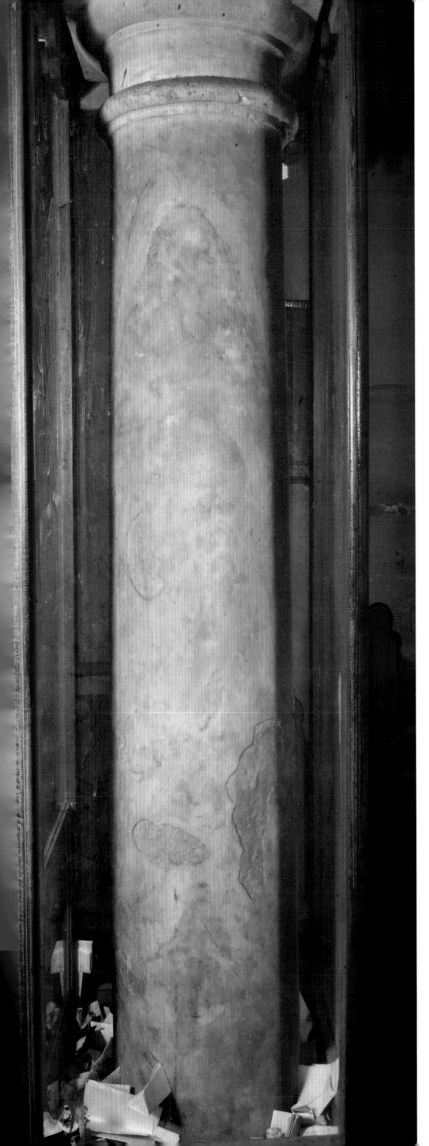

View of the interior, facing southeast. Note the varying heights of the columns. At the back is the shrine containing the relics of St. Cyrus, St. John, and St. George. The icons of the shrine all date to the nineteenth century and are painted in what is known as the Jerusalem style.

The encased column surrounded by notes containing prayers and petitions.

A nineteenth-century icon of the saintly brothers, by Anastasi al-Rumi, in its original frame.

The nineteenth-century "Jerusalem style" icons in the shrine. Left to right: St. Barsum the Naked with the serpent, the Virgin and Child, and St. George, spearing the dragon.

Nineteenth-century icons representing St. Theodore, the Sacrifice by Abraham, Sts. Isidore and Victor.

The modern bell tower of the church.

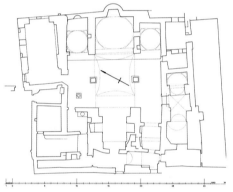

Plan of the Church of the Archangel Michael.
Note maze of rooms surrounding the church area.
Courtesy Dr. Peter Grossmann.

The screen of the central altar room.
On the curtain an embroidery of
the Archangel Michael.

The Church of the Archangel Michael al-Qibli
(*Dayr Malak Michael al-Qibli*)

The Church of the Archangel Michael is located in an enclosure called the Southern Monastery of the Archangel Michael (*Dayr Malak Michael al-Qibli*).

The Archangel Michael—leader of the heavenly host, intercessor for mankind, protector of the faithful—is held in the highest regard in Egypt. He is the angel of the Lord, who welcomes souls into Heaven and defeats the powers of evil. Countless churches and chapels are dedicated to him. The stories of his deeds and intercessions are numerous. In the calendar of saints, he is commemorated on the twelfth day of every Coptic month.[252] Since early Christian times, springs and waters have been dedicated to St. Michael, and in Egypt he is particularly connected with the Nile. Alfred Butler says that a shrine in this church with a painting of St. Michael was deeply venerated by all the Copts in Cairo: "His influence is thought specially potent in controlling the rise of the Nile."[253]

The *History of the Patriarchs* tells the story of the saintly monk Bulus (Paul) ibn Raga, who built the Church of St. Michael under Patriarch Philotheus (d. 1003).[254] It is not known whether or not an older church existed at the site. Indeed, only a few of the events that have taken place at this church over the centuries have come down to us.

Patriarch Gabriel III was patriarch for a very short time (1268–71), during years of intrigue around the patriarchal throne. According to the fourteenth-century Christian historian al-Mufaddal, he was installed as patriarch in the Church of St. Michael the day before his enthronement in the Hanging Church.[255] Thirteenth- to fourteenth-century calendars of saints mention the commemoration of the priest and martyr Ptolemy in this church on 6 Khihak/2 December.[256] Unfortunately, nothing more is known about the martyr or his feast.[257] Thirteenth- to eighteenth-century manuscripts, now preserved in libraries in France and England, once belonged to the church's library.[258]

Father Vansleb went to the Church of St. Michael on the evening of 17 July 1672; he spent the night there and attended mass in the early morning.[259] At the beginning of the eighteenth century, the church was rebuilt by Mu'allim Lutf Allah Abu Yusuf (d. 1720).[260] The English bishop Richard Pococke, who traveled the Near East from 1737 to 1742, remarked that the "Convent of Saint Michael" was uninhabited. A priest went there every Sunday to officiate.[261] It is not known when the complex was abandoned; likewise, nothing is known about what this church looked like before the eighteenth-century reconstruction. At present, a basilican ground plan, with several modifications and additional elements, can still be recognized. Several walls of the present church building include parts of the older construction.[262] A modern bell tower is decorated with a wrought-iron image of the archangel.

The interior of the haykal with the eastern niche and a small synthronon. Christ, in the center, is accompanied by two archangels and the Twelve Apostles.

FOLLOWING PAGES:
The interior of the church; view toward the southeast.

THE COPTIC MUSEUM

Gawdat Gabra

THE COPTIC MUSEUM

AT THE CLOSE OF THE NINETEENTH CENTURY, there were three major museums in Egypt. Located at Giza, Alexandria, and Cairo (in al-Hakim Mosque), these museums were repositories for the material heritage of Egypt from its pharaonic, Greco-Roman, and Islamic histories. Missing from this schema was a museum devoted to Egypt's rich Coptic heritage.

As far back as 1899, Ya'qub Nakhla Rufayla, in his Arabic-language history of the Copts, had expressed a desire for the wise men of the nation to assume responsibility for Coptic monuments, landmarks, and artifacts. He hoped that this material culture might be preserved, much like Islamic Egyptian cultural artifacts, in a special hall. Rufayla strongly urged the educated Coptic laity to preserve the surviving Coptic monuments and manuscripts and to petition the patriarch for a centralized location for the collection and display of Coptic artifacts.

At about the same time, Max Herz, head of the technical section of the Comité de conservation des monuments de l'art arabe (hereafter Comité), wrote to its president, Husayn Fakhri Pasha, and suggested that a Coptic museum be established. The letter also encouraged the patriarch to designate a storeroom for the collection and preservation of endangered Coptic artifacts. In January 1902, Husayn Fakhri Pasha informed the Comité that the patriarch had promised to collect the extant Coptic artifacts in a one-room annex beside the Hanging Church (al-Mu'allaqa). On 2 June 1907, Hanna Bey Bakhoum advised the Comité that the patriarch had ordered them to prepare an inventory of the artifacts in the churches. Despite the Comité's interest, however, nothing further was accomplished.

The legacy of Coptic art, with its rich history of monuments, manuscripts, and artifacts, might have been lost to posterity were it not for the passion of one man. Murqus Simaika Pasha had been born into a respected, prosperous Coptic family of Cairene notables in 1864. A beneficiary of the reforms of Patriarch Cyril IV (1854–61), he was educated at the patriarchal school, where he learned Coptic, Greek, English, and French. Simaika cultivated excellent relations with scholars who studied the heritage of Christian Egypt: Somers Clarke, Jean Clédat, and Johann Georg, Duke of Saxony. Alfred Butler and Josef Strzygowski had become his personal friends, and thus, inspired by Butler's essential study of Egypt's Coptic Churches, Murqus Simaika became interested in preserving Coptic churches and beginning a Coptic museum. In the winter of 1908, Simaika prevailed upon Patriarch Cyril V and obtained silver Gospel caskets and liturgical vessels bearing fourteenth- and fifteenth-century Coptic and Arabic inscriptions. Getting the patriarch to agree to raise LE180 for the protection of these artifacts was Simaika's greatest achievement.

The side garden and staircase of the old wing of the Coptic Museum as it once was.

OPPOSITE:
Front staircase leading to the old wing of the Coptic Museum as it appears today.

FOLLOWING PAGES:
The entrance to the Coptic Museum after its most recent renovation and inauguration in 2006.

Portriat of Marcus Simaika Pasha. Photograph courtesy of Dr. Samir Simaika.

With the support of Patriarch Cyril V, Simaika acquired architectural elements and artifacts from private collections from Rosetta to Khartoum, in addition to items from monasteries, churches, old palaces, and private homes. The first hall for the exhibition of what would become the world's largest collection of Coptic art was inaugurated on 14 March 1910 in the presence of Patriarch Cyril, Fakhri Pasha, Herz Pasha, and Boinier Pasha.

Simaika chose a distinctively appropriate location for the museum in the symbolically significant historical setting of the Roman Fortress of Babylon, surrounded by Cairo's oldest churches. He succeeded in his fund-raising campaign, compiling an imposing list of private contributors before the first annual state subsidy was approved. Simaika's efforts ensured that a substantial portion of Coptic heritage was salvaged for posterity. Although the Coptic Museum started as a church museum and is of course reflective of Egypt's Christian heritage, it has unquestionable national significance in documenting the history of Egypt; it belongs to all the people of Egypt and to visitors from around the world who are interested in Egypt's unique contributions to art, religion, and history. The museum's rich holdings document the unique place of Coptic art within Egypt's artistic heritage, from its pharaonic roots through interaction with Greco-Roman, Byzantine, and Islamic art. It is also interesting to note that of Egypt's four major museums—the Egyptian, Greco-Roman, Coptic, and Islamic—only the Coptic Museum had an Egyptian founder and first director.

In 1920, Sultan (later King) Fouad, an ardent supporter of cultural and charitable projects, visited the Coptic Museum and left a donation of LE500. He visited again in 1923, this time bringing King Victor Emmanuel III of Italy and his queen; this high-profile visit resulted in considerable publicity for the museum. A decade later, the time was ripe for the museum to achieve national status with government funding, and in 1931 the Department of Antiquities assumed responsibility for the collections. At that time, the museum only consisted of what is now known as the Old Wing, a fine piece of architecture with a roof made of decorated antique timber. To decorate the galleries, Simaika combined architectural elements such as magnificent arches and fascinating mashrabiya work he had retrieved from older edifices, as well as beautifully carved and painted ornamental ceilings.

Excavations were carried out at several archaeological sites. Of special significance were those of Flinders Petrie and Edouard Naville in Heracleopolis Magna (Ahnas); Gayet in the city and necropolis of Antinoé (Ansina); Clédat, Emile Chassinat, and Jean Maspero in the Monastery of St. Apollo at Bawit; James E. Quibell in the Monastery of St. Jeremiah at Saqqara; and Petrie in Oxyrhynchus (al-Bahnasa). These excavations yielded a vast number of Late Antique and Coptic monuments that enriched not only the collections of the Egyptian Museum in Cairo and the Greco-Roman Museum in Alexandria, but also the collections of several European institutions.

Initially, Simaika had intended to transfer the Coptic holdings in the Egyptian Museum to the Coptic Museum and obtained the necessary funding for a larger new wing to house them. Unfortunately, the Second World War delayed his ambitious project, and he died in 1944 without seeing it completed. Simaika's crucial role was honored during the inauguration ceremony for the New Wing in 1947. A bust of the founder graces the museum's entrance, and a memorial plaque, set on the façade at the instigation of the "Government of His Majesty King Farouk I," commemorates Simaika's name in Coptic, Arabic, and English as the founder of the Coptic Museum, who devoted his life to the preservation of Coptic monuments.

The architecture of the New Wing carefully preserves the architectural style of the Old Wing. The ceilings of the New Wing are made of beautifully carved woodwork, and there are picturesque fountains and windows of stained glass in some galleries. The most striking feature of the Coptic Museum lies in the aesthetic continuity of the exhibited works within their architectural setting. The objects are at home in this museum, especially in the Old Wing.

By 1966, however, the entire structure of the Old Wing had deteriorated and was in immediate need of restoration. Consequently, the Old Wing was closed that year. The museum had antiquated methods of exhibition and lighting, primitive showcases and flooring, and lacked the simplest museum facilities. In

Modern carving of fish on the staircase within the new wing. In Coptic art the fish is used as a symbol of Christianity.

1984 the walls were shored up, galleries on the upper floor of the Old Wing were renovated, and comparatively modern methods of exhibition were introduced. President Hosni Mubarak opened the renovated museum with its new display on 8 March 1984. The museum's reputation made it a 'must' on the itineraries of heads of state—kings and presidents alike—as well as official delegations. Among the distinguished visitors were King Carl XVI Gustaf of Sweden and Queen Silvia, who expressed a great interest in the collection. Helmut Schmidt, chancellor of Germany, was so thoroughly impressed on his visit to the museum that after his retirement, I had the honor of accompanying him and his wife twice through the galleries.

Unfortunately, corresponding restorations planned for the lower floor of the Old Wing, which houses the manuscript section, as well as construction of a research library, had to be postponed and were only taken up again in the 1980s. Between 1986 and 1998, the Old Wing was rebuilt from the foundations up, but without any alteration in its appearance. The entire block, including the manuscript section, a library, and one of the galleries for woodwork, was painstakingly reconstructed, square meter by square meter. The process was slow, but highly effective, especially in terms of structural stability.

In 1991, a few months prior to a massive earthquake that damaged many monuments in Cairo, another project to strengthen the Old Wing's foundations was initiated. The collapse of the building with its priceless collections was averted thanks to the structural reconstruction carried out the few years before the earthquake and the reinforcement of the foundations, completed only months before the catastrophe. There was some minor damage from the 1992 earthquake, and cracks appeared in some walls as a result of groundwater seepage. This problem too was eventually resolved (see the Introduction) making it possible in 2003 to attend to the superstructure, with its magnificently painted wooden ceiling, stained-glass windows, and picturesque fountains on the grounds. At Zahi Hawass's invitation, I selected objects from the holdings of the museum, supervised their installation in the renovated galleries of the Coptic Museum, and prepared the labels and additional informative material for visitors.

The museum remained closed for some time while the extensive renovations were carried out. Finally, on 25 June 2006, President Mubarak officially reopened the museum, with its completely new installation of the world's largest and most comprehensive collection of Coptic art and artifacts.[1] To coincide with the opening, the American University in Cairo Press published a volume on the artistic treasures in the museum and the churches of Old Cairo, along with an illustrated guide to the museum and churches.

The Coptic Museum preserves hundreds of splendid artifacts that were once integrated within the fabric of Old Cairo. These artifacts belonged to the Fortress of Babylon, to churches within or outside that fortress, and to Fustat. The following eight pieces have been chosen to represent the invaluable artistic heritage of Old Cairo during the Late Antique and medieval periods.

Interior views of the exhibition areas of the Coptic Museum with magnificantly restored painted and inlaid ceilings and stained-glass windows.

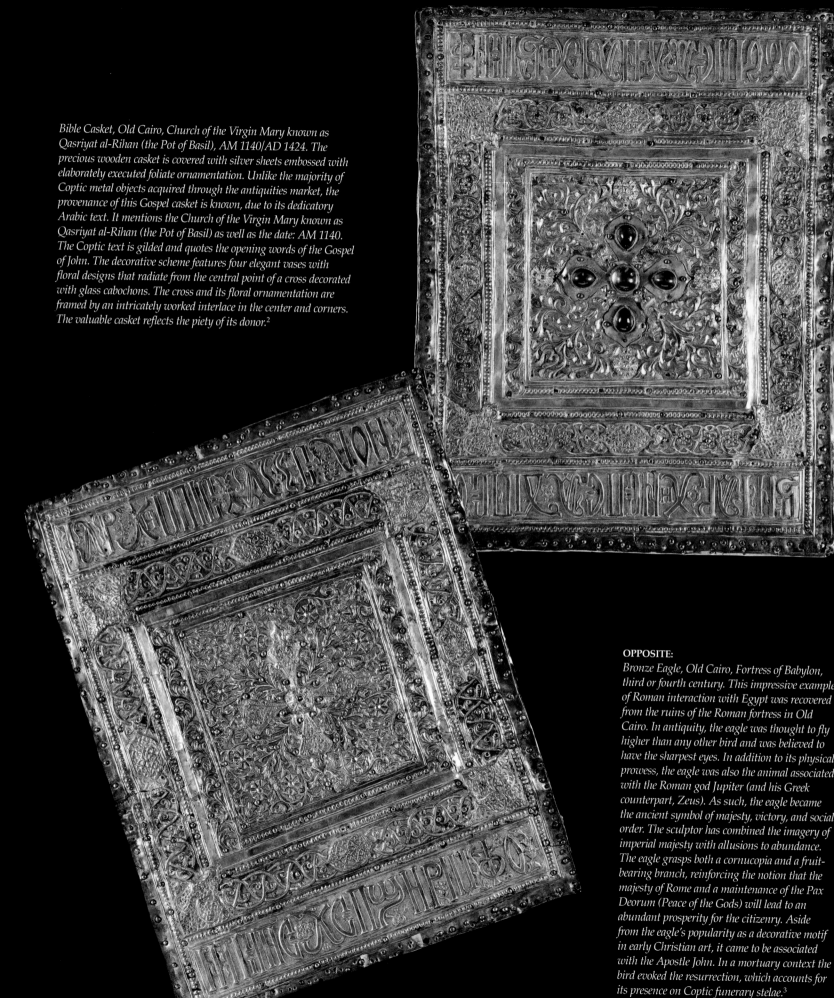

Bible Casket, Old Cairo, Church of the Virgin Mary known as Qasriyat al-Rihan (the Pot of Basil), AM 1140/AD 1424. The precious wooden casket is covered with silver sheets embossed with elaborately executed foliate ornamentation. Unlike the majority of Coptic metal objects acquired through the antiquities market, the provenance of this Gospel casket is known, due to its dedicatory Arabic text. It mentions the Church of the Virgin Mary known as Qasriyat al-Rihan (the Pot of Basil) as well as the date: AM 1140. The Coptic text is gilded and quotes the opening words of the Gospel of John. The decorative scheme features four elegant vases with floral designs that radiate from the central point of a cross decorated with glass cabochons. The cross and its floral ornamentation are framed by an intricately worked interlace in the center and corners. The valuable casket reflects the piety of its donor.[2]

OPPOSITE:

Bronze Eagle, Old Cairo, Fortress of Babylon, third or fourth century. This impressive example of Roman interaction with Egypt was recovered from the ruins of the Roman fortress in Old Cairo. In antiquity, the eagle was thought to fly higher than any other bird and was believed to have the sharpest eyes. In addition to its physical prowess, the eagle was also the animal associated with the Roman god Jupiter (and his Greek counterpart, Zeus). As such, the eagle became the ancient symbol of majesty, victory, and social order. The sculptor has combined the imagery of imperial majesty with allusions to abundance. The eagle grasps both a cornucopia and a fruit-bearing branch, reinforcing the notion that the majesty of Rome and a maintenance of the Pax Deorum (Peace of the Gods) will lead to an abundant prosperity for the citizenry. Aside from the eagle's popularity as a decorative motif in early Christian art, it came to be associated with the Apostle John. In a mortuary context the bird evoked the resurrection, which accounts for its presence on Coptic funerary stelae.[3]

Altar, Old Cairo, Church of Sts. Sergius and Bacchus (Abu Sarga), fifth century. In the Christian celebration of the Eucharist, altars evolved from simple wooden tables to highly elaborate and decorated pieces. The open form of this example, the earliest wooden altar to have survived from Egypt, is reminiscent of an earlier style. Its design imitates an arcade. Of the twelve columns, eight featuring oblique fluting remain. The archivolts are decorated with stylized myrtle foliage. The shells and crosses that decorate the spandrels may symbolize the rebirth of the soul after baptism. The altar is displayed in the gallery of the Churches of Old Cairo under a wooden dome. The latter dates to the Fatimid period and originally belonged to the Hanging Church.[4]

Icon with St. Antony and St. Paul of Thebes, Old Cairo, Monastery of St. Mercurius (Abu Sayfayn), AM 1493/AD 1777. This icon depicts the visit that St. Antony (d. 356) paid to the hermit St. Paul of Thebes (d. ca. 340). The two saints are identifiable by the names written in Coptic flanking their ornate halos. Both St. Antony and St. Paul of Thebes lived in retreat in the Eastern Desert near the Red Sea and are considered founders of eremitical monasticism in Egypt. This icon, which illustrates their story, was painted in AM 1493/AD 1777 and dedicated to the Monastery of St. Mercurius in Old Cairo. The bread-bearing crow alludes to an anecdote associated with these two saints: St. Paul of Thebes survived on bread brought to him by a crow, half a loaf at a time. On the occasion of St. Antony's visit, the crow miraculously provided a whole loaf. The toy-like lions at the feet of the saint allude to another anecdote describing how, upon the death of St. Paul, a pair of lions appeared and dug the grave in which St. Antony laid him to rest. While St. Paul is dressed in a tunic of plaited palms, St. Antony is wearing a monk's habit and holding a tau-staff and a scroll with an Arabic inscription that exhorts "his beloved children to keep all his commandments." The icon has been attributed to Yuhanna al-Armani, one of the most talented icon painters of that time.[5]

The Four Gospels Dedicated to the Hanging Church (al-Mu'allaqa), AM 988/1272 CE. Coptic illustrated manuscripts represent an important part of Egypt's Christian art of the thirteenth and fourteenth centuries. Although a considerable number of Coptic Gospel books in the Bohairic dialect are preserved in some of the monasteries and the ancient churches of Egypt, and in many museums and libraries all over the world, illustrated manuscripts are comparatively rare. The frontispiece of this Gospel of St. Mark is drawn carefully with geometric designs enclosing floral ornament. The title of the Gospel is framed by rich foliate decoration. The marginal decoration consists of stylized undulating scrolls and bunches of grapes. Despite the Islamic flavor of Coptic ornamentation of the thirteen and fourteen centuries, this manuscript and others like it from that period prove that Coptic scribes and painters were quite capable of producing magnificent manuscripts whose quality rivaled that of contemporaneous Islamic manuscripts.[6]

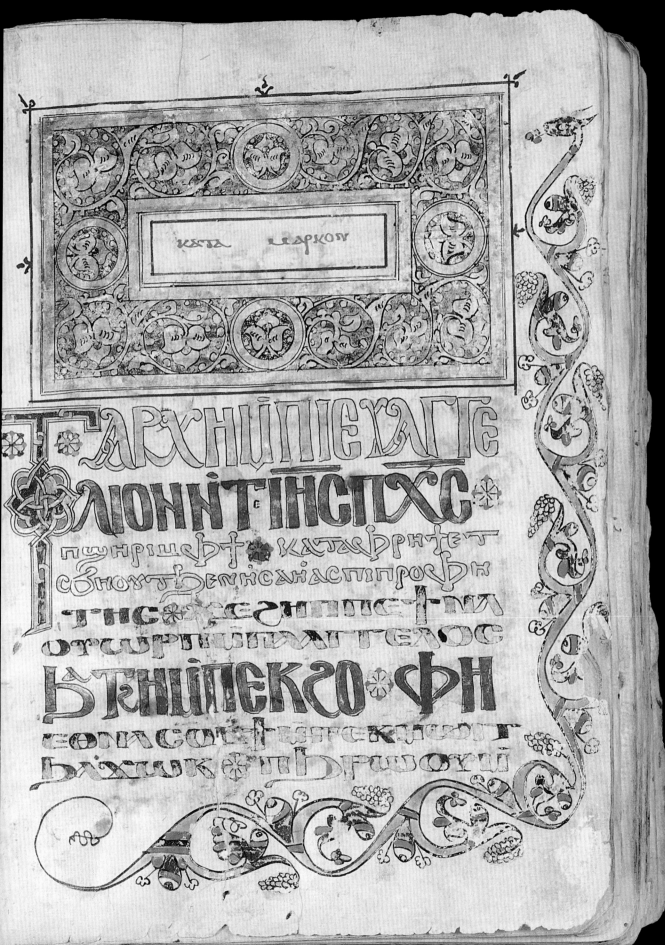

Leaves of a Richly Carved Door, Old Cairo, Church of St. Barbara, sycamore and pine, early sixth century. During restoration work carried out in the early twentieth century, this door was found sandwiched between two walls. It is the most significant door that has survived from the Roman and Byzantine periods in Egypt. The upper panels show the bust of Christ within a wreath carried by two angels in full flight. The scene is flanked by two men set against torsated columns with curtains. They carry a book adorned with a cross and probably represent evangelists with the Gospels. On the other panels the figures of Christ, St. Mark, Christ in a mandorla, the Virgin Mary, and the twelve apostles are depicted. The panels on the back of the door are engraved with vine scrolls springing from vases. They show a close stylistic connection with early-sixth- century Constantinopolitan art.[7]

Lintel with the Entry into Jerusalem and the Ascension, Old Cairo, the Hanging Church (al-Mu'allaqa), sycamore, eighth century. From the fourth century onward, both Western and Eastern Christian communities tended to combine the Entry into Jerusalem with the Ascension. Here the chronologically earlier episode occupies more than a quarter of the available space and is relegated to the left end of the frieze. Christ, riding an ass, is depicted beardless and unhaloed. While one man spreads a cloak on the ground in front of the ass, another hails Christ by waving a palm frond. Behind him stands the "daughter of Zion" mentioned in the Gospel of St. John, 12:15. The brickwork structures representing Jerusalem's city walls at the far left, and visible behind and between the figures over the entire length of the frieze, may also have been intended as an evocation of the Roman Fortress of Babylon, the actual setting of the Hanging Church. In the representation of the Ascension, Christ appears in the mandorla supported by two angels, but he is accompanied by only two of the four apocalyptic creatures: the lion and the ox. The nearest figure to the right of Christ is the Virgin Mary. The apostles occupy the relatively small remaining space to the left of Christ. The Greek inscription, a hymn to Christ, was dedicated by Abba Theodore and Deacon George. A part of the hymn reads: "Holy, holy, holy are you, O Lord: heaven and earth are full of your holy glory, because they are full of your greatness." According to recent studies, the date

*Basket Capital with a Looped Cross, Fustat,
marble, fifth or sixth century. The name
'basket capital' evokes, as one might imagine,
the resemblance of the convex-sided capital to
a basket. The lower part of the two-zone capital
has been incised in imitation of wickerwork,
strengthening the resemblance. A chevron-
patterned band surrounds the base of the
capital. The corners of the upper section are
decorated with doves, perched for flight, and
the spaces are filled with a wreathed looped
cross symbolizing the triumph of Christianity.
A similar column capital decorates the mihrab
of the Ibn Tulun Mosque (see below), which
might have been brought from Fustat.*[9]

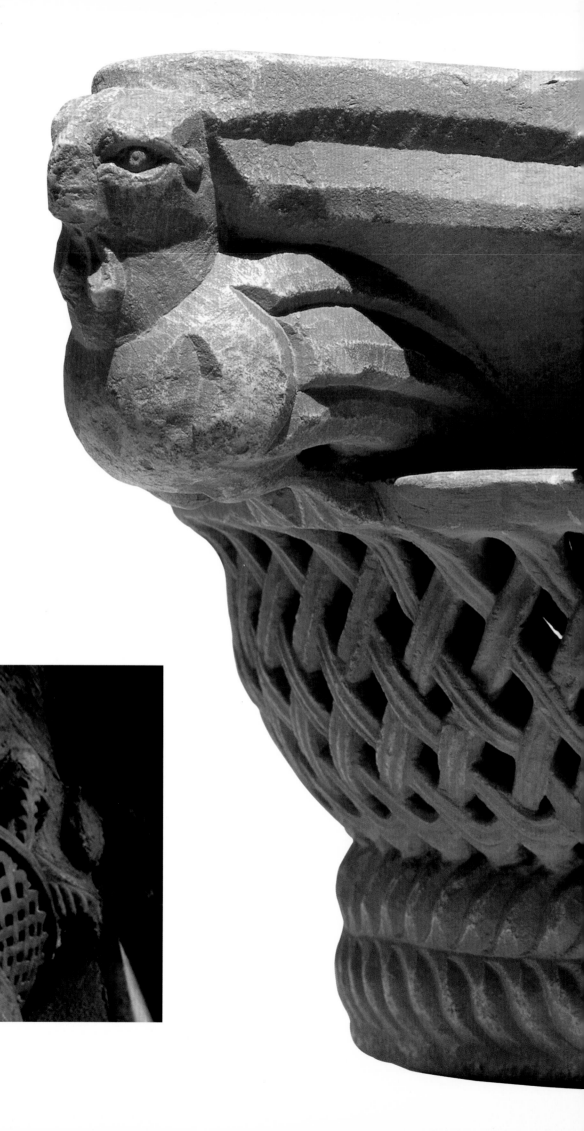

266

THE ISLAMIC HERITAGE OF OLD CAIRO

Tarek Swelim

THE LOST CITY OF FUSTAT

THE ARRIVAL OF THE ARAB GENERAL 'AMR IBN AL-'AS in Egypt in 640 would turn out to have a tremendous impact on this already ancient country, and indeed to mark the dawn of new era: the Islamic period. At the time of the Arab invasion, Egypt had been a province of the Byzantine Empire, ruled from Constantinople. Its main administrative center was Alexandria, a port on the Mediterranean whose easy access for trade ships from across the region made it Egypt's commercial center as well. Alexandria had of course also long been known as a great center of learning due to its famous library, storehouse of all the knowledge of the classical world until its destruction in a series of fires starting in the first century BCE. When 'Amr invaded, Alexandria was referred to as the city adjunct to Egypt, rather than the city of Egypt. Both physically and culturally, Alexandria was Mediterranean in character, and the Arab general knew it would not be a suitable center from which to rule and administer Egypt. Control of Egypt had to come from along the river Nile itself.

Just south of where the Nile splits into its Rosetta and Damietta branches stood the Fortress of Babylon, originally built by the Roman emperor Diocletian around 300. As well as being a military fort, the settlement served as an important harbor: all goods transported north and south along the Nile had

Across the Nile from the fortress, on the Island of Roda, stood a Nilometer. This important device measured the level of the floodwaters: the degree of flooding corresponded to the size and quality of the crops and was thus used as the basis for determining annual rates of taxation. (Ola Seif, after Kubiak 1987 and Yeomans 2006)

OPPOSITE PAGE:
The Nilometer on Roda Island, the Mosque of 'Amr, and Babylon on the mainland.

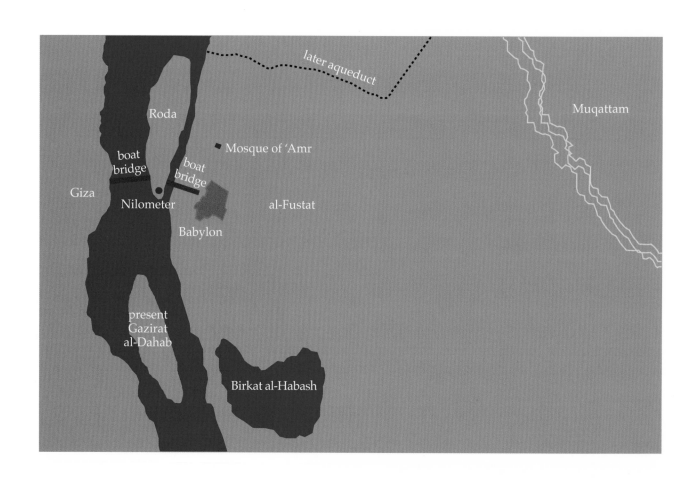

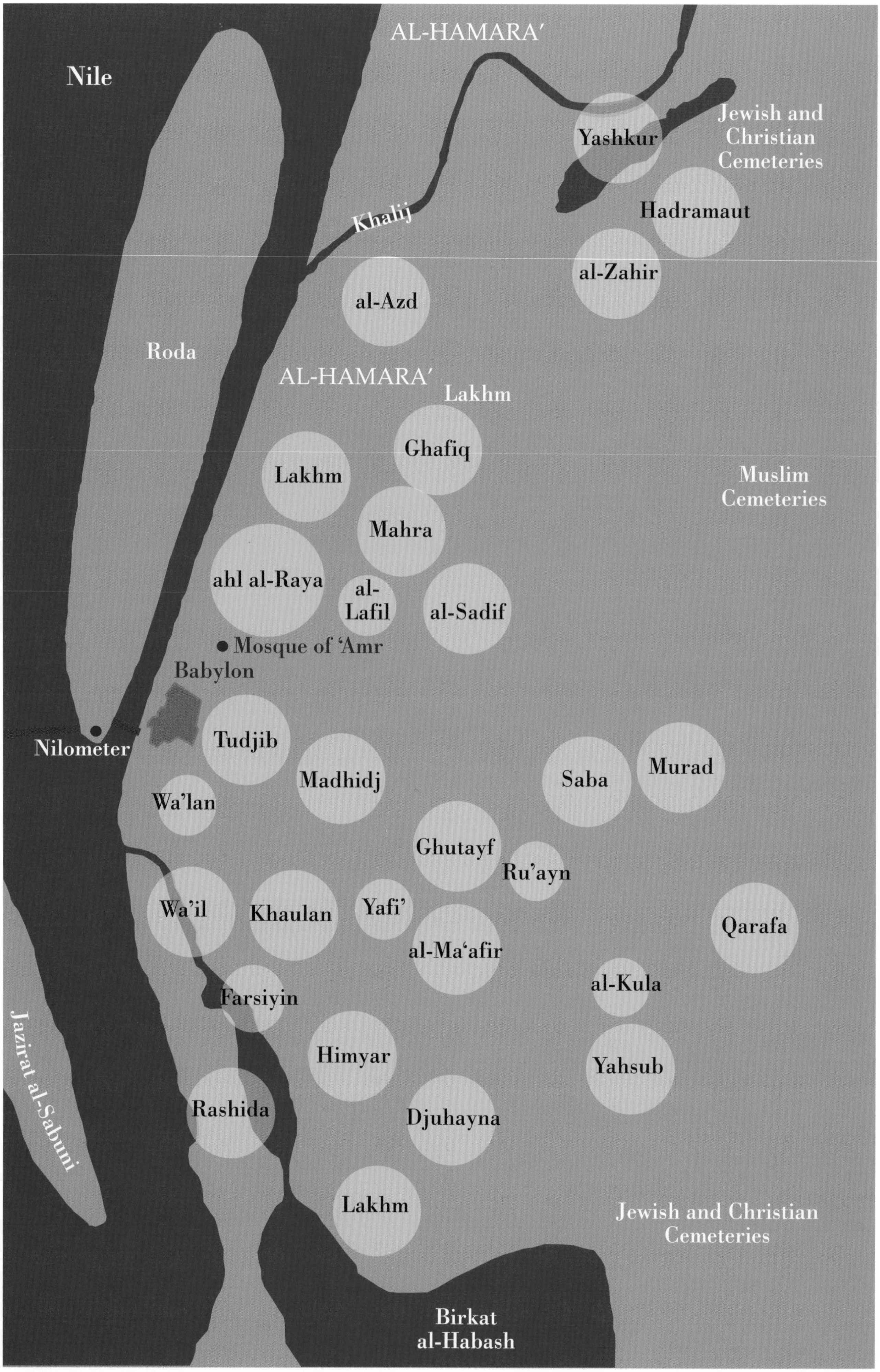

AL-HAMARA'

Nile

Khalij

Yashkur

Jewish and Christian Cemeteries

Hadramaut

al-Zahir

al-Azd

Roda

AL-HAMARA'

Lakhm

Ghafiq

Lakhm

Muslim Cemeteries

Mahra

ahl al-Raya

al-Lafil

al-Sadif

● Mosque of 'Amr

Babylon

Nilometer

Tudjib

Madhidj

Saba

Murad

Wa'lan

Ghutayf

Ru'ayn

Wa'il

Khaulan

Yafi'

Qarafa

al-Ma'afir

al-Kula

Farsiyin

Himyar

Yahsub

Rashida

Djuhayna

Lakhm

Jewish and Christian Cemeteries

Birkat al-Habash

Jazirat al-Sabuni

Map showing the various ethnic groups and tribes that expanded out of the military camp town into a city proper. (Ola Seif, after Kubiak 1987 and Yeomans 2006)

to pass through this fulcrum, where customs duties were levied on nearly everything. Across the Nile from the fortress, on the Island of Roda, stood a Nilometer (p. 271). This important device measured the level of the floodwaters: the degree of flooding corresponded to the size and quality of the crops and was thus used as the basis for determining annual rates of taxation. Economic and political programs in Egypt were thus closely tied to water levels: when they were high, the economy flourished, but when the river was low, the economy declined, affecting agriculture and tax revenue and ultimately leading to civil unrest. If this became sufficiently troubling, the military would intervene and take charge, sometimes even overthrowing the ruler of the moment. The Nilometer was therefore a crucial building to control, together with the Fortress of Babylon on the east bank.

The Fortress of Babylon had been built to protect the heavy traffic on the Nile at this strategic point. Moreover, it not only controlled shipping along the Nile, but also stood on the canal built by the Roman emperor Trajan in the second century CE to link the Nile to the Red Sea. (See the chapters "The Fortress of Babylon in Old Cairo" and "The Jewish Heritage of Old Cairo.") 'Amr understood the importance of taking this well-built and fortified settlement; he laid siege to it for six months until finally his Arab army conquered and Egypt was claimed as an Islamic province. The area where the Arabs had camped during their assault on the fortress was called 'al-Fustat,' probably derived from the Byzantine Greek word *phossatom*, meaning 'entrenchment.'[1] And thus the settlement of Fustat became the first Islamic capital of Egypt.

It would have been logical for 'Amr to choose Alexandria, with its wealth and splendid architecture, as his capital city, but several factors disposed him—and the Arab caliph 'Umar—against such a choice. Neither caliph nor general wanted the hardened soldiers of the Arab army to be softened by Alexandria's seductive luxuries. The caliph had also given 'Amr explicit instructions to "put no water between yourselves and me. . . . When I travel to you from Medina, my horse must take me directly to the place where I join you."[2] Other reasons were more obviously strategic: Because Alexandria was a Mediterranean seaport, its defense would require a well-equipped, up-to-date navy, which 'Amr and the Arabs did not have. And the site of the Fortress of Babylon was attractive for a number of reasons: its control of the Nile, its location opposite the Roda Nilometer, and its proximity to Trajan's canal, which assured Caliph 'Umar that the rich goods from Egypt could easily be transported to Medina.

The Arabs called the Fortress of Babylon Qasr al-Sham' (The Palace of the Candles), and according to André Raymond, it must have resembled traditional Egyptian towns.[3] The population of the fortress comprised mainly Copts and Jews. The area included old churches, like the Church of Sts. Sergius and Bacchus (*Abu Sarga*) and the Hanging Church (*al-Mu'allaqa*), as well as the Ben Ezra Synagogue. It had markets, a port on the Nile, and towered fortifications. Two of the towers flanked the opening of Trajan's canal, which traversed the fortress.[4]

Earlier sources have always linked the Fortress of Babylon to Trajan. Modern archaeological works, however, have proved that the actual fortress dates back to the time of Diocletian and that the connection to Trajan is not to the fortress but rather to the canal: the Amnis Trajanus, named for the emperor himself.[5] Trajan's canal promptly became the main trade route between East and West, allowing the export of bulky goods from Egypt in return for Indian spices and luxury goods, such as Mediterranean and Egyptian wines.[6] Trajan also built a magnificent stone harbor on the site of the Fortress of Babylon, its entrance flanked by the two massive walls beneath the present-day churches of St. George (*Mari Girgis*) and Sts. Sergius and Bacchus.[7]

Trajan's reasons for digging the canal were purely connected to his economic interests in the Near East. Wanting to have full control of the trade routes, his main obstacle was the rise and power of the Nabateans, whose capital was the city of Petra in what is today the Kingdom of Jordan. The Nabateans controlled the trade traffic in every direction, in part by ensuring vital safety of passage to merchant caravans traveling through their territory. There was an alternative trade route over the Red Sea, but piracy made that voyage far riskier than the overland route through the Nabatean kingdom. For Trajan to gain control over the Nabateans, he had simply to curb the power of the pirates in the Red Sea and thus make the sea route viable, which would ultimately divert the trade routes. Instead of making their arduous way through the rough, rocky mountains of Jordan, merchants could more easily move their goods by ship: starting at the port of Aqaba, sailing down the Red Sea coast to the port of Safaga and/or later to Suez, and then sailing along Trajan's canal to join the Nile valley at Babylon/Old Cairo/Fustat. The strategy worked, and in the year 106, Trajan annexed the Nabatean kingdom to Rome. This was important for his reorganization of the eastern provinces, as it allowed the construction of the Via Nova

Traiana—an adaptation of the ancient trans-Levantine trail running from Aqaba to Damascus, known as the King's Highway.[8]

The canal fell into disuse sometime between 300, when Diocletian constructed the Fortress of Babylon to guard its entrance, and the Arab conquest in 641. Its strategic location was probably among the reasons why 'Amr chose it as the location for his Islamic capital. The historian Ibn Abd al-Hakam refers to a letter from Caliph 'Umar to 'Amr in which he commands that the canal be re-dug as a matter of urgency so that Egyptian corn can be sent to Arabia to alleviate the famine there. Peter Sheehan notes that this account is particularly interesting because it reveals that Egypt opposed re-excavation of the canal because it had previously been a tool of Egypt's economic exploitation.[9] The opposition was evidently fruitless: the tenth-century chroniclers al-Farqan and al-Kindi refer to the canal being re-excavated.[10] After the Arab conquest, the canal was renamed Khalig Amir al-Mu'minin (the Canal of the Commander of the Faithful), and was no doubt a major factor in the spectacular growth of Fustat. Eventually, although the timing is uncertain, it fell out of use again: this may have occurred around 750, concurrent with the end of Umayyad rule; or perhaps in 767–68, when parts of the city's southern districts were sacked and burned to prevent their falling into the hands of the Abbasids; or indeed the canal might have stayed closed for some time after Caliph al-Mansur blocked it to prevent supplies from reaching rebels in Medina.

It is interesting to note that the canal was still active during the tenth century: the historian al-Muqadassi wrote in 985 that cereals were still giving life to the Hijaz via the town of Belbeis. This may have stopped, however, by the middle of that century.

The famous Khalig al-Misri was a section of the canal to the north of Fustat that would become the western border of the medieval city of al-Qahira. During the outbreak of cholera in 1896, this part of the canal was filled in and made into a road, which today is known as Port Said Street in modern downtown Cairo.[11]

Today, the early Arab Muslim settlement is almost impossible to locate because the Nile has shifted five hundred meters to the west since the time of the Arab conquest. Raymond says that it was more "a loose conglomerate of tribal concessions rather than a truly organized urban settlement."[12] At the time of the founding of Fustat, one would have encountered first the relatively narrow alluvial plain along the Nile, a low area (amal asfal) with a few higher locations where the fortress and the mosque of 'Amr were located. East of the settlement was a rocky plateau—a high area called Amal Fawq, where the lake of 'Ain al-Sira and the mound of Kawm al-Jarih are located, with Gebel Yashkur to the north and the Muqattam Hills on the east. To the south was the Lake of Bikat al-Habash. To the west was the Nile, which flowed past the Mosque of 'Amr and the Fortress of Babylon.

Over time, Fustat expanded from a military camp town into a city proper. It was composed of various ethnic groups and tribes, listed by Kubiak as follows (p. 272): One of the main groups was the 'people of the flag or standard' (ahl al-raya), who numbered about five hundred and were members of the Quraysh tribe; they were settled in the area around the Mosque of 'Amr. Another tribe, called 'the companions' (ansar), occupied the land to the south and the central area between the mosque and the fort. Other Arab tribes included the Tudjib, Lakhm, al-Latif, al-Sadif, Khaulan, Madhidj, Murad, Saba, Yashkur, Ghafiq, Mahra, Rashida, Qarafa, al-Azd, al-Zahir, Hadramawt, Himyar, Wa'il, and Wa'lan (p. 272). To the north were mostly non-Arabs, such as native Egyptians, Nubians, Ethiopians, Persians, Greeks, and Jewish converts; other nationalities who had come to Egypt with the Arab armies; and remnants of the Byzantine army.[13] In all, there were probably between thirty and forty tribal units in Fustat. Each group was granted an allotment of land whose size and location reflected the tribe's social, ethnic, and economic status.[14]

The population of Fustat grew quickly as a result of high birth rates and immigration from Arabia and al-Sham. By the late seventh century, during the reign of the Umayyad caliph Mu'awiya (661–80), the population had grown to forty thousand. Instead of a military camp, Fustat was now a town with all aspects of urban life. Bankers, clerks, administrators, merchants, and artisans from across the Islamic world were making a decent and respectable living in Fustat.[15] During Caliph Mu'awiya's reign, Fustat also had a dynamic building boom: an estimated five hundred houses were built in those years, including one hundred villas and palaces.[16] Excavations at Istabl 'Antar by R.P. Gayraud and by Kubial reveal that by the 740s, the population of the city had reached around two hundred thousand, not counting the slaves, clients, and Copts.[17]

As it grew in size and population, the city of Fustat developed into an international capital. Its main sources of income were trade and the export of agricultural goods. Its location just east of the Trajan canal and its bridge, made up of a line of boats, opposite the Nilometer allowed ships coming from the East and the Red Sea to bring goods from as far as India and China, as well as North Africa and Andalusia. Fustat was a bustling city and a melting pot of Eastern and Western cultures.

Good communication between East and West contributed to Fustat's success. Messages between Babylon and Medina could be transmitted in less than a week, allowing Caliph Umar to maintain close ties with his armies in Egypt. It also cemented his desire to re-excavate Trajan's canal so that Egypt's surplus agricultural produce could be shipped to Arabia and other parts of the empire.[18]

The Persian traveler Nasir-i-Khusraw visited Fustat in the eleventh century and described it as having buildings fourteen stories high, with roof gardens and ox-drawn water wheels to irrigate them. He included long passages about the city's thriving markets and noted that its wealth was impossible to count or estimate—indeed, he added, if he tried to list or describe it, his words might not be believed.[19]

In contrast, the physician Ibn Radwan (1068) thought that the streets of Fustat were too narrow for their high buildings. He commented that the hills to the east and north blocked the city's ventilation to such an extent that the air became stagnant and polluted, particularly from the furnaces and a multitude of steam baths.[20]

In 1168–69, the crusader king Amalric, of the Latin kingdom of Jerusalem, attacked Fustat. He encamped in the area south of the city, whereupon the Fatimid vizier, to prevent the crusading army from conquering Fustat and looting its riches, set it on fire. Al-Maqrizi says that for fifty days, the sky above the city was clogged with smoke.[21] The deliberate burning of Fustat must have affected the Mosque of 'Amr, although no records of specific damage exist.

After the fire, Fustat was abandoned and became essentially a garbage dump. Old and modern photographs show the miserable, dilapidated state into which it eventually fell (pp. 276–77). In its abandonment, it also became a popular source for illegal digging by the sabbakhin, who were seeking sibakh, or rich nitrogenous soil, as fertilizer as well as searching for artifacts.[22]

Archaeological finds show that despite its decline, Fustat continued to be used for centuries, although textual documentation dwindles after the fifteenth century. The early-twentieth-century excavations by Ali Bey Bahgat, undertaken over twelve years, exposed streets and quarters with the foundations of their buildings. In addition, thousands of artifacts and pottery shards were discovered from all periods of Islamic history and from the diverse cultures of the Islamic world, as well as great quantities of Chinese ceramics and Spanish ware. Bahgat's findings, together with Gabriel's, are elaborated in their 1921 publication, *Fouilles d'al-Foustat*.[23] Further excavations were carried out by Wladislaw Kubiak and George Scanlon, which are outlined in the numerous articles of the Preliminary Reports.[24] Scanlon proved he could date a revival of glazing in Egypt to about 700. Among his other great finds was the superb lustred glass goblet made for the Abbasid governor 'Abd al-Samad ibn 'Ali in 778, which showed that the technique was Egyptian in origin.[25] Scanlon also worked with Ralph Pinder-Wilson on Fustat glass of the early Islamic period[26] and published wonderful material on the pits of Fustat,[27] describing the city's highly sophisticated water and sewerage systems (pp. 278–79).

Additional excavations were carried out by teams of different nationalities (p. 279). The excavations of the French team, headed by R.P. Gayraud, at Istabl 'Antar revealed hydraulic works, including an aqueduct and reservoirs, as well as tombs in the area where Yemeni tribes lived; the findings were published in the Annales Islamologiques of the Institut français d'archéologie orientale (IFAO).[28] Several Egyptian teams, mostly headed by 'Abd al-Rahman, 'Abd al-Tawwab, and Ibrahim 'Abd al-Rahman, have carried out a number of works since the 1970s. The Japanese team from Waseda University, which excavated the elite district of Ahl al-Raya close to the Mosque of 'Amr, found a wealth of ceramics from different periods.[29] Additional textiles, woodwork, glass weights, metalwork, and coins have been unearthed and documented by Jere Bacharach, shedding light on the high level of culture and sophistication the inhabitants of Fustat once enjoyed.[30]

After the fire, Fustat was
abandoned and became essentially
a garbage dump. It eventually fell
into a miserable, dilapidated state.
Abandoned, it became a popular
source for illegal digging by people
seeking rich nitrogenous soil as
fertilizer, as well as people
searching for artifacts.

OPPOSITE PAGE TOP:
*The pits of Fustat, the city's highly
sophisticated water and sewerage systems.*

THIS PAGE TOP AND BELOW:
*Excavations were carried out by teams of
different nationalities. The excavations
of a French team at Istabl 'Antar revealed
hydraulic works, including an aqueduct
and reservoirs, as well as tombs in the
area where Yemeni tribes lived.*

THE MOSQUE OF 'AMR IBN AL-'AS

I N THE CENTER OF FUSTAT, near the Fortress of Babylon, 'Amr ibn al-'As had a mosque built in his name, adjacent to his house (p. 271). The Mosque of 'Amr, as it became known, was the first mosque in Egypt, and indeed all of Africa. Nothing of the original mosque survives except for a few decorative elements. It began as a much smaller building than the restored version that stands in Fustat today. Since its construction, the mosque has undergone innumerable restorations, enlargements, and additions, and has been torn down and rebuilt multiple times. The result is that the mosque we see today has been completely remade over the centuries, and in terms of architectural fabric is effectively a newly built mosque on the same site as the one originally founded by 'Amr (see general view, pp. 282–83).

The Original Mosque

In comparison to the present structure, the original Mosque of 'Amr was very small. It was a rectangular building of 50 by 30 cubits (22.8 meters x 13.7 meters) and served a congregation of seven hundred men,[31] who gathered there on Fridays from the Ahl al-Raya quarter of Fustat (pp. 271 and 272).[32] In plan, it resembled the Mosque of the Prophet Muhammad in Medina, which was built of mud bricks and palm logs. There were six entrances on three walls; the fourth wall—the qibla, which faced Mecca—had no openings. A modest ceiling of palm trunks split in half was supported by other palms, used as columns. The original interior was a large columned hall *(riwaq)*, without the kind of open courtyard *(sahn)* that exists in the mosque today. The original structure had no minaret for the call of prayer, nor did it have a mihrab (the niche that serves to indicate the direction of Mecca); four columns served that function instead.[33]

Doris Behrens-Abouseif believes that the first mosque designers did not identify the orientation of Mecca with a concave mihrab; instead, the presence of four columns suggests that a flat niche might have been used, with two pairs of columns flanking it.[34]

Additions and Restorations in the Early Islamic Periods

In 664, a year after the death of 'Amr ibn al-'As, a tomb was added to the mosque on the eastern corner of the building, said to have been the tomb of 'Amr's son 'Abd Allah.[35] In 673, Maslama Ibn Mukhallad, the governor of Egypt, ordered four short, squat minarets to be constructed at the four corners of the mosque.[36] These small minarets were the first of their kind in Egypt and resembled the short towers at the corners of the Roman *temenos* of the Great Umayyad Mosque of Damascus. Minarets were then added to all subsequent mosques in Fustat. In the pre-minaret age, the times for prayers were announced with a *naqus*, a kind of bell used by the Copts of Egypt.[37]

The Mosque of 'Amr was enlarged in various ways in 698, although none of these changes were recorded by historians (see p. 281 for the later additions). In 710, Qurra ibn Sharik, governor of Egypt, added a semicircular mihrab to the mosque. Yet more work was undertaken in 750, nothing of which has been recorded.

A *ziyada* (additional open area, with a wall to delimit it) was added to the mosque in 791, on the northwestern side, the area of which was called Rahbat Musa (p. 281). Another two *ziyada*s were added at later dates, as

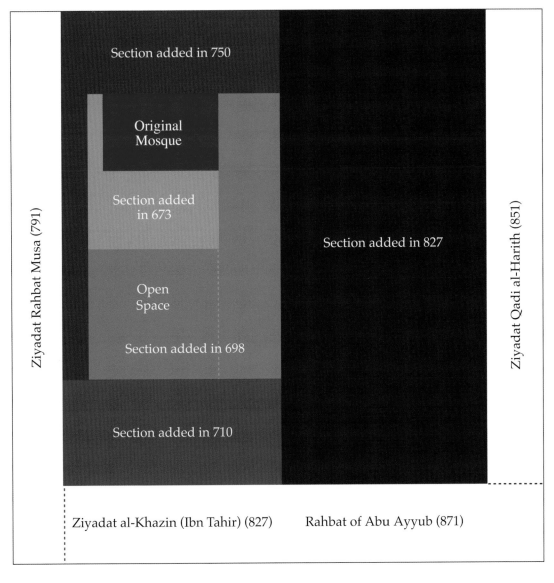

Section added in 750

Original Mosque

Ziyadat Rahbat Musa (791)

Section added in 673

Open Space

Section added in 698

Section added in 710

Section added in 827

Ziyadat Qadi al-Harith (851)

Ziyadat al-Khazin (Ibn Tahir) (827)   Rahbat of Abu Ayyub (871)

The Mosque of 'Amr was enlarged in various ways in 698, although none of these changes were recorded by historians. (Ola Seif, after Creswell 1979 and Yeomans 2006)

FOLLOWING PAGES:
The mosque we see today has been completely remade over the centuries, and in terms of architectural fabric is effectively a newly built mosque on the same site as the one originally founded by 'Amr.

described below, none of which survive. The current ones are a modern creation and are referred to as the *haram* of the mosque. The original mosque had no *ziyada*, perhaps because the Muslim population at that time was still small and the extra space was thus unnecessary. It seems logical that as the Muslim population grew, the mosque needed to be enlarged, thereby necessitating the addition of the *ziyada*s on three sides.

'Abd Allah ibn Tahir made the most significant enlargement in 827, which brought the mosque to its present size. Ibn Tahir was appointed governor of Egypt by Caliph al-Ma'mum. The historian al-Maqrizi records that Ibn Tahir ordered the mosque to be doubled in size, with an addition to the southwest,[38] and that his additions included the great mihrab and all the area on the southwest side, as well as the second *ziyada*—Ziyadat al-Khazin.[39] Ibn Tahir added thirteen doors to the mosque, each with a different name:[40] five on the northeast wall, three on the northwestern side, four on the southwestern side, and one for the mosque's preacher *(khatib)* on the qibla side.[41] There is nothing, however, to indicate precisely where this qibla wall door was located, whether it was next to the main mihrab or to one side or the other. Historians add that the mosque had 378 columns. 'Abd Allah ibn Tahir did not stay long in Fustat, returning to Baghdad only a few months after he arrived; works in the mosque of 'Amr were therefore completed by his successor, 'Isa ibn Yazid al-Jaludi.[42] According to Creswell, this was the last recorded enlargement made in the mosque proper; "the period of growth of the mosque was ended," although the *ziyada*s would yet be added.[43]

In 851–52, the third *ziyada* was added, named after a judge *(qadi)* who was probably attached to the mosque named al-Harith, hence its name Ziyadat Qadi al-Harith. Creswell believes this was added on the southwest wall.

The Mosque of 'Amr in the Tulunid and Ikhshidid Periods

When Ahmad ibn Tulun became the governor of Egypt in 869, he founded a new capital for Islamic Egypt called al-Qata'i' and built a large mosque there to serve as the new imperial mosque, representing his new Tulunid regime. A couple of years later, in 871–72, the Ziyadat al-Khazin was added to the Mosque of 'Amr. It later became known as Rahbat Abu Ayyub. There are no records of architectural changes being made to the Mosque of 'Amr during the reign of Ibn Tulun. This is not surprising, as it is known that Ibn Tulun was undertaking heavy building activities for his new capital in order to further his political program of becoming an independent state, separate from the Abbasid caliphate.

In 888, in the reign of Ibn Tulun's son Khumarawayh, a fire broke out in the Mosque of 'Amr that destroyed three of its windows and some of the columns. The windows must have been part of Ibn Tahir's earlier enlargement of the mosque. The ruler took charge of all repairs, for which he paid 6,400 dinars.[44]

After the fall of the Tulunid dynasty in 905 and the Abbasid invasion of Egypt, the city of al-Qata'i' was leveled to the ground. The subsequent rulers of Egypt, the Ikhshids, briefly attempted to revive the glory of the Tulunid period. We know little about the Mosque of 'Amr during that period except that, in 936–67, the majority of the *riwaq* column capitals were gilded, and collars were placed at the junction of the column shafts and capitals.[45] It is interesting to observe that, in spite of the fact that gold and silver were considered unholy by conservative interpreters of the Islamic tradition, they were extensively used in the mosque during this period.[46]

Records show that in 947–48, the *qadi* of the mosque had a room constructed on the roof for use by the muezzins.[47] This was not a common feature of Cairene mosques at that time. In subsequent years, however, similar structures were built on the roof of the Ibn Tulun Mosque after its endowment deed (*waqfiya*) was usurped by Sultan Lajin in 1296; this also led to the construction of a bridge linking the roof of the mosque to its spiral minaret.

These rooftop rooms, which have since been removed, were intended to facilitate the muezzins' calculation of the specific times for the call to prayer (*adhan*), and to hold the equipment needed for this purpose. The roof was also used as an ambulatory: people would circumambulate it as they do holy shrines in order to receive baraka, or blessings. Waterwheels were used to lift water to the roof for drinking, cleaning, ablutions, and for use in latrines.[48]

The Mosque in the Fatimid Period

In 969, the Fatimids conquered Egypt under the command of General Gawhar al-Siqilli (the Sicilian), who arrived in Egypt from the city of Mahdiya in what is now Tunisia. He founded a new capital for Islamic Egypt and called it al-Qahira—later known as Cairo. This was to become a fortified city built to protect the Fatimid caliph and his entourage, with two large palaces adorned with fantastic goods and a rich treasury. The area being urbanized was the extension of Fustat to the north, where the city of al-Qata'i' had previously stood. The Fatimid rulers claimed to be direct descendants of Fatima—the daughter of the Prophet Muhammad and wife of Imam 'Ali, the Prophet's cousin and youngest convert to Islam. 'Ali was to become the fourth of the 'Rightly Guided Caliphs' after the Prophet's death. Civil wars broke out between Muslim communities after the death of 'Ali and the martyrdom of his son al-Husayn. The followers of 'Ali, known as the Shi'a (meaning the faction of 'Ali), were expelled from Arabia and fled in different directions. Those who fled to Tunisia became known as the Fatimids.

The Fatimids were followers of the Isma'ili sect of Shi'ism and had an ambitious program to spread their doctrine throughout the Muslim world. The majority of the Egyptian population followed the opposing, earlier Sunni doctrine, making Egypt a prime target for the spread of Shi'i thought, politics, and military authority. Soon after the Fatimid invasion of Egypt and the founding of al-Qahira, a new program of teachings was established in the Mosque of al-Azhar by a famous vizier known as Ya'qub ibn Kilis, a Jewish convert to Islam. He is credited with the formation of the madrasa system at al-Azhar in 989.

According to Behrens-Abouseif, modern excavations at the Mosque of 'Amr support the case that it was an important center for religious teaching and a venue for political leaders to hold assemblies and engage in civic and legal activities. The archaeological findings at the *qibla riwaq* (arcaded hall directed toward Mecca) indicate the existence of small structures that al-Maqrizi describes as *zawiyas* (teaching chapels) built within the mosque, each having its own latrine.[49]

The Fatimids paid attention to the Mosque of 'Amr as a means of gaining popularity among the Egyptian people. They built small domed tombs—shrines—over the burial places of the Prophet Muhammad's descendants, including al-Husayn, Sayyida Zaynab, Sayyida Ruqayya, Sayida Aisha, and many more. These memorials became the focus throughout the region for *mulids*, festivals marking the anniversaries of the saints' deaths. These festivities became very popular among local Egyptians, particularly in rural areas, enabling the ruling Fatimids quickly to gain popular support.

Apart from the small holy shrines, the Fatimids also built important mosques throughout the city of al-Qahira, such as the mosques of al-Azhar, al-Hakim, al-Aqmar, and Salih Tala'i'. These mosques were mostly for the use of the Fatimids and their armies; Egyptians did not pray there, using instead the large space of the Ibn Tulun Mosque, which they had restored in order to administer the land taxes (*kharaj*) from its pulpit (*minbar*).

The Mosque of 'Amr continued to be used; the historian al-Muqaddasi visited it in 985 and noted that its walls were decorated here and there with mosaic patterns.[50] The existence of the mosaics is confirmed by the account of another historian dating from 997, which notes that the mosque was replastered and whitewashed and a great quantity of mosaic removed.[51] The removal of mosaic decoration is unusual, and one might thus surmise that mosaics were by that time no longer fashionable in Egypt. Mosaics were rare in the Cairene mosques and are found only in the mausoleum of Shagar al-Durr (1250), the main mihrab of Sultan Lajin in the Ibn Tulun Mosque (1296), the madrasa/mausoleum of Amir Aqbugha in the al-Azhar Mosque (1339–40), and the *mihrab* of

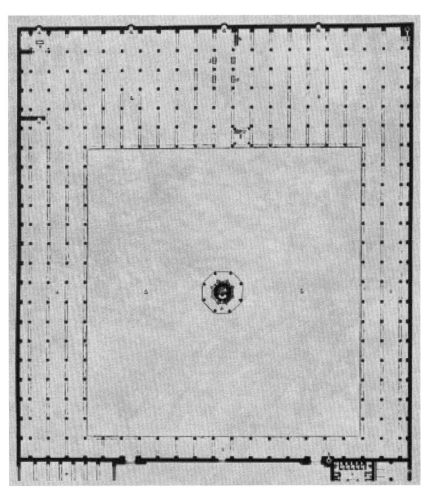

The only known mayda'a *in the Mosque of 'Amr is shown in the plan of Pascal Coste, and was probably added by Murad Bey in 1798.*

the Madrasa of Sultan Qalawun (1284–85). Alternatively, the removal of mosaic decoration in the Mosque of 'Amr may indicate that it had been damaged beyond restoration by fire or ill-treatment. Or it might be that mosaics were simply no longer a métier used in Egypt. Certainly during the Byzantine period the city of Alexandria had had some of the best mosaicists, but with the decline of the city as a productive industrial center, the craftsmen may have gone elsewhere in the Islamic world: mosaics remained popular in Palestine, for instance, and the region of al-Sham.

In 988–89, the Mosque of 'Amr gained even greater importance when the Fatimid vizier Ibn Kilis, by order of Caliph al-'Aziz bi-Illah, built a fountain (*fawwara*) in the middle of the *sahn*. This was not, however, a typical fountain: it was built under the dome of the *bayt al-mal*, the provincial treasury.[52] As vizier, Ibn Kilis was in charge of the economy and finances of Egypt. Locating the treasury in the Mosque of 'Amr sent the message that the wealth of the caliphate belonged not to the Fatimid caliph and his entourage, but rather to the people of Egypt. The fountain added both a popular and an aesthetic element to the treasury edifice. A *fawwara* is different from a *mayda'a*, or ablution place, which would have been constructed somewhere outside the mosque; there is no mention, however, of a *mayda'a* in the historical records. The only known *mayda'a* in the Mosque of 'Amr is shown in the plan of Pascal Coste (illustration on this page), and was probably added by Murad Bey in 1798 as discussed below.

The historian Ibn Duqmaq describes the dome of the *bayt al-mal*, which he says was built by the *mutawalli* of Jerusalem and was surrounded by wooden roofing that Creswell suggests served as an awning.[53]

The Ibn Tulun Mosque encompassed the first *fawwara* in Egypt, which was destroyed by fire in 986 and rebuilt two years later. The *fawwara* at Ibn Tulun was domed, but not intended for the treasury. The precedent for having a treasury in a mosque comes from the Great Umayyad Mosque of Damascus, where an octagonal dome supported on thick columns rises above the ground; there is no *fawwara* beneath it. The *fawwara* of Ibn Kilis combined the features of Ibn Tulun and the Great Umayyad Mosque. Siting the treasury in the middle of the Mosque of 'Amr, where local Egyptians went to pray, was a strategic move on the part of Ibn Kilis and the Fatimid caliph, consolidating as it did a relationship of confidence between the new Shi'ite regime and the majority Sunni Egyptian population.

Over the years, the Mosque of 'Amr sustained a great deal of damage. It is believed that at some point, one of its minarets collapsed, because a new minaret was added in 1052 on the eastern corner of the mosque, over what is now the so-called Tomb of Shaykh Abdallah ibn 'Amr. Today the tomb is covered by a dome.

During the reign of the eccentric Fatimid caliph al-Hakim bi-Amr Illah, the mosque gained even greater stature. In 1013 he bought the mosque for 100,000 dinars from the descendants of 'Amr ibn al-'As and added a great chandelier, decorated with seven hundred lamps and 22,000 dirhams of silver. Historians note that this chandelier was so large it could not be carried through the doors of the mosque, requiring the construction of a temporary opening. In addition, al-Hakim replaced some of the wooden columns in two *riwaq*s with stone ones, painted red and green.[54] By this time, there were seven *riwaq*s or porticoes on the front of the mosque, seven on the back, five on the east side, and five on the west side.

Caliph al-Hakim was eager to buy Cairo's older mosques, and he also bought the Ibn Tulun Mosque from that ruler's descendants. The motives for these purchases are unclear, as is much surrounding the reign of this unstable ruler. Why would he spend such extravagant sums to buy those two great mosques, which had been imbued with importance by his Fatimid predecessors? In fact, he had built a large mosque in his own name outside the early walls of al-Qahira, at Bab al-Futuh. Again there is reason to believe that it was another effort to gain popularity among the Egyptian people. Al-Hakim was known to be involved in numerous intrigues between the Sunnis and Shi'a, between the Jews and the Egyptian Copts; he did not have a single, straightforward policy and thus remained to a large degree mysterious.

In 1046, the Fatimid caliph al-Mustansir added silver decoration to the mihrab and some columns of the mosque. The following year, the Persian traveler and adventurer Nasir-i-Khusraw arrived in Fustat and left a good description of its streets and houses. He visited the Mosque of 'Amr and expressed his admiration for the building. He records that it was known as the Bab or Taj al-Jawami'—Gate or Crown of all Mosques[55]— and writes that "the qibla wall was entirely paneled with white marble on which was engraved, in beautiful characters, the entire text of the Qur'an. Every night more than one hundred lamps were lit." Khusraw also notes that the chief judge *(qadi al-qudah)* held his court inside the mosque during his time, and Creswell believes that this situation remained unchanged four hundred years later, based on a remark by al-Maqrizi that the court usually sat on Tuesdays and Thursdays.[56]

Some time later a new decorative program was again imposed on the Mosque of 'Amr, following an innovation originally expressed elsewhere in Cairo: in the Ibn Tulun Mosque (these additions were made to the Mosque of 'Amr before completion of Ibn Tulun Mosque), a wooden frieze running along the walls below the ceiling is said to have contained the entire text of the Qur'an, and the same decoration is said to have been applied to the qibla wall of the Mosque of 'Amr. Nothing of this remains, however, in either mosque, and it is difficult to imagine how all the text might have been inscribed on the qibla wall in the Mosque of 'Amr.

In 1050, al-Maqrizi notes that a *maqsura*, or wooden screen, and a mihrab carved of teak wood, flanked by two sandalwood columns, were made for the use of the mosque's imam.[57]

Portable wooden mihrabs were popular in Egypt. Wonderful masterpieces of woodwork, they were brought out for prayers and then replaced in storage. They could also be used for major occasions, as in the holy month of Ramadan. The Museum of Islamic Art in Cairo has three superb examples of such portable mihrabs with exquisite and intricate carvings.[58] It is believed that these mihrabs were used outside in the *sahn*, as the mosque had a mihrab set within its qibla wall: when worshipers congregated in the open to pray, they needed a qibla orientation and used a portable mihrab to indicate it.

Over the years, the Mosque of 'Amr must have suffered damage to both its decoration and its fabric. It is believed that at some point, one of its (probably four) minarets collapsed, because a new minaret was added in 1052 on the eastern corner of the mosque, over what is now the so-called tomb of Shaykh Abdallah ibn 'Amr. Today the tomb is covered by a dome that evidently postdates the collapsed minaret (pp. 286–87).

Low Nile flow during the 1160s created great difficulties for the Fatimids. Internal civil strife combined with external threats from the crusaders, who had established their Latin kingdoms along the western coast of Palestine and al-Sham, brought chaos to Egypt and its Fatimid rulers. This included King Amalric's attack on Fustat in 1168–69, which led to the burning of the city.

The Fatimids were desperate and requested assistance from the Zangid Atabeks of al-Sham. The popular general Shirkuh, who was under the command of Nur al-Din Zangi, was asked to come and restore order to Egypt. In Shirkuh's army was his nephew Salah al-Din Yusuf (later known as Saladin of the Crusades). After their arrival in Egypt, they had the Fatimid vizier arrested and eventually executed. Shortly afterward, in 1169, Shirkuh suddenly died and Salah al-Din assumed control. Amalric retreated to Jerusalem. It is worth noting that Fustat was neither invaded nor destroyed by the crusaders: it was the Fatimids who caused it to be burned. It fell into ruins, never to regain its former prominence.

The Mosque in the Ayyubid Period

The accession of Salah al-Din in Egypt saw the end of the Fatimid dynasty and the birth of the Ayyubid. Egypt reverted to Sunnism, and Salah al-Din launched new restoration projects in the Mosque of 'Amr. On the qibla side, the columns were scraped, its walls replastered, and its marble pavement repaired. He also ordered the renewal of the mihrab with the addition of marble panels in the fashion of the time, and had his name inscribed upon it. In this he followed the example of Amir al-Afdal Shahinshah, who had done the same when he commissioned a mihrab for the Ibn Tulun Mosque; it was an act that signified the authority of the new regime.

An inscription on one of the columns in the qibla riwaq *is attributed to the famous scholar Imam al-Shafi'i—the founder of the fourth school of Sunni law, and probably dates to the Ayyubid period.*

Al-Maqrizi tells us that the famous scholar Imam al-Shafi'i—the founder of the fourth school of Sunni law, who lived and died in Egypt (767–820) and was buried in his mausoleum in the Southern Cemetery— taught at the mosque of 'Amr during the eighth century.[59] An inscription on one of the columns in the *qibla riwaq* is attributed to him (see right), and probably dates to the Ayyubid period. No further restoration was made to the mosque during the Ayyubid period until its end in 1250.

Subsequently, however, the attention of the authorities turned elsewhere and the mosque began to deteriorate yet again. With the construction of Cairo's Citadel, all administrative affairs were transferred there; al-Qahira's walls were opened to the Egyptian public. For the first time, the population entered the great palaces of Bayn al-Qasrayn, and all their treasures were looted. Old Cairo and the area of Fustat became a ghost city, and the Mosque of 'Amr was ignored; it was probably rarely used during this period.

When the historian Ibn Sa'id al-Maghrabi visited the mosque between 1241 and 1250, he described it thus:

> I entered, and saw a great mosque, of ancient structure, without decoration, or any pomp in the mats which ran round part of the walls and were spread on the floor. And I observed that the people, men and women alike, made a passage of it . . . passing through from door to door to make a short-cut . . . and the roads and corners and walls were covered with cobwebs; and children played about the court; and the walls were written upon with charcoal and red paint in various ugly scrawls written by the common people.[60]

The Mosque in the Mamluk Period (1250–1517)

The disorder continued. The French king Louis IX (St. Louis) attacked Egypt at the head of a crusade. He was met by the last Ayyubid sultan, Salih Nagm al-Din Ayyub, whose army of Mamluks captured the crusader king in the town of Mansura in the Nile Delta. Salih fell ill and died, and his wife, Shagar al-Durr, who was of Armenian origin, became queen of the Mamluks. She married one of her husband's generals in order to legalize her position as queen, but was assassinated shortly thereafter. The successor to the throne was Amir/Sultan Qutuz, who feared that Egypt was at risk of Mongol invasion; the Mongol Hulago had invaded and destroyed the city of Baghdad, capital of the Abbasid caliphate, and was already sweeping through al-Sham and Palestine. Qutuz allied himself with his great rival, Amir Baybars; together they defeated the Mongols at the battle of 'Ain Jalut (in what is now the Palestinian West Bank) in 1260. On the way to Egypt, Baybars asked Qutuz to reward him with the governorship of Acre (in Palestine), but Qutuz refused. Baybars took matters into his own hands and had Qutuz assassinated. Upon entering al-Qahira, Baybars was received as a great military general and victorious leader. He was acknowledged as Sultan Baybars I of the Mamluks in al-Qahira, which continued as the capital of the empire.

During this period the heart of the city of al-Qahira—the area of Bayn al-Qasrayn—began to be urbanized. The old Fatimid palaces were destroyed, as were their cemeteries. New religious and funerary institutions replaced the Fatimid structures. Among the buildings that still survive are the madrasa and mausoleum of Sultan Salih Nagm al-Din Ayyub, which were built on the remains of the eastern palace. Adjacent to it to the north, Sultan Baybars I also built his great madrasa, of which only part still remains. Opposite was the monumental complex of Sultan Qalawun, who served as the right hand and second-in- command after Sultan Baybars I, and who succeeded him.

This brief chronology highlights the instability of the period. In addition, the center of religious teachings had now shifted to the newly founded institutions in the Bayn al-Qasrayn area and the al-Azhar Mosque. Despite these new institutions, the Mosque of 'Amr was given special importance because the structure was under threat of destruction.

In 1303, an earthquake struck and many buildings were destroyed. Amir Salar restored the mosque the following year. It is believed that he also added a stucco mihrab façade on the northwest side of the mosque, which is probably the same mihrab that is on the main street façade of the mosque today.

In 1268, Sultan Baybars I ordered the chief *qadi* to restore the mosque. The *qadi* inspected it and had a number of rooms that had been built on the roof cleared away. Also after consulting with the architect, the *qadi* gave orders to stop the water of the *fawwarat al-fisqiya* (the fountain in the middle of the *sahn*), as it was causing damage to the foundations of the mosque. This restoration resulted in the complete demolition and rebuilding of the northwest wall. Some columns were removed and replaced and the arches above rebuilt, other columns were repolished, and the whole mosque was replastered.[61]

The mosque must have fallen into neglect some time after that, because during the reign of Sultan Qalawun in 1288, more repairs were carried out, including the removal of dust and refuse that had accumulated in the area of the *ziyada*.[62]

In 1303, during the reign of Sultan Qalawun's son, al-Nasir Muhammad, an earthquake struck and many buildings were destroyed. Amir Salar restored the mosque the following year. Creswell believes that Amir Salar also added a stucco mihrab façade on the northwest side of the mosque,[63] which is probably the same mihrab that is on the main street façade of the mosque today (p. 290).

Ibn Duqmaq mentions that the Mosque of 'Amr had five minarets: two on the south and three on the north.[64] The one on the south corner, he writes, was called the minaret of 'Arafa. (Subsequently, in the Ottoman period, this one was attributed to Murad Bey.) On the east corner was the Great Minaret, while on the north corner was one that had been newly built. The fourth minaret was called al-Sa'ada (happiness). Next to it, on the west corner and over the door leading to the roof of the mosque, was the fifth minaret, which had been restored. According to Creswell, these minarets must have been built before 1399: Ibn Duqmaq died in 1406 and his chronicles do not mention the 1399 works of Burhan al-Din.[65]

The finial of the 'Arafa minaret does not resemble in its architectural form and details the minarets of the Mamluk period. Early Mamluk minarets usually end with a finial shaped like an incense burner (*mabkhara*), while those built after the Mosque of Maridani, that is, after 1340, generally had onion-shaped finials. The minaret of 'Arafa, meanwhile, is capped with a pencil-shaped top, no doubt from the Ottoman period. Two minarets were added to the mosque by Murad Bey during his restoration of 1798–99; this is probably one of them. The minaret of 'Arafa must have collapsed or fallen into ruins during the Ottoman period and therefore been rebuilt and/or restored by Murad Bey. It is also possible that the lower octagonal shaft dates from the Mamluk period, and Murad Bey's addition consisted of only the upper part to the pencil-shaped finial.

None of the remaining four minarets mentioned by Ibn Duqmaq is still standing, but the date of their collapse is not known. The Great Minaret, which was on the western corner of the mosque, has been replaced by an Ottoman-style dome—the mausoleum of the so-called Tomb of Shaykh Abdallah ibn 'Amr (pp. 286–87).

A mosque with five minarets is in itself remarkable; Cairene mosques usually had just one or two. The only mosque that had more than two minarets is the Mosque of al-Azhar, which is understandable due to its importance as an intellectual center of Muslim scholarship. That the Mosque of 'Amr had five minarets signifies its importance as a center of worship in Cairo during the Mamluk period.

Al-Maqrizi says that the mosque fell yet again into a ruinous state: "its arches were out of the perpendicular, and it was on the point of collapsing."[66] He adds that after the death of Sultan Barquq in 1399, the important people of that time were occupied by other business and pleasure, implying that the mosque was very much neglected. Into this vacuum stepped the chief of the merchants, Burhan al-Din, who decided to restore the mosque at his own expense, with financial support from his contemporaries. The whole *qibla riwaq* was demolished and rebuilt, and the weak points in the walls were repaired and plastered until, in al-Maqrizi's words, "it became new again." This restoration started in 1399 and was completed in 1401–1402.[67]

The next restorations of the mosque, recorded by the historian Ibn Iyas, were those by Sultan Qaytbay (1468–96); they were carried out in two phases to repair the walls and the roof. Sultan Qaytbay was a great patron of architecture and one of the most prolific builders of the entire Mamluk period, comparable to the Roman emperor Hadrian in his zeal for architectural patronage. Among Sultan Qaytbay's most famous achievements were his funerary complex in the northern cemetery and his imposing and impressive *wakala*s (commercial buildings used as hotels for traveling merchants): one behind Bab al-Nasr and the other behind the al-Azhar Mosque. Moreover, it was by order of Sultan Qaytbay that the fort in Alexandria was built overlooking the ancient Royal Harbor on the site of the famed Lighthouse of Pharos, and using the stones of the Lighthouse in its construction.

The Mosque in the Ottoman Period (1516–1798)

The Ottoman Turks defeated the Mamluks in 1516, at the battle of Marg Dabiq (near the city of Halab in what is now Syria). The Ottomans declared the end of the Mamluk empire, and all its territories came under their rule in 1517. The city of al-Qahira, having been an imperial capital for centuries, now became merely a province of the Ottoman Empire.

Creswell says that the French diplomat Caesar Lambert reported that a certain Bayram Bey restored the mosque in 1627,[68] but it is not clear which parts of the mosque were restored. Maillet, who visited Egypt and the mosque between 1692 and 1708, describes it as being well kept and decorated with various kinds of marble, granite, and porphyry.[69] Unfortunately, none of these rare and expensive materials survives. In 1737, Richard Pococke drew a plan of the mosque, which Creswell dismisses as inaccurate.[70]

Restoration Work by Murad Bey

The most significant restoration of the Mosque of 'Amr during the Ottoman period was that of Murad Bey in 1798–99. The historian al-Jabarti describes the mosque's state of dilapidation, noting that its roof, as well as some of its *riwaq*s, had collapsed to the extent that no one was using the mosque.[71] According to al-Jabarti, Murad Bey spent large sums of money that he had "taken impiously and employed unrighteous, and he set up its corners *(arkan)* and strengthened its construction, and arranged its columns and perfected its decoration, and built two minarets to it, and restored the whole roof with sound wood, and plastered the whole of it; and when it was finished, the result was the best imaginable." In addition, new mats were spread on the floor and lamps hung from the ceiling.

Marcel's *Égypte*

Only a few months later, in 1798, Bonaparte led his army of soldiers and savants on the famous expedition to Egypt. The scholars came to study Egypt and record everything they saw; their findings were published as the monumental volumes of the *Description de l'Égypte*. Marcel, one of the most prominent scholars, subsequently published his own separate volume, *Égypte*. He recounts that Murad Bey had levied a heavy tax on the Jews of Egypt, and they, in exchange for canceling the order, disclosed that 'Amr had buried treasure under the foundations of his mosque.[72] It was this search that prompted Murad Bey's restoration. An iron case containing a Qur'an manuscript written in Kufic script was uncovered. Marcel says that he bought a few leaves of this manuscript from the sheikh of the mosque and published them. Creswell studied the pages and concluded that because they bore diacritical marks, they should be dated a couple of centuries later than the time of 'Amr, and thus that Marcel's story was really closer to legend than fact.[73] The British traveler W.G. Browne, who visited Cairo between 1792 and 1796, gives a different version, suggesting that the books were discovered in a sycamore chest in a cellar as the mosque foundations were being cleared.[74] He says nothing about the taxing of the Jews. Creswell does note, however, that the leaves to which Marcel refers almost certainly existed until at least 1809, for when Seetzen was shown a little dark room on the north side of the mosque, the floor was buried a foot deep in enormous parchment leaves covered with great Kufic writing.[75]

Creswell believes that the arrangement of the Mosque of 'Amr during his time (that is, before its most recent restoration) was the result of the works carried out under Murad Bey, based on the ground plan drawn by the French architect Pascal Coste a few years after the French expedition.[76]

The Plan of Pascal Coste (1818–26)

The ground plan drawn by Pascal Coste between 1818 and 1826 (p. 285) shows a large rectangular building with three entrances on its street façade. There is a square courtyard with a *fawwara* in the middle and surrounded by *riwaq*s on four sides. The *riwaq*s are arranged so that there is one aisle on the northwestern side and three on the southwestern. Of these latter, the one closest to the exterior wall is narrower than the other two. The northeast side has four aisles, again with the one closest to the wall being narrower than the others. Six aisles run along the *qibla riwaq*. The arches of the *qibla riwaq* are shown running perpendicular to the qibla wall; today they run parallel to the *qibla riwaq*. The plan also shows a domed building at the east corner of the mosque, supposedly the tomb of Shaykh Abdallah, the son of 'Amr ibn al-'As. In the plan, a platform supported on columns *(dikka)* is shown along the main axis of the mihrab and facing the *sahn*, just as it appears today. The plan also shows a *mayda'a* on the outside of the west façade, which is on the main street. Two minarets appear on the plan: one next to the *mayda'a* on the main façade, and the other on the south corner. Both of these minarets still survive (pp. 282–83, 293, 296–97). At the time it was drawn, Pascal Coste's plan was the most accurate representation of the mosque.

Murad Bey's extensive restoration of 1798–99, completed just a few years before Pascal Coste drew his plan, was the largest undertaken since the enlargement carried out by Ibn Tahir in 827. More repairs were made in 1849, during the reign of Muhammad 'Ali Pasha, although it is not known exactly what was restored at that time. Sa'id Pasha (1854–63) removed the northeastern *riwaq*. In 1873 the Ministry of Waqfs drew a new plan that was published by Corbet in 1890 and so supplanted Coste's.[77]

During the khedivial or royal period, almost every ruler made a point of praying in the Mosque of 'Amr on important occasions, and both King Fuad and the late King Farouk often attended Friday prayers. After the 1952 Revolution, the presidents of Egypt—Muhammad Naguib, Gamal Abdel Nasser, and Anwar Sadat—did not pray in the mosque, probably because it was so closely associated with the royal family. The only Egyptian president to have prayed in the Mosque of 'Amr was Hosni Mubarak, during the inauguration of the building after its 2002 restoration. During and after the 25 January 2011 Revolution, the Mosque of 'Amr was a central point of gatherings after Friday prayers, from which protesters would begin their marches to Tahrir Square in downtown Cairo.

The Mosque of 'Amr Today

At present, upon approaching the mosque (pp. 282–83), one climbs down a short flight of steps in order to reach the level of the building: the urban build-up has raised the street level higher than its original foundation. The steps are directly in front of the main entrance of the mosque and form a passage that serves as both a gathering place and a buffer between the street activities and the mosque. This area is quite spacious and encircles the mosque on four sides.

Walking through the passage to the far right end, one arrives at a platform with steps leading up to it. This platform runs along the entire southwestern façade and continues around the whole circumference of the mosque. A few steps lead up to the men's ablution block, which is arranged conveniently for the worshipers to perform their ablutions before prayers, five times a day; toilets are situated next to the ablution block. The same area also incorporates the main offices and quarters of the servants and administrators of the mosque— the sweepers, cleaners, and so on. At the far eastern corner of the building is a large transformer, which supplies the mosque with electricity. The passage continues around the southeastern façade (the exterior of the qibla wall) of the mosque; there is nothing of significance in that area. After turning left to follow the mosque's northwestern façade, however, one comes into view of the women's ablution block.

The passage mentioned above is modern and dates back to the 2002 restoration. It is interesting to note that the *ziyada*s mentioned by historians in descriptions of the original mosque were similar in form and function and surrounded the mosque on three sides; each had a different name. This arrangement was a fashion in early archaic mosques of the time: it is present in the Ibn Tulun Mosque and was later echoed in the mosques of al-Azhar and al-Hakim. The contemporary passage still acts as a modern form of *ziyada*, surrounding the building with services for the worshipers and workers of the mosque. The only exception is that this feature now runs along all four sides of the mosque instead of only three.

The modern *ziyada* protects the mosque and its walls from urban encroachment and everyday abuse, which one witnesses in relation to most of the Islamic buildings in Cairo. It creates a feeling of spaciousness around the mosque, allowing passersby better to appreciate its walls and their decorative windows. Finally, it induces a greater sense of deference for this ancient building—the first mosque ever to be built in Egypt and Africa.

The Main Street (Northwestern Side)

The mosque's main façade (pp. 282–83) has four entrances, three of which are arranged symmetrically. The central one, which serves as the main entrance, is large and projects outward; the other two are much smaller. A fourth entrance is situated farther along the right-hand side. The façade is almost all new.

The top of the main entrance is raised higher than the rest of the roof and surmounted by stepped crenelations. Its door is set in a recess, flanked by columns on both sides, with a pointed arch above it and tiers of *muqarnas* (alveole) decorations. Both sides of this projecting entrance are decorated by niches in the Fatimid style found in the Mosque of al-Aqmar. Overall, the decorative composition of this entrance recalls the style of the Fatimid and Mamluk periods, such as that in the Mosque of al-Hakim and later that of Sultan Baybars I, in what today is the Cairene district of al-Dahir.

A minaret with an octagonal shaft, a balcony supported by tiers of muqarnas, *and a short, circular shaft surmounted by a pencil-shaped finial, typical of the Ottoman period is found above the smaller entrance to the right of the main entrance.*

Windows pierce the entire upper section of the southwestern façade (pp. 295, 296–97); most of them are new, as can be seen in the window above one of the entrances on the main façade.

The two smaller entrances are arranged symmetrically on either side of the main entrance. The one on the right (south) side is topped by a minaret with an octagonal shaft, a balcony supported by tiers of *muqarnas*, and a short, circular shaft surmounted by a pencil-shaped finial, typical of the Ottoman period (p. 293). The minaret, as mentioned above, is attributed to the 1798 restorations of Murad Bey.

An imposing stucco mihrab lies between this entrance and the last one, located to the right of the façade (p. 290). The mihrab's decoration dates it to the Mamluk period, more particularly to the restorations of Amir Salar in 1304.[78]

The last entrance (p. 294) was originally used by worshipers entering the mosque after they had performed their ablutions. Pascal Coste's plan of the mosque (p. 285) shows that there was once an ablution block next to this entrance;[79] it was installed by the Ministry of Waqfs and must eventually have been removed, though the date of its removal is unknown.

The Southwestern Façade

Windows pierce the entire upper section of the southwestern façade (pp. 295, 296–97); most of them are new, as can be seen in the window above one of the entrances on the main façade (p. 294). They are shaded by stucco grilles with geometric designs, and each one is flanked by a squat column on each side. Each column has a wooden transom that runs across the span of the window and is decorated in floral patterns in the Coptic style. The design of the windows has changed somewhat since Creswell's time: he describes the same arrangement, but a beam is set traversely on each column and the arch springs from it. Then above the latter is another, larger one, set parallel to the wall face which cuts off the tympanum of the lower part of the window, each part being filled with a stucco grille.[80] These must have been removed during the last restoration of the mosque. Above the transverse beams was a wooden transom that ran across the span of the window, similar to the current design.

The southwestern façade is also new except for its southern extremity, which still bears the original fired-brick wall. The façade as a whole is a flat, continuous wall with one entrance for male worshipers to use after

Several of the original windows have survived in the older section of the wall and have recently been restored. At that south corner is another minaret, similar to that on the main façade and also attributed to the works of Murad Bey in 1798.

The southeastern façade is pierced by windows. They are different from those on the other walls: their overall shape is the same, but each is flanked by two tall, narrow openings. This curious arrangement of triplet windows is unique, and they have no stylistic parallel.

using the new ablution block. Window grilles similar to those on the main façade pierce the wall, but in a slightly different arrangement (p. 295). Their spandrels have shallow, niche- like decorations with pointed arches and are flanked by column-like decorative elements, which are flat and unadorned. Creswell tells us that the original column-like elements alternated between a lobed and a tri-lobed design. They had been walled up at some point, but he managed to convince Mahmud Effendi Ahmad, the architect of the Comité de conservation des monuments de l'art arabe, to expose them again.[81] Several of the original windows have survived in the older section of the wall and have recently been restored. At that south corner is another minaret, similar to that on the main façade and also attributed to the works of Murad Bey in 1798 (pp. 296–97).

The window arrangement on the façade of the Mosque of 'Amr had a direct influence on the façade of the Ibn Tulun Mosque, though it also copies elements from the Great Mosque of Samarra.[82]

The Southeastern Façade

The southeastern façade is built entirely of fired brick (pp. 286–87), indicating that it too is part of the old edifice. It is uniformly built except for its eastern extremity, which Creswell describes as having "very rough and ugly buttresses."[83] The upper part of the wall is again pierced by windows, but they are different from those on the other walls (illustration this page): their overall shape is the same, but each is flanked by two tall, narrow openings. This curious arrangement of triplet windows is unique; according to Creswell, they have no stylistic parallel. He dates them to the period before Murad Bey's restorations and suggests that they could very possibly be from that undertaken by Burhan al-Din in 1399.[84] Old photographs of the mosque (p. 299) reveal that these windows were walled up sometime in the nineteenth century and uncovered in the 1930s.[85]

At the eastern corner of the mosque, where the southeastern façade ends, there is a domed building attributed to Shaykh Abdallah ibn 'Amr ibn al-'As, which will be discussed in greater detail below (pp. 286–87)

The Northeastern Façade

The northeastern façade (pp. 286–87) has an older section built of fired brick at its southern extremity and a newer stone-built section. It boasts an entrance in front of the existing women's ablution block, and windows similar to those on the opposite corresponding wall again pierce the entire wall.

The interior of the Mosque of 'Amr retains little of its original form. One enters the mosque through the main central entrance to find a large *riwaq*, which was completely rebuilt in 2002 by the Supreme Council of Antiquities (SCA). The columns in the *riwaq* resemble their ancient cousins and bear Corinthian-style capitals; their shafts, however, are made of concrete. The columns support semicircular arches, which in turn support a wooden ceiling.

The arches resting on columns set directly along the four transepts in front of the four entrances are perpendicular to the *sahn* (pp. 300–301); the rest of the arches in the *riwaq* are set parallel to it. The floors are covered with wall-to-wall carpet, decorated to look like small prayer rugs one next to the other.

It is clearly a very large *riwaq* and has long seats for the disabled, weak, and / or older visitors and worshipers in the mosque—quite an innovation among the mosques of Cairo today (p. 302). On the right and left are bookcases belonging to the mosque library. To the left of the *riwaq* there is a cabinet in which several burial shrouds are kept to be given free of charge to the poor when a family member dies (p. 302). This is only one of the charitable services the mosque provides to the poor; it is not a common feature of older mosques, although it has become prevalent in contemporary Cairene mosques of social and cultural importance.[86]

One leaves this magnificent space to walk into a large square-shaped open courtyard, or *sahn* (pp. 304–305), with an imposing *fawwara* in the middle. As mentioned above, the Mosque of 'Amr did not initially have such a courtyard; it was added long after the original edifice was built. The courtyard today has been restored heavily with the addition of a glittering marble floor.

Mosquée au Vieu Caire

Old photographs of the mosque reveal that the windows on the southeastern façade were walled up sometime in the nineteenth century and uncovered in the 1930s.

The arches resting on columns set directly along the four transepts in front of the four entrances are perpendicular to the sahn; the rest of the arches in the riwaq are set parallel to it.

The riwaq is large enough to accommodate long seats for the disabled, weak, and/or older visitors and worshipers in the mosque—quite an innovation among the mosques of Cairo today.

To the left of the riwaq there stands a cabinet in which several burial shrouds are kept to be given free of charge to the poor when a family member dies. This is only one of the charitable services the mosque provides to the poor.

FOLLOWING PAGES:
The Mosque of 'Amr did not initially have a courtyard or the imposing fawwara; it was added long after the original edifice was built. The courtyard today has been restored heavily with the addition of a glittering marble floor.

The columns in the riwaq or arcades on the lateral sides of the mosque resemble their ancient cousins and have Corinthian-style capitals; their shafts, however, are made of concrete. The columns support semicircular arches running parallel to the sahn.

The arches in the qibla riwaq *are set parallel to the* sahn; *in Murad Bey's 1798 restoration (above) they ran perpendicular to the qibla wall. The original arches were removed and the new columns rebuilt during the 2002 restoration (opposite). The changed orientation of the arches is evident when compared to an earlier photograph taken from the same angle.*

The *riwaq*s or arcades on the lateral sides have the same type of columns, with Corinthian-style capitals supporting semicircular arches running parallel to the *sahn* (pp. 306–307).

It is interesting to see that the arches in the *qibla riwaq* are set parallel to the *sahn*, since in Murad Bey's 1798 restoration they ran perpendicular to the qibla wall (p. 308). The original arches were removed and the new columns rebuilt during the 2002 restoration. The changed orientation of the arches (p. 309) is evident when compared to an earlier photograph taken from the same angle as that on page 308.

For the general public, the 2002 restoration gave the Mosque of 'Amr a spacious, grand atmosphere, especially in the area of the *qibla riwaq* (pp. 309, 310). For someone familiar with the mosque before its restoration, however, and for the student of the Islamic architecture of Cairo, the changes can be very awkward and disturbing from an aesthetic point of view. Among the mosque's unique features were its unusual arcades running perpendicular to the qibla wall rather than parallel to it, as they do today. These had given the mosque a distinct character of its own and made the mosque easily recognizable in nineteenth-century paintings. For instance, in Jean-Léon Gérôme's 1827 masterpiece, Prayer in the Mosque of 'Amr (p. 311), the arches and their columns, as well as the architectural details of the mosque are quite accurately copied. The arches are shown to be perpendicular to the qibla wall and joined by tie beams that spring from wooden transverse beams directly above the Corinthian columns. Standing at the same spot and angle as the presumptive viewer in Gérôme's painting (p. 311), it is easy to see how the *qibla riwaq* has been altered by the 2002 renovations.

While they might be disturbing, however, the changes are not in themselves bad. It is important to note that they were intended to restore the mosque to its original form, which predates the restoration of Murad Bey. That reason by itself would justify the mosque's 'new' look. Moreover, it would be unfair to suggest that the mosque has totally lost its character as a result of these changes; they have rather added a new element that reflects the mentality of the period when the restoration was carried out.

On the far right (south) side of the *riwaq*, there are columns adjacent to the wall (pp. 312–13). These are Corinthian columns with wooden transverse beams above them, which are decorated with floral motifs that resemble purely Coptic designs. Above those beams are other tie beams, which run across the entire span of the arches. These are also finely decorated. According to Creswell, these are the earliest existing decorative pieces found in Islamic Egypt.[87] One may therefore assume that these carvings are the earliest existing decorative pieces found in the Islamic architecture of Egypt.

The decoration of the transverse and tie beams is evidently inspired by similar designs found in the Dome of the Rock in Jerusalem and the Great Umayyad Mosque of Damascus. While in these original mosques the beams are very highly decorated, in the Mosque of 'Amr they are much simpler. They also recall acanthus-leaf designs in the fifth-century Monastery of St. Simeon the Stylite, north of Aleppo.[88]

A door in the far right corner leads to a staircase to the roof by which one can reach the second minaret of Murad Bey (barely seen on p. 310).

The qibla wall has three mihrabs, each with its own smaller *minbar*, the central one being larger than the other two *minbars*—the pulpit from which the imam delivers the Friday sermon—on the right-hand side (pp. 314–15).

Meanwhile, on the far left (eastern) corner of the *riwaq*, there is a square space covered by a dome and enclosed by a wooden *maqsura* (p. 316); unusual triple columns of the Corinthian order support the dome at two points. This was known as the Mausoleum of Abdallah, the son of 'Amr ibn al-'As, who was regarded as a holy saint and therefore called a shaykh. There is no evidence, however, that this man ever came to Egypt or is buried in the mosque. Similarly, not all the *mashhad*s (shrines) of the Prophet's family were burial places; some were built merely to preserve the memory of those people.

According to Julius Franz Pasha, Abdallah's mausoleum was erected by Abbas Pasha I sometime during his reign (1849–54). As mentioned earlier, a dome had been built in the same place in 664. The present structure is built on the nineteenth-century model of dome architecture in Cairo, which uses the hemispherical-shaped domes that were common throughout the Ottoman Empire. The walls on the interior of the dome are plain. The dome itself is supported by an interesting style of squinches, not commonly used in Cairo before.

The mosque has a long wooden *maqsura*, which is used today to separate men from women during prayer times (p. 317). A large square *dikka* lies in the *qibla riwaq* facing the *sahn* (p. 317). The *dikka* served as a platform on which someone—the *muballigh*, or deliverer—would stand to repeat (or deliver) the words of the imam during Friday prayers for worshipers too far away to hear him. The *dikka* in the Mosque of 'Amr appears to be an old one that was brought from elsewhere and reused. It resembles that of the Khanqah of Sultan Farag ibn Barquq in the Northern Cemetery and others of the Mamluk period.

Conclusions

Although the present mosque stands on the same location as the original edifice, nothing of the original building remains except for a few columns and several wooden beams at the windows. Since the enlargement carried out by Ibn Tahir, the size of the mosque has remained fairly constant, but most of the walls and columns, minarets, mihrabs, and *fawwara* are relatively new.

The mere fact that this was the first mosque to have been built not just in Egypt, but in all of Africa, makes the area a holy site for modern Egyptians. It is unique among the early mosques of Cairo, for it is still very popular, and people go there in large numbers to pray every Friday. This popularity stands in stark contrast to that of the ninth-century Ibn Tulun Mosque, to name just one example, which sees far

The arcades running perpendicular to the qibla wall rather than parallel to it gave the mosque a distinctive character of its own and made it easily recognizable in nineteenth-century paintings. For instance, in Jean-Léon Gérôme's 1871 masterpiece, Prayer in the Mosque, the arches and their columns, as well as the architectural details of the mosque, are quite accurately copied. The arches are shown to be perpendicular to the qibla wall and joined by tie beams that spring from wooden transverse beams directly above the Corinthian columns. Standing at the same spot and angle it is easy to see how the qibla riwaq has been altered by the 2002 renovations (opposite and below). Given in 1887 to the Metropolitan Museum of Art in New York by Catherine Lorillard Wolfe.

FOLLOWING PAGES:
The Corinthian columns adjacent to the wall on the far right side of the riwaq have wooden transverse beams above them, which are decorated with floral motifs that resemble purely Coptic designs. Above those beams are other tie beams, which run across the entire span of the arches. These are also finely decorated.

The qibla wall has three mihrabs, each with its own minbar — *the pulpit from which the imam delivers the Friday sermon—on the right-hand side.*

On the far left (eastern) corner of the riwaq, there is a square space covered by a dome and enclosed by a wooden maqsura; unusual triple columns of the Corinthian order support the dome at two points. This was known as the Mausoleum of Abdallah, the son of 'Amr ibn al-'As, who was regarded as a holy saint and therefore called a shaykh.

The mosque has a long wooden maqsura, *which is used today to separate men from women during prayer times. A large square* dikka *lies in the* qibla riwaq *facing the* sahn. *The* dikka *served as a platform on which someone—the* muballigh, *or deliverer—would stand to repeat (or deliver) the words of the imam during Friday prayers for worshipers too far away to hear him.*

less use than the Mosque of 'Amr despite being located in a very densely populated district of Cairo. Indeed, the Ibn Tulun Mosque has probably been regarded with some degree of disdain since the time of its construction: although it is considered to be an early Islamic monument, Ahmad ibn Tulun was merely a political ruler, not a religious one like 'Amr ibn al-'As, and so inspires less devotion. Al-Azhar, one of the other great mosques of Cairo, is similarly regarded as a political institution more than a religious or holy one: because of its role as the center of Sunni Muslim scholarship, it became a locus of political authority among its teachers and students.

Nor is it considered to be an early Islamic monument. In contrast, the fact that General 'Amr himself was a contemporary of the Prophet Muhammad and his companions undergirds the holy character of the mosque built in his name and memory. Moreover, 'Amr was the Muslim general who defeated the Byzantines and drove them from Egypt once and for all and introduced Islam to Egypt, whence it spread across North Africa and into the heart of the continent. The Mosque of 'Amr is therefore a memorial to early Islam, the Arab conquest, and the beginning of a new era in the history of Egypt.

Students of Islamic arts rarely used to study the architecture of this mosque because it is relatively new. Before its restoration, the building was dilapidated and aesthetically uninviting. With the most recent renovations, however, the mosque has been virtually rebuilt, and its unique features and history are sure to encourage students of Islamic art to visit and admire this memorable building.

GLOSSARY

ambon: pulpit of a church; a priest or bishop preaches from the ambon

architrave: a horizontal lintel or beam resting on the capitals of (a row of) columns

arkan: corners that support part of a building

bayt al-mal: a financial institution responsible for the administration of taxes in Islamic states; the Treasury

cenobitic community: monks or nuns living together in an organized monastic community, sharing prayer and work

ciborium: (pl. ciboria) painted wooden canopy sheltering a church altar

deesis: (Gr. 'entreaty') a representation of Christ accompanied by his mother Mary and St. John the Baptist, who intercede for mankind

dikka: platform supported on columns

durqa'a: a central hall (see *qa'a*)

fawwara: fountain in the middle of a courtyard

Hadith: narrations concerning the words and deeds of the prophet Muhammad

haykal: altar room of a church

iconostasis (Gr. Orthodox): a wooden screen that partitions off the sanctuary of a church; decorated with icons.

iwan: a vaulted hall or space, walled on three sides with one side completely open

katib: scribe or secretary; a high official whose modern equivalent would be a minister, secretary of state, or deputy secretary of state

kharaj: land taxes

khurus: a transverse space reserved for the clergy between the altar room(s) and the nave of the church

laqqan: basin in the floor of a church, used for the ceremony of foot washing on Maundy Thursday, the Feast of St. Peter and St. Paul, and the ceremony of the Blessing of the Water on the Feast of Epiphany

mabkhara: finial of a minaret shaped like an incense burner

madrasa: an educational institution for the teaching of the four schools of Islamic law, as well as jurisprudence and different sciences

mandorla: an almond-shaped halo enclosing a whole person in a religious painting

maqsura: wooden screen

mashhad: Muslim shrine built to preserve the memory of the dead; some *mashhad*s are actual burial places

mashrabiya: projecting window that features wooden latticework made up of intricately turned wood, connected without nails

mayda'a: washing area for ablutions before prayer

Melkites: Christians accepting the decrees of the Council of Chalcedon of 451; they support Christ's two separate human and divine natures after the Incarnation

mi-étage: half-story

mihrab: a niche that serves to indicate the direction of Mecca

minbar: pulpit of a mosque

muballigh: deliverer (repeater) of the words of the imam for worshipers too far away to hear the imam at prayer

muezzin: man who calls Muslims to prayer from the minaret of a mosque

mulid: festival marking the anniversary of a saint's death

muqarnas: vaulting technique using brackets and dome segments

mutawalli: official appointed to care for a shrine

naos: the area of a church in which the laity assembles; the nave, and, when present, the side aisles and return aisle

naqus: a kind of bell used to call worshipers to prayer before minarets were used

narthex: transverse vestibule of a church

Nilometer: a small building with gauges for measuring the water level of the Nile *opus sectile:* a type of marble mosiac work

Pachomian: Pachom or Pachomius (d. 346) is regarded as the founder of cenobitic monasticism in Egypt; he organized his community around work and prayer, and drew up the first monastic rules

qa'a: central reception hall of Egyptian buildings, with a covered central space *(durqa'a)* and one or more *iwan*s (vaulted or flat-roofed extensions)

qadi: judge

qadi al-qudah: chief judge

qibla riwaq: arcaded hall facing toward Mecca

riwaq: an arcaded hall supporting a ceiling

soffit: the underside of an architectural structure, such as an arch

spolia: reused building elements

squinch: an architectural element to effect a transition between a square bay and part of a dome or drum, consisting of a small arch placed across a corner with a convex shape behind the arch

Synaxarion: calendar of saints and feasts, containing biographies of saints and martyrs and various biblical and other commemorations; the liturgy contains a daily reading of the Synaxarion, commemorating the saint or feast of that specific day

synthronon: a bench or raised platform for the clergy set against the east wall of the apse in a church, usually incorporating a bishop's throne

tamav: Coptic for 'mother,' as Tamav Irene, mother superior of Abu Sayfayn Convent

wakala: lodging house built for traveling merchants

waqfiya: an endowment deed

zawiya: teaching chapel built within a mosque

ziyada: an open area in a courtyard with a wall to define the space

NOTES

Notes to the Introduction

1 See chapter on the Coptic Museum.
2 Gabra 1999. In 1994 a Middle Kingdom offering stand made of quartzite, which bears the name of a high priest of Heliopolis, was found during the restoration of the Church of St. Barbara (see Gabra 1995). An intact granite naos inscribed with the name of Nectanebo I (380–363 BCE), whom the text calls "Beloved of Atum, who is in front of the chamber of the gods," stands in the cafeteria behind the Greek church. It may originally have belonged to a temple at the site; alternatively, it may have been brought there from Heliopolis (Gabra 2012).
3 See chapter on the Coptic Museum.
4 Heikal 1983, 180f.
5 For example, see P. Lambert 1994, 17, 26, 37.
6 Gabra 1993.
7 P. Lambert 1994; Grossmann, Le Quesne, and Sheehan 1994; Grossmann, Jones, Noeske, Le Quesne, and Sheehan 1998; see also Gabra 2002, 173.
8 Gabra 1999, 150.
9 Gabra and Eaton-Krauss 2007a, 2007b.
10 Gabra 2002.

Notes to the Fortress of Babylon in Old Cairo

1 Hartung 2007. For predynastic Heliopolis see Debono and Mortensen 1988.
2 Kohler 2008.
3 Butler 1914, 15–22; Maspero and Wiet 1919, 139– 41; Jomer 1965; see also Coquin 1974, 8f., 27f.; Goitein 1983, 6, 10f.
4 Becker 1993, 148.
5 Yoyotte 1954, 84f., 114f.; Yoyotte 1973, 33f.; de Meulenaere 1975.
6 Gardiner 1947, 143.
7 Sheehan 2010, 30.
8 Gomaa 1982; Gardiner 1947, 131–44; Raue 1999, 28, note 5.
9 Drioton 1953; Sheehan 2010, 30.
10 Yoyotte 1954, 84–115, especially 111–15; de Meulenaere 1975; see also Heiden 2002; Sheehan 2010, 31.
11 For example: Montet 1957, 157; Kakosy 1977.
12 Sheehan 2010, 30, note 62; see also Kees 1977, 100.
13 Ball 1942, 18, 28.
14 Ball 1942, 82. For other classical geographers and a discussion of the subject see Redmount 1995.

15 Posener 1936, 48–87; Posener 1938, 271; see also Sheehan 2010, 36f.
16 Sidebothman and Wendrich 2001–02, 23; Bagnall and Rathbone 2004, 278; Gabra 2010, 47.
17 Sheehan 2010, 35.
18 Sheehan 2010, 40.
19 Toussoun 1925, 234; Jomer 1965, 957; cf. Kubiak 1987, 60, 118f.; Sheehan 2010, 39.
20 Toussoun 1922, 175; see also Kubiak 1987, 119, note 58; Sheehan 2010, 52.
21 Becker 1993, 147; Sheehan 2010, 49.
22 Sheehan 2010, 49.
23 Charles 1981, 55f (ch. 72, 16–19).
24 Grossmann, Le Quesne, and Sheehan 1994.
25 Grossmann, Jones, Noeske, Le Quesne, and Sheehan 1998; see also Sheehan 1994; Sheehan 2010, ch. 3.
26 For example, see Bagnall and Rathbone 2004, 87.
27 For Diocletian see Jones 1964, vol. 1, 37–76.
28 Heinen 1991, 945; Rowlandson 1996, 63f., 68, 121.
29 Bagnall 1993, 330–32.
30 For example, see Bowman 1986, 77f.
31 Mustafa and Jaritz 1984–85; Abdel Wareth and Zignani 1992.
32 el-Saghir, Golvin, Redde, Hegazy, and Wagner 1986; see also Bowman 1986, 54. For the military fortifications of Diocletian in Egypt, see Grossmann 2002, 351f.
33 Zosimus 1887, vol. 2, 34; Jones 1964, vol. 1, 52. For the military reforms of Diocletian see Campbell 1994, 232, 235–40.
34 Bowman 1986, 45; see also Davis 2004, 34–36.
35 Cody 1991, 434; Gabra 2008, 70f.
36 What follows is based on Grossmann, Le Quesne, and Sheehan 1994; Grossmann, Jones, Noeske, Le Quesne, and Sheehan 1998; Sheehan 1994; Sheehan 2010, ch. 3.
37 Sheehan 2010, 63; see also Gabra 1990.
38 See *Description de l'Égypte* 1994, vol. 5, pl. 20; Ch. Coquin 1974, pl. 2; P. Lambert 1994, 55, 61, Fig. 1.19.
39 Munier 1943, 19.
40 See chapter on the Coptic Museum.
41 See Kubiak 1987, 106, note 89; Sheehan 1994, 58.
42 See Butler 1902, 244–46; Kubiak 1987, 50f.

Notes to the Jewish Heritage of Old Cairo

1 Porten 1968.
2 Josephus, *Antiquities* 13.62–73.iii.1–3.
3 Tosefta Sukkah 4.6, ed. Zuckermandel, p. 198.
4 Fuks 1953, 131–58.
5 Ben-Sasson 1976, 362–63; Stillman 1979, 153–58.
6 P. Lambert 1994, 49–63, 253.
7 P. Lambert 1994, 80–84.
8 Reif 2000, 104–105.
9 The title *dhimmi* ('people of the contract') was used to describe Jews and Christians (and some other minorities) whose lives were protected by the Muslims and who were, in return for their loyalty to an Islamic government, granted a better status than heretics or non-believers but not one that was equal to that of Muslims.
10 Goitein 1964, 83–84.
11 Goitein 1964, 85; P. Lambert 1994, 225.
12 Lim and Collins 2010.
13 Reif 2000, 70–97.
14 Reif 2009, Cambridge University Library (hereafter, CUL) T-S Ar.5.1.
15 CUL T-S 8J22.27; see Goitein 1967–88, 3.186.
16 CUL T-S 10J4.11, T-S K25.205; see Goitein 1967–88, 3.169.
17 CUL T-S 16.278, T-S 13J20.9; see Goitein 1967–88, 3.220-22.
18 CUL T-S 13J21.10; see Kraemer 1991, 247–48.
19 CUL T-S NS J2 and T-S 12.425; see Goitein 1971, 83–110, and Goitein 1967–88, 2.188.
20 CUL T-S Ar.53.65 and Or.1081 J4; see Goitein 1971, 92–93, and Goitein 1967–88, 2.182.
21 Babylonian Talmud *Gittin*, 45a; see Goitein 1967– 88, 5.373–76.
22 Goitein and Friedman 2008, 52–89.
23 CUL T-S 13J18.8; see Goitein 1967–88, 1.219.
24 CUL T-S 12.515; see Mann 1931–35, 1.360–61.
25 Reif 2000, 195–96 and 205–206.
26 Jewish Theological Seminary of America, ENA 2.II.41a; see Goitein 1975, 47–50.
27 CUL, T-S 8J22.25; see Goitein and Hacker 1980, 170–72.
28 Goitein 1967–88, 2.160–61.
29 CUL T-S 12.608; see Goitein 1967–88, 2.219.
30 Isaacs and Baker 1994; Lev and Amar 2008.
31 Bohak 2008.
32 Reif 2010, ch. 27.
33 For bibliographical details, see Reif 2000, 119.
34 Reif 2000, 121–48.

Notes to the Christian Heritage of Old Cairo

1 See references in Ch. Coquin 1974, 173–76. Sheehan 2010, figs. 3–4.

2 den Heijer 1996, 69–77, with earlier literature. The editions used are those by B.T.A. Evetts (*HPE*) and by various authors for the Societe d'archeologie copte (*HPC*).

3 den Heijer 1993, 1994, and 1996, 77–80; Zanetti 1995. Translations: Evetts and Butler 1895; al- Suryani 1992.

4 Wustenfeld 1845; Evetts and Butler 1895, 305–46.

5 References by church in Ch. Coquin 1974.

6 Vansleb 1671 and 1677 (English translation: Vansleb 1678); on his life and travels see Delahaye 2003, with earlier literature.

7 Vansleb 1671, 200–203.

8 Vansleb 1677, 236–45 (English translation, Vansleb 1678, 142–48).

9 Mayeur-Jaouen 1992.

10 Cairo, College de la Sainte Famille, Archive Jullien.

11 Johann Georg, Duke of Saxony 1914, 1930, and 1931. On Prince Johann Georg and his collection see Heide and Thiel 2004.

12 Munier 1943, 19.

13 Burmester 1955, 24; Grossmann 1991, 317–18; van Loon in Gabra and van Loon 2007, 112. Recent archaeological research has confirmed this hypothesis: Sheehan 2010, 88.

14 *HPE* III, 106; Munier 1943, 25.

15 *The History of the Churches and Monasteries in Egypt*, fol. 37b (Evetts and Butler 1895, 121). According to Ch. Coquin 1974, 22, this is the only source designating the Church of Abu Sayfayn an Episcopal church. Cf. Burmester 1955, 16 (repeated in Ishaq 1991, 1613).

16 R.-G. Coquin 1991; Gabra 2008, 221.

17 Grossmann 2002, 505–507; van Loon in Gabra and van Loon 2007, 100.

18 *HPC* II-ii, 136.

19 Grossmann 2002, 66; Sheehan 2010, 79–80.

20 Sheehan 2010, 85–87.

21 A *katib*—scribe or secretary—was a high official, equivalent to the modern minister, secretary of state, or deputy secretary (Sellheim and Sourdel 1978).

22 Grossmann 2002, 77–78.

23 Grossmann 2002, 95–100. Churches of this type can be extended by adding more bays and corresponding *haykal*s.

24 *HPE* IV, 406–08; also found in *The History of Churches and Monasteries of Egypt* fol. 23b (Evetts and Butler 1895, 84–86).

25 Sheehan 2010, 92.

26 McKenzie 1992, 17–18; Sheehan 2010, 82.

27 McKenzie 1992, 17–18, 45.

28 Altar: Gabra and Eaton-Krauss 2007b, 195, no. 125. Doors: Gabra and Eaton-Krauss 2007b, 215–17, no. 133. Altar screen St. Barbara: Jeudy in Snelders and Jeudy 2006, 114–22; Jeudy 2007b, 125–29.

29 Jeudy in Snelders and Jeudy 2006, 119.

30 Sheehan 2010, 82, 99.

31 Butler 1884, vol. 1, frontispiece, 251; Jullien 1887, 546; Jullien 1889, 223, also published in Ch. Coquin 1974, pl. II; Ch. Coquin 1974, pl. IX–X. The ruins and rubbish mounds were in plain sight until the end of the nineteenth century: al- Maqrizi (Evetts and Butler 1895, 328), Vansleb (1677, 131, 237; 1678, 81, 143) and Butler (1884a, vol. 1, 250).

32 Sheehan 2010, 99–100.

33 Grossmann 2002, 94–95.

34 MacCoull 1996.

35 Atiya 1991.

36 References for the various churches in Ch. Coquin 1974.

37 Middeldorf Kosegarten 2000.

38 Jeudy 2004, 82–86.

39 Z. Skalova directed these restoration projects; see Skalova in Skalova and Gabra 2006, 160, 178.

40 The influence was mutual. Themes, iconography, and compositions were introduced into European art through contacts with artists working in a Christian environment in the Middle East.

41 Lezine 1972, 72–79, 115–20; Revault and Maury 1977, 77–83.

42 Sheehan 2010, 95.

43 Paris, Bibliotheque nationale de France, Ms. Ar. 132, dated 1629 (Salmon 1903, 25, 44).

44 Sheehan 2010, 95, 108–10, figs. 44, 46, 53, and pls. 10 and 36.

45 CCMAA 1903, 31 and 66; CCMAA 1910, 125–26 and pl. VII.

46 CCMAA 1906, 126.

47 Ch. Coquin 1974, 18–25.

48 Motzki 1991; Gabra, in Gabra and van Loon 2007, 106–107; Guirguis 2008, 39–43.

49 Guirguis 2008: 43–44.

50 Skalova in Skalova and Gabra 2006, 132–33, figs. III.54 and III.56; 219–27, nos. 23–27.

51 The Ark or "Throne of the Chalice" (Arabic: *Kursi al-Kas*), a small wooden casket in which the chalice is kept until Holy Communion (Gabra 2008, 101–102). For an inventory of chalice thrones, see van Moorsel 1991.

52 Skalova in Skalova and Gabra 2006, 137–40. Most recently on the life and work of Yuhanna al- Armani and Ibrahim al-Nasih: Guirguis 2008.

53 Gabra in Gabra and van Loon 2007, 140–45.

54 Johann Georg, Duke of Saxony 1914, 10. The photographs of the prince (1914, figs. 29–31) show that the panels were not in the same position as today.

55 van Moorsel, Immerzeel, and Langen 1994, 39; Jeudy 2004, 76.

56 Butler 1884, vol. 1, 75–270.

57 Somers Clarke 1896, 66–67.

58 In 1961, the responsibilities of the Comite were taken over by the Egyptian Antiquities Organization (now the Supreme Council of Antiquities). For the early history of the Comite, see Reid 1992; El-Habashi and Warner 1998, 81– 82.

59 Somers Clarke 1896, 66. Later, Somers Clarke became a member of the Comite and repeatedly reported demolition, neglect, and destruction of churches and monasteries all over Egypt, advising registration of monuments and restorations. See, for example, CCMAA 1915–19, 527–28 (Reid 1992, 66).

60 CCMAA 1895, 85–86.

61 Sheehan 2010, 121–22, 128.

62 CCMAA 1897, 12–13 and 103–108; Reid 1992, 66.

63 Herz 1914, 191–94; El-Habashi and Warner 1998, 85.

64 Sanders 2008, 12–16 (with further literature) discusses the various views on preservation and conservation in Europe and Egypt.

65 Published in Patricolo, Monneret de Villard, and Munier 1922b.

66 Somers Clarke 1896, 64: "none but the poorest now live in Old Cairo."

67 Donald Malcolm Reid noticed this phenomenon for Islamic monuments (Reid 1992, 64–65).

68 For example, CCMAA 1901, 3, 34; CCMAA 1903, 25.

69 Sheehan 2010, 136 and fig. 62.

70 Sheehan 2010, xiii, 1.

71 Sheehan 2010, 137–42.

72 Guirguis 2008, esp. 13–15.

73 Sheehan 2010, fig. 24.

74 *HPE* IV, 519–22; Cf. Ch. Coquin 1974, 66–67.

75 This miracle, with various details, is described in, for example, the *History of the Patriarchs* (*HPC* II- ii, quote on 144), *The History of the Churches and Monasteries of Egypt* and the Synaxarion, the Calendar of Saints (den Heijer 2004, 49–57).

76 R.-G. Coquin 1991, 1912–13.

77 Ch. Coquin 1974, 69–73.

78 Ch. Coquin 1974, 66–69.

79 Vansleb 1677, 237–38 (1678, 143–44).

80 Guirguis 2008, 42.

81 Butler 1884, vol. 1, 208–28, 235, note 1: Butler noted that, revisiting in 1884, the effect of the restoration was less disastrous than imagined.

82 Guirguis 2008, 119, note 174: "The *nazir al-kanisa* (pl. *nuzzar*) was the official in charge of overseeing the administrative and financial affairs of a church." Cf. CCMAA 1895, 42–43.

83 Inscriptions: e-mail from G. Gabra, 1 August 2010.

84 Described by Somers Clarke 1896, 64–65. Cf. Sheehan 2010, 122–23 and figs. 65–66.

85 Somers Clarke 1896, 64, quoted in Sheehan 2010, 23.

86 Jullien 1887, 559 (reprinted in Jullien 1889, 228). "The whole place thoroughly rearranged, like a French cathedral fresh from the hands of M. Viollet le Duc" according to Somers Clarke (1896, 64). Eugene-Emmanuel Viollet le Duc (d. 1879) was a French restoration architect and theorist, known for 'over-restoration' of French Gothic churches. He advocated a 're-creation' of monuments, to restore a monument to the state it was meant to be, even if the outcome was a building that never had existed in reality. (Dictionary of Art Historians: http://www.dictionaryofarthistorians.org/violle tleduce.htm).

87 Johann Georg, Duke of Saxony 1914, 6–9; cf. CCMAA 1899, 39; CCMAA 1912, 34–35.

88 For the activities of the CCMAA from 1897 to 1910, see Herz 1914, 195. CCMAA 1915–19, 192–94, 412–13, 416. For the lintel, see Gabra and Eaton-Krauss 2007b, 206–11, no. 129, and van der Vliet 2007, with earlier literature. Later, minor repairs were carried out: CCMAA 1927–29, 93, 127; CCMAA 1941–45, 16, 23; CCMAA 1946–53, 354–55. Cf. Ch. Coquin 1974, 69, with corrections.

89 Guirguis 2008, 87–89.

90 Sheehan 2010, 138.

91 Sheehan 2010, 139.

92 The Latin translation is published in J.P. Migne, ed., *Patrologia Graeca* 111, 1119 (cited in Ch. Coquin 1974, trans.: 118, text: 133–34). Vansleb (1677, 239; 1678, 144) wrote that, according to Sa'id ibn Batriq, a Coptic secretary to 'Abd al-'Aziz built the Church of St. Sergius. Grossmann 2002, 414; Grossmann 2006, 9. Cf. Sheehan 2010, 89.

93 De Lacy O'Leary 1937, 248; Papaconstantinou 2001, 186–87. The Coptic calendar year is based on the ancient Egyptian solar calendar. It consists of twelve months of thirty days with five more days (six in a leap year) of the intercalary month. Depending on leap years, the year starts on 11 or 12 September with the month of Tut, followed by Babeh, Hathor, Kihak, Tubeh, Amshir, Baramhat, Baramuda, Bachans, Baunah, Abib, Nasi, and Misra. The names of the months are derived from Egyptian gods or from festivals that took place in the relevant period. The intercalary days are called 'the delayed days' or 'the little month.' This calendar regulated the agricultural schedule in the Nile valley before the building of the High Dam in Aswan and survives in Coptic liturgy and *synaxaria*, calendars of saints (Wissa Wassef 1991).

94 Grébaut 1927, 553; Cf. Ch. Coquin 1974, 93.

95 Vatican Library, Cod. Vat. Copt. 62, fol. 211–43, especially fols. 228–29 (Porcher 1914, 350–52); Ch. Coquin 1974, 93–94; manuscript dates to the ninth or tenth century.

96 *HPC* III, 171, 210.

97 Ch. Coquin 1974, 98–100.

98 *HPC* II-ii, 136; cf. Grossmann 2002, 414.

99 See references in Ch. Coquin 1974, 99.

100 Jullien 1887, 545 (reprinted in Jullien 1889, 225). Cf. Sheehan 2010, fig. 57.

101 Sheehan 2010, 89–90 and figs. 40–42.

102 Salmon 1903, 64–68; cf. Habib 1967a, 32.

103 Ch. Coquin 1974, 97–98.

104 Sheehan 2010, 93–95, figs. 12, 43, 56, and 58, and pls. 9, 32–33, and 42. Grossmann (2006) argues for a late-thirteenth-century date for the building of the crypt, after remodeling of the nave.

105 Sheehan 2010, 107–108 and pls. 16–17. The painting in the southern *haykal* is a second layer, repeating the same subject (Milward Jones 2006; Bolman 2006). On the basis of stylistic parallels it might be dated to around 1200. Bolman assigns a somewhat later date to this painting, in comparison to the paintings in the Old Church of the Monastery of St. Antony near the Red Sea. However, in my view, the angels and the face of Christ show much closer similarities

to paintings in the upper-floor chapels and gallery in the Church of St. Mercurius, which can be dated to the renovation after the fire of 1168 (van Loon 1999, 27–30). In view of this idea, Sheehan's arguments do not contradict an earlier date.

106 Sheehan 2010, 107.

107 Middeldorf Kosegarten 2000, 58–59.

108 Ch. Coquin 1974, 171–72.

109 See references in Ch. Coquin 1974, 100–102. Cf. Sheehan 2010, 115.

110 Sheehan 2010, 118–19.

111 Butler 1884, vol. 1, 181–203, (with plan) 185; Jullien 1887, 545–59 (reprinted in Jullien 1889, 226–27 and illustration on 225); Sheehan 2010, 119 and fig. 59.

112 For the activities of the CCMAA from 1897 to 1910, see Herz 1914, 191. CCMAA 1912, 35; CCMAA 1915–19, 194–95. Later, minor repairs: CCMAA 1930–32, 273; CCMAA 1941–45, 136; CCMAA 1946–53, 213, 299, 356. Cf. Ch. Coquin 1974, 95–96 (with corrections) and Sheehan 2010, 130–32 and figs. 71–72.

113 Sheehan 2010, 138–40.

114 Ch. Coquin 1974, 109–13.

115 Gabra and Eaton-Krauss 2007b, 195, no. 125.

116 Jeudy 2004, 75 and pl. 10; Sheehan 2010, pl. 37.

117 Papaconstantinou 2001, 135–36. On the saints see most recently Boutros 2008.

118 Kratchkowsky and Vasiliev 1924, 779.

119 De Lacy O'Leary 1937, 98; Meinardus 1972–73.

120 Salmon 1903, 64–66.

121 Salmon 1903, 44.

122 Ch. Coquin 1974, 117–18.

123 Ch. Coquin 1974, 124–25. Fourteenth-century western pilgrims also reported relics of St. Barbara in the Hanging Church. Possibly only some of her relics had been transferred (Ch. Coquin 1974, 80).

124 Grossmann 2002, 417.

125 Butler 1884, vol. 1, 235–46; quote on 236.

126 Habib 1967a, 38–39. The dates were read by Dr. Munier, librarian of the Egyptian Museum.

127 Inv. no. 778: Jeudy in Snelders and Jeudy 2006, 114–22; Jeudy 2007b, 125–29.

128 Johann Georg, Duke of Saxony 1914, 9.

129 Coptic Museum, inv. no. 738 (Gabra and Eaton-Krauss 2007b, 216–17, no. 133).

130 Johann Georg, Duke of Saxony 1930, 14.

131 For the activities of the CCMAA from 1897 to 1910, see Herz 1914, 194. CCMAA 1915–19, 195–99; CCMAA 1920–24, 33–34; CCMAA 1927–29, 53, 127; CCMAA 1950–52, 299, 356; Patricolo, Monneret de Villard, and Munier 1922b; Cf. Ch. Coquin 1974, 120, with corrections; Grossmann 2002, 417, and Sheehan 2010, 95, 111, 131–32 and figs. 36 and 73–74.

132 Skálová, in Skálová and Gabra 2006, 176–79. Although it was completely blackened at that time, Johann Georg (1914, 9 and photo 27; 1930, 14) was struck by its quality.

133 Grossmann 2002, 417.

134 CCMAA 1910, 35.

135 See "The Church of Sts. Sergius and Bacchus," note 92.

136 De Lacy O'Leary 1937, 140–45; Papaconstantinou 2001, 69–71.

137 Sheehan 2010, 90.

138 Sheehan 2010, 138–39.

139 Butler 1884, vol. 1, 248. Cf. CCMAA 1897, 105. Adeline Jeudy claims that the hall also burned down in the nineteenth century (Jeudy 2007a, 219). Only the church is reported to have burned down; to my knowledge, the hall is not mentioned.

140 Lézine 1972, 115–20; Revault and Maury 1977, 77–83.

141 For the activities of the CCMAA from 1897 to 1910, see Herz 1914, 194. CCMAA 1927–29, 93–94; CCMAA 1930–32, 273; CCMAA 1941–45, 217–18. Cf. Ch. Coquin 1974, 134.

142 Lézine 1972, 120; Revault and Maury 1977, 79–80. Ground plans before and after restoration: Revault and Maury 1977, figs. 25–26.

143 Gabra in Gabra and van Loon 2007, 106–107.

144 Burmester 1955, 36. Greek Orthodox Period: *HPC* II-ii, 171, cf. Ch. Coquin 1974, 141.

145 Habib 1967a, 44; Meinardus 1994, 30. Although hymns liken the Mother of God to a great many precious objects and sweet-smelling plants, I have not found basil among them (Muyser 1935). Basil is used in the Coptic Orthodox ceremony for the consecration of a baptistery (Wissa Wassef 1971, 157–58).

146 *HPC* II-ii, 108.

147 Vansleb 1677, 240 (1678, 145).

148 Guirguis 2008, 86–87 and color plates 5, 8, 11, 16c; Atalla 1998, vol. 2, 138–42, with further literature. Seven other icons cannot be identified with certainty. Guirguis hesitates about assigning the commission of the rebuilding and refurbishment to Mu'allim Salib 'Abd al-Masih. However, this is confirmed by a note in a manuscript dated 1778 in the library of the church (Khater and Burmester 1973, vii–viii, cf. Ch. Coquin 1974, 141).

149 Habib 1967a, 45–48.

150 For the activities of the CCMAA from 1897 to 1910, see Herz 1914, 192. CCMAA 1915–19, 199–200; CCMAA 1941–45, 16, 24, 136; CCMAA 1946–53, 300. Cf. Ch. Coquin 1974, 141.

151 Gabra and Eaton-Krauss 2007b, 187.

152 Sheehan 2010, 110–11, 139 and pl. 6.

153 On the chains of St. George, see Meinardus 2002, 86–88.

154 For the doors: Jeudy 2007a, 218.

155 Lézine 1972, 72–79; O'Kane 2000, 152–54; Jeudy 2007a; Sheehan 2010, 110.

156 Sheehan 2010, 108–10, figs. 44 and 53, and pls. 10 and 36.

157 Vansleb 1677, 241 (1678, 146).

158 Jullien 1887, 572 (reprinted in Jullien 1889, 232–33).

159 Sheehan 2010, 116–17.

160 St. George's Convent, Old Cairo 1992, 1997.

161 CCMAA 1900, 118–19 and pl. IX.

162 For the activities of the CCMAA from 1897 to 1910, see Herz 1914, 193–94. For plans

before and after the CCMAA restoration, see Lézine 1972, figs. 5–7. Major restoration on the ceiling and the lower part of the walls followed in the early 1950s: CCMAA 1946–53, 144, 257, 300. Cf. Ch. Coquin 1974, 147–48, with corrections.

163 Sheehan 2010, 132–35 and fig. 75.

164 Sheehan 2010, 95.

165 St. George's Convent, Old Cairo 1992, 1997.

166 Jomard was a member of Napoleon's retinue of scholars who arrived in Egypt in 1798. They compiled the vast work *Description de l'Egypte* (1821–30). Panckoucke 1829, 466.

167 Ch. Coquin 1974, 155, 160. According to Meinardus 1977, 283, at that time the Nilometer was rediscovered by Father Arsenius Kacoyiannis.

168 Ch. Coquin 1974, 157.

169 Ch. Coquin 1974, 158; Sheehan 2010, 118.

170 Vansleb 1677, 241–42 (1678, 146).

171 Ch. Coquin 1974, 162–63. Richard Pococke (first half of the eighteenth century) relates the same treatment as Father Jullien (see below, Pococke quoted in Meinardus 2002, 87).

172 Meinardus 1977, 283.

173 Ch. Coquin 1974, 163–66; Meinardus 1977, 284.

174 Chester 1872, 127.

175 Butler 1884, vol. 1, 158–65.

176 Jullien 1887, 570–71 (reprinted in Jullien 1889, 230–31).

177 Somers Clarke 1896, 61.

178 For the nineteenth-century writers cf. Sheehan 2010, 123–27 and figs. 6 and 67.

179 CCMAA 1909, 63–64. Later repairs: CCMAA 1941–45, 46–47, 137, 166–67. Cf. Ch. Coquin 1974, 156; Sheehan 2010, figs. 32–33.

180 Sheehan 2010, 136 and figs. 5 and 76.

181 Grossmann 1991, 320.

182 Sheehan 2010, 136 and pls. 11–12, 30, and 46.

183 Gabra in Gabra and van Loon 2007, 124–27.

184 De Lacy O'Leary 1937, 201–202; Papaconstantinou 2001, 145–46.

185 *The History of the Churches and Monasteries of Egypt*, fol. 34b (Evetts and Butler 1895, 116; cf. Ch. Coquin 1974, 27).

186 *The History of the Churches and Monasteries of Egypt*, fol. 37b (Evetts and Butler 1895, 122; cf. Ch. Coquin 1974, 30).

187 See references in Ch. Coquin 1974, 23–24.

188 Vansleb 1671, 201. At the same time, he calls the Church of the Virgin in Harat Zuwayla the patriarchal church, and says that the Church of the Virgin in Harat al-Rum was designated a patriarchal residence (Vansleb 1671, 200–201). Patriarch John VIII (1300–20) chose Harat Zuwayla as his residence, while Matthew IV (1660–75) moved the seat to Harat al-Rum (R.-G. Coquin 1991; Gabra 2008, 221). In his second book, Vansleb noted a patriarchal cell above the Church of Abu Sayfayn (1677, 131; 1678, 81).

189 Vansleb 1677, 131, 242 (1678, 80–81, 146)

190 Butler 1884, vol. 1, frontispiece; Jullien 1889, 223; also published in Ch. Coquin 1974, pl. II.

191 Jullien 1887, 584 (reprinted in Jullien 1889, 233).

192 Butler 1884, vol. 1, 144.

193 *The History of the Churches and Monasteries of Egypt*, fol. 35b (Evetts and Butler 1895, 117).

194 *The History of the Churches and Monasteries of Egypt*, fols. 34b–37b (Evetts and Butler 1895, 116–22).

195 van Loon 1999, 24–30; Grossmann 2002, 505–507; van Loon in Gabra and van Loon 2007, 100–105.

196 *HPC* II-ii, 140–45.

197 *The History of the Churches and Monasteries in Egypt*, fol. 37b (Evetts and Butler 1895, 121). According to Ch. Coquin 1974, 22, this is the only source designating the Church of Abu Sayfayn as a bishop's church.

198 See references in Ch. Coquin 1974, 21–23.

199 See references in Ch. Coquin 1974, 21 and 24–25.

200 See references in Ch. Coquin 1974, 23–24.

201 *HPC* IV-ii, 222. Cf. McKenzie 1992, 153.

202 Vansleb 1677, 341–44; description of the church: 242–44 (1678, 205–207 and 146–48).

203 Guirguis 2008, 84.

204 For the activities of the CCMAA from 1897 to 1910, see Herz 1914, 191–92 (Cf. Ch. Coquin 1974, with corrections). A plaque to commemorate this achievement was placed in the church. For the text, see CCMAA 1910, 122.

205 Fissures and cracks in walls and domes were repaired, and other repairs were carried out on the ancient wooden altar screens (CCMAA 1933–35, 217; CCMAA 1941–45, 16, 23, 136).

206 These restoration projects were directed by Z. Skálová. For a bibliography on the subject see the Skálová bibliography in Skálová and Gabra 2006, 272–73.

207 Much of Shenute's literary corpus survives and is an endless source of information about various aspects of fifth- and sixth-century monastic life in the Sohag region, as well as on his theological views. His work is being edited and studied by an international group of scholars under the direction of Prof. Stephen Emmel (University of Münster, Germany). This project is part of the Consortium for Research and Conservation in the Monasteries of the Sohag Region (dir. E.S. Bolman), including restoration work in the Monastery of St. Bishay (the Red Monastery), and survey and excavations around the Church of St. Shenute in the White Monastery. For a short overview, see van Loon in Gabra and van Loon 2007, 284–87.

208 *HPE* III, 106–12.

209 cf. Ch. Coquin 1974, 40.

210 Wüstenfeld 1845, 65.

211 P. Grossmann, unpublished manuscript.

212 Burmester 1955, 49–50; cf. Ch. Coquin 1974, 40–41.

213 Butler 1884, vol. 1, 135, 143–46, and figs. 8–9. This situation is documented in detail on the plans of the CCMAA (1897, pls. VI–VII).

214 The previous state is discussed and documented in CCMAA reports. For the activities of the CCMAA from 1897 to 1910, see Herz 1914, 193. CCMAA 1915–19, 200–207; CCMAA 1933–35, 218; CCMAA

1941–45, 16), 136. Cf. Ch. Coquin 1974, 41 with corrections.

215 Burmester (1955, 52), Habib (1967a, 77–78), and Meinardus (1994, 44) described three upper chapels, which included a baptistery, as "ruined" and "dismantled." According to Butler, they were dedicated to St. George, St. Philotheus, and the Virgin. Valuable wooden altar screens, described by Butler (1884a, vol. 1, 143–44) were removed and, on the orders of Patriarch Cyril V (1874–1928), transferred to other churches.

216 Meinardus 2002, 61.

217 al-Kindi (d. 961) and al-Maqrizi (d. 1442); Wüstenfeld 1845, text 23, 50; trans. 57–58, 119. Cf. Ch. Coquin 1974, 49–50.

218 Guirguis 2008, 84–85.

219 Guirguis 2008, 85, 87.

220 van Moorsel, Immerzeel, and Langen 1994, 20–21 (no. 11–12), 35 (no. 34).

221 Jeudy 2004, 75–76 and pl. 13.

222 For the activities of the CCMAA from 1897 to 1910, see Herz 1914, 195.

223 Butler 1884, vol. 1, 149.

224 CCMAA 1933–35; CCMAA 1949–50, 214. Cracks in the dome over the altar and the supporting arches were repaired, and the exterior covered with a new layer of plaster. Cracks in the baptistery were repaired. CCMAA 1951–52.

225 "The Convent" 2008, 26–27

226 Butler 1884, vol. 1, 28; Cf. Ch. Coquin 1974, 57.

227 van Doorn-Harder 1995, 58–59, 81–82; "The Convent" 2008, 31–45.

228 "The Convent" 2008, 56–67, 99–105.

229 "The Convent" 2008, 85–98, 106–107.

230 van Doorn-Harder 1995, 171.

231 Butler 1884, vol. 1, 250. Also described by the Muslim historian al-Maqrizi ((d. 1442); Evetts and Butler 1895, 328) and Father Vansleb (1672: Vansleb 1677, 132 (1678, 81)).

232 Chester 1872, 134; Butler 1884, vol. 1, 264, 268–69.

233 For the activities of the CCMAA from 1897 to 1910, see Herz 1914, 191, 193, 195; Church of the Virgin: CCMAA 1961, 356; Dayr al-Amir Tadrus, wall: CCMAA 1946–53, 300; Abu Qir wa Yuhanna: CCMAA 1961, 213–14, 299.

234 *HPC* II-ii, 210–11.

235 An attempt has been made by Butler 1914, 47–48.

236 *HPC* II-iii, 361.

237 Ch. Coquin 1974, 183.

238 Vansleb 1671, 203. For a discussion on the interpretation of Babylon in this verse, see Davis 2004, 4–5.

239 Vansleb 1677, 132 (1678, 81).

240 Guirguis 2008, 42.

241 Jeudy 2004, 75–76 and pl. 12.

242 Grossmann 1982, 105, 136, 160; Grossmann 1991, 323; al-Suryani 1996, 124; Sheehan 2010, 137.

243 Meinardus 2002, 58–59. For the Church of St. Simeon in Muqattam, see Gabra in Gabra and van Loon 2007, 188–93.

244 Ch. Coquin 1974, 191–93.

245 Papaconstantinou 2001, 96–100.

246 *HPC* II-iii, 290.

247 Grossmann 1982, 211–12; Grossmann 1991, 323.

248 Papaconstantinou 2001, 135–36. On the saints, see most recently Boutros 2008.

249 Meinardus 2002, 40.

250 Ch. Coquin 1974, 199.

251 Meinardus 2002, 58–59.

252 Van Esbroek 1991.

253 Butler 1884, vol. 1, 269.

254 *HPC* II-ii, 151–69, esp.163–64 and 167.

255 Blochet 1920, 451. *The History of the Patriarchs* does not mention his consecration and enthronement (*HPC* III-ii/iii, 228–29).

256 See references in Ch. Coquin 1974, 207. Correction: the manuscript in Rome (dated 1343) calls the martyr Hippolytus instead of Ptolemy.

257 Ptolemy or Ptolemeus is mentioned as one of the companions of St. Cyrus and St. John, martyred in Damanhur (14 Baunah/8 June; Papaconstantinou 2001, 135).

258 See references in Ch. Coquin 1974, 210, 213–14.

259 Vansleb 1677, 236 (1678, 142–43).

260 *HPC* III-ii/iii, 287; Ch. Coquin 1974, 206; Meinardus 1994, 58; Guirguis 2008, 42.

261 Quoted in Butler 1914, 56.

262 P. Grossmann, unpublished manuscript.

Notes to the Coptic Museum

1 Rufayla 1899; Simaika 1930; Gabra 1999; Ormos 2001; Reid 2002, 258–85; Gabra and Eaton-Krauss 2007b, 1–5, 257.

2 Habib 1967a, 77 (no. 180), pl. 44; Bénazeth and Gabra 1989, 75–76; Gabra 1993, 84–85 (no. 30); Gabra and Eaton-Krauss 2007b, 187; 275, no. 1565.

3 Gabra 1993, 86 (no. 31); Gabra and Eaton-Krauss 2007b, 32f.; 270, no. 1510.

4 Habib 1967a, 102 (no. 236), pl. 57; Coquin 1974, 110; Gabra 1993, 93 (no. 38); Gabra and Eaton-Krauss 2007b, 194f, 276, no. 1172.

5 Koptische Kunst 1963, 294 (no. 237); Habib 1967a, 68 (no. 147), pl. 37; Bénazeth and Gabra 1989, 76–77; Gabra 1993, 83 (no. 29); van Moorsel, Immerzeel, and Langen 1994, 16–18 (for the painter), 36–37 (no. 35), pl. 8b; Skálová and Gabra 2003, 137–40; Török 2005a, 258–59 (no. 193); Gabra and Eaton-Krauss 2007b, 94 f., 272 f., no. 3418.

6 Simaika 1939, 7 (Bibl. 92); Leroy 1974; Atalla 2000, front cover view, 100, 102; Gabra and Eaton- Krauss 2007b, 123–25, 273 (manuscript library no. 92).

7 Patricolo, Monneret de Villard, and Munier 1922a, 45–47 and passim, figs. 18, 20–21, 27–28, 34–35; Koptische Kunst 1963, 261 (no. 144); Habib 1967a, 110 (no. 262), pls. 66–60; Severin 1977, 252, pl. 286a–c; Hunt 1998; Gabra 1993, 102–103 (no. 45); Severin 1998, 322; Török 2005b, 325, 328–29, fig. 148; Gabra and Eaton-Krauss 2007b, 216–17, 276, no. 738.

8 Habib 1967a, 107–108 (no. 255), pl. 63; Severin 1977, 252, pl. 287a–b; Gabra 1993, 96 (no. 41); Hunt 1998, 48; Severin 1998, 322; Török 2005b, 351–58, pls. 168–76; van der Vliet 2007; Gabra and Eaton-Krauss 2007b, 206–11, 276, no. 753.

9 Kautzsch 1936, 164, pl. 32 (523); Simaika 1937, 13, pl. 27 (with incorrect Inv. No. 3507); Atalla 1998, vol. 2, 91; Gabra and Eaton-Krauss 2007b, 42, 270, no. 38.

Notes to the Islamic Heritage of Old Cairo

1 Raymond 2000, 11.

2 al-Maqrizi 1959, vol. 1, 296, quoted in Raymond 2000, 12.

3 Raymond 2000, 12. A second, smaller fortress abutted the south side and later became the observatory.

4 See the axonometric reconstructions showing the relationships between the southwest corner of the Trajanic harbor and the later Fortress of Babylon, also showing their relationships with the Hanging Church. In addition, a comparison can be made between the towers of the Roman fortress of Babylon and the entrance of Trajan's canal, in Sheehan 2010, figs. 24, 27.

5 Sheehan 2010, 42.

6 Sheehan 2010, 35, and figs. 24, 27.

7 Sheehan 2010, 58.

8 Sheehan 2010, 41.

9 Sheehan 2010, 52.

10 Sheehan 2010, 52.

11 Sheehan 2010, 57, note 2.

12 Raymond 2000, 14.

13 Kubiak 1987, 62–63; Yeomans 2006, 16; Raymond 2000, 14.

14 Raymond 2000, 14; Kubiak 1987, 67–71.

15 Yeomans 2006, 17.

16 Yeomans 2006, 26; Kubiak 1987, 96–97.

17 Raymond 2000, 18.

18 Yeomans 2006, 15.

19 Behrens-Abouseif 1989, 6.

20 Quoted in Behrens-Abousief 1989, 7.

21 al-Maqrizi 1959, vol. 1, 338–39, quoted in Raymond 2000, 75.

22 Bacharach 2002, 3.

23 Bahgat and Gabriel 1921.

24 Scanlon and Kubiak 1964–78.

25 Kubiak 1987, 9.

26 Scanlon and Pinder-Wilson 2001.

27 Scanlon 1974, 60–78.

28 For these excavtions, see Gayraud 1991.

29 Bacharach 2002, ix.

30 Bacharach 2002.

31 Kubiak 1987, 129; he argues that it was not used for 1,200 men.

32 Yeomans 2006, 16.

33 According to the Arabic historian al-Qalqashandi (d. 1418), in *Subh al-a'sha fi sina'at al-insha'*.

34 Behrens-Abouseif 1989, 47.

35 Creswell 1979, vol. 2, 178.

36 Behrens-Abouseif 1989, 48.

37 Behrens-Abouseif 1989, 48.

38 al-Maqrizi 1959, vol. 2, 253, quoting Ibn 'Abd al-Hakam 2002, 132; Ibn Duqmaq 1893, 65; all cited in Creswell 1979, vol. 2, 171.

39 Yaqut, al-Maqrizi, and Suyuti mention that the Ziyadat al-Khazin was built by Abu

Bakr al- Khazin in AH 357/968 CE, that the latter died before it was completed, and that his son 'Ali completed it in 358/969. Creswell 1979, vol. 2, 171, note 2.

40 Ibn Duqmaq names only eight of these doors, as follows: on the east side from south to north, Bab al-Sharabiyin, Bab Zawiyat Fatima, Bab 'Amr, Bab al-Halawaniyin, and Bab al-Jani'z; on the west side, the third and fourth from the south were called Bab Suq al-Ghazl and Bab al-Akhfaniyin; Bab al-Khatib, on the south side, was also called Bab al-Zizalakhta (or Zinzalakhta), from a mango tree that grew there. See Ibn Duqmaq 1893, 59.

41 Creswell 1979, vol. 2, 171, after al-Maqrizi 1959, vol. 2, 253, who was quoting a writer called Ibn al-Mutawwaj (d. 1329).

42 Ibn Duqmaq 1893, 60; al-Maqrizi 1959, vol. 2, 253; both from Ibn al-Mutawwaj, cited by Creswell 1979, vol. 2, 171.

43 Creswell 1979, vol. 2, 171.

44 Ibn Duqmaq 1893, 7, al-Maqrizi 1959, vol. 2, 250; mentioned by Creswell 1979, vol. 2, 172.

45 Ibn Duqmaq 1893, 67; al-Maqrizi 1959, vol. 2, 249, mentioned by Creswell 1979, vol. 2, 172.

46 Behrens-Abouseif 1989, 49.

47 Behrens-Abouseif 1989, 49.

48 Behrens-Abouseif 1989, 50.

49 Behrens-Abouseif 1989, 50.

50 al-Muqqadasi 1967, 198–99; Creswell 1979, vol. 2, 304.

51 Creswell 1989, 304, mentions it was Yaqut al- Hamawi in Mu'jam al-Buldan, vol. 3, translated and annotated by Wadie Jwaideh (Leiden: Brill, 1959), 899. However, I could not locate this source at the time of writing this chapter.

52 al-Maqrizi 1959, vol. 2, 249; mentioned in Creswell 1979, vol. 2, 172.

53 Ibn Duqmaq 1893, 68; al-Maqrizi 1959, vol. 2, 254; mentioned in Creswell 1979, vol. 2, 172.

54 Ibn Duqmaq 1893 and al-Maqrizi 1959; mentioned by Creswell 1979, vol. 2, 172.

55 Nasir-i-Khusraw, *Safar Nameh, Relation du Voyage de Nasiri Khusraw* (Paris, 1881), 147 and note 1.

56 Creswell 1979, vol. 2, 173.

57 al-Maqrizi 1959, vol. 2, 251. These were used in summer, and were usually removed in winter.

58 The first mihrab is that of al-Amir at the Mosque of al-Azhar (1126). The second is that of Sayyida Nafisa (1138–46), added during the reign of al- Hafiz. The third is that of Sayyida Ruqayya (1154–60), added during the reign of Salih Tala'i'.

59 al-Maqrizi 1959, vol. 2, 255.

60 al-Maqrizi 1959, vol. 1, 341; vol. 2, 29–35, as quoted in Creswell 1979, vol. 2, 174, note 1.

61 Ibn Duqmaq 1893, 69; al-Maqrizi 1959, vol. 2, 251; both cited in Creswell 1979, vol. 2, 174

62 Ibn Duqmaq 1893, 69; al-Maqrizi 1959, vol. 2; both cited in Creswell 1979, vol. 2, 74.

63 The date of this stucco mihrab is discussed in Creswell 1979, vol. 2, 174.

64 Ibn Duqmaq 1893, 61; translated in Creswell 1979, vol. 2, 174.

65 Creswell 1979, vol. 2, 175.

66 al-Maqrizi 1959, vol. 2, 253; mentioned and translated by Creswell 1979, vol. 2, 174.

67 al-Maqrizi 1959, vol. 2, 253; mentioned and translated by Creswell 1979, vol. 2, 174.

68 Creswell 1979, vol. 2, 175 and note 7; C. Lambert, cited in Creswell 1979, vol. 2, 176.

69 *Description de l'Egypte* 1798, 196–97; Creswell 1979, vol. 2, 174.

70 Creswell 1979; al-Maqrizi 1959, 176; Pococke 1743–45, 28 and plate XI.

71 al-Jabarti 1880, vol. 2, 170, 5–23; in Corbet 1890, 790; Creswell 1979, vol. 2, 176–77.

72 Marcel 1848, 248–49.

73 Creswell 1979, vol. 2, 177, note 1.

74 Browne 1799, 80; mentioned by Creswell 1979, vol. 2, 177.

75 Creswell 1979, vol. 2, 177, note 1.

76 Coste 1839, pl. I; in Creswell 1979, vol. 2, 177–78.

77 Creswell 1979, vol. 2, 179.

78 Creswell 1979, vol. 2, 174.

79 Seen in Creswell's plan, fig. 168, opposite p. 188, in Creswell 1979, vol. 2.

80 Creswell 1979, vol. 2, 180.

81 Creswell 1979, vol. 2, 181.

82 Creswell 1979, vol. 2, 181.

83 Creswell 1979, vol. 2, 182.

84 Creswell 1979, vol. 2, 188.

85 I would like to thank the staff of the Rare Books and Special Collections Library of the American University in Cairo for providing me with these valuable photographs from their K.A.C. Creswell Photo Collection Archives, which are copies of the originals located at the Ashmolean Museum at Oxford University.

86 Such as the mosque shrines of Sayyida Zaynab and Sayyida Nafisa, as well as many others.

87 Creswell 1979, vol. 2, 184, and note 3; Creswell 1989, 308; Behrens-Abouseif 1989, 48.

88 Yeomans 2006, 24.

BIBLIOGRAPHY

AI: *Annales islamologiques*

ASAE: *Annales du Service des antiquités de l'Egypte,* Cairo

BARCE: *Bulletin of the American Research Center in Egypt*

BIE: *Bulletin de l'Institut d'Egypte,* Cairo

BIFAO: *Bulletin de l'Institut Français d'Archéologie Orientale,* Cairo

BSAC: *Bulletin de la Société d'Archéologie Copte*

BSFE: *Bulletin de la Société française d'égyptologie,* Paris

CE: *Coptic Encyclopedia,* ed. A. Atiya, New York

CdE: *Chronique d'Egypte,* Brussels

ECA: *Eastern Christian Art*

EI: *The Encyclopedia of Islam,* Leiden and London

JNES: *Journal of Near Eastern Studies,* Chicago

MIFAO: *Mémoires publiés par les membres de l'Institut français d'archéologie orientale,* Cairo

PO: *Patrologia Orientalis*

SAK: *Studien zur Altägyptischen Kultur,* Hamburg

SKCO: *Sprachen und Kulturen des christlichen Orients,* Wiesbaden

Abdel Wareth, U., and P. Zignani. 1992. "Nag al-Hagar: A Fortress with a Palace of the Late Roman Empire; Second Preliminary Report." *BIFAO* 92:185–210.

Atalla, N.S. 1998. *Coptic Icons,* vols. 1 and 2. Cairo.

———. 2000. *Illustrations from Coptic Manuscripts.* Cairo.

Atiya, A.S. 1991. "Literature, Copto-Arabic." *CE* 5:1460–67.

Bacharach, J. 2002. *Fustat Finds.* Cairo.

Bagnall, R.S. 1993. *Egypt in Late Antiquity.* Princeton, NJ.

Bagnall, R.S., and D.W. Rathbone, eds. 2004. *Egypt from Alexander to the Early Christians: An Archaeological and Historical Guide.* Los Angeles.

Bahgat, 'A., and A. Gabriel. 1921. *Fouilles d'al-Foustat.* Paris.

Ball, J. 1942. *Egypt in the Classical Geographers.* Cairo.

Becker, C.H. 1993. "Misr (C)." *EI* 7:146–52.

Behrens-Abouseif, D. 1989. *Islamic Architecture in Cairo: An Introduction.* Cairo.

Bénazeth, D., and G. Gabra. 1989. "L'Egypte copte," in *Egypte Egypte: Chefs-d'oeuvre de tous les temps* (exh. cat.; Institut du monde arabe), F.M. Ricci, ed. Paris.

Ben-Sasson, H.H., ed. 1976. *A History of the Jewish People.* London.

Blochet, E. 1920. "Al Moufazzal ibn Abil-Fazzaîl: Histoire des sultans mamlouks." *PO* 14:375–672.

Bohak, G. 2008. *Ancient Jewish Magic: A History.* Cambridge, UK.

Bolman, E.S. 2006. "The Newly Discovered Paintings in Abu Serga, Babylon, Old Cairo: The Logos Made Visible." *BARCE* 190:14–17.

Boutros, R. 2008. "Le culte des saints Cyr et Jean chez les Coptes à la lumière des sources hagiographiques arabes," in *Alexandrie médiévale,* eds. J.-Y. Empereur and C. Décobert, vol. 3, 115–44. Cairo.

Bowman, A. 1986. *Egypt after the Pharaohs.* London.

Browne, W.G. 1799. *Travels in Africa . . . 1792–98, London, 1799.* London.

Burmester, O.H.E. 1955. *A Guide to the Ancient Coptic Churches of Cairo.* Cairo.

Butler, A.J. 1884. *The Ancient Coptic Churches of Egypt,* 2 vols. London.

———. 1902. *The Arab Conquest of Egypt and the Last Thirty Years of the Roman Dominion.* Oxford.

———. 1914. *Babylon of Egypt: A Study in the History of Old Cairo.* Oxford.

Campbell, B. 1994. *The Roman Army, 31 BC–AD 337.* London.

CCMAA. The bulletins of the Comité de conservation des monuments de l'art arabe are cited by bulletin year, not the year of publication. All bulletins, published in Arabic and French (1882–1961), are available at http://www.islamic-art.org/comitte/comite.asp.

Charles, R.H. 1981. *The Chronicle of John (c. 690 AD), Coptic Bishop of Nikiu, Being a History of Egypt before and during the Arab Conquest, Translated from Hermann Zotenberg's Edition of the Ethiopic Version.* Reprint of the London 1916 edition. Amsterdam.

Chester, G.J. 1872. "Notes on the Ancient Christian Churches of Musr el Ateekah, or Old Cairo, and Its Neighbourhood." *Archaeological Journal* 29:120–34.

Cody, A., O.S.B. 1991. "Calendar, Coptic." *CE* 2:433–36.

"The Convent of the Great Martyr St. Philopater Mercurius 'Abi Seifein' for Nuns, Old Cairo." 2008. *Tamav Erene and Glorious Horizons in Monastic Life,* Part 1. Cairo.

Coquin, Ch. 1974. *Les édifices chrétiens du Vieux-Caire.* Bibliothèque d'études coptes 11. Cairo.

———. 1991. "Church of Abu Sayfayn." *CE* 2:549–52.

Coquin, R.-G. 1991. "Patriarchal Residences." *CE* 6:1912–13.

Corbet, E.K. 1890. "The History of the Mosque of Amr at Old Cairo." *Journal of the Royal Asiatic Society,* October, 759–800.

Coste, P. 1839. *Architecture Arabe, ou Monuments du Kaire, Mesurés et dessinés de 1818 à 1825.* Paris.

Creswell, K.A.C. 1979. *Early Muslim Architecture.* 2 vols. New York.

———. 1989. *A Short Account of Early Muslim Architecture,* ed. James Allen. Cairo.

Davis, S.J. 2004. *The Early Coptic Papacy: The Egyptian Church and Its Leadership in Late Antiquity.* Vol. 1 of The Popes of Egypt series. Cairo.

De Lacy O'Leary. 1937. *The Saints of Egypt in the Coptic Calendar.* London and New York (Reprint Amsterdam 1974).

Debono, F., and B. Mortensen. 1988. *The Predynastic Cemetery at Heliopolis. Archäologische Veröffentlichungen* 63. Mainz am Rhein.

Delahaye, G.-R. 2003. "Johann Michael Vansleb (1635–1679): Voyageur en Egypte et en Orient pour le compte de la Bibliothèque royale." *Le Monde Copte* 33:113–22.

Description de l'Egypte. Etat moderne, vol. 1, 1809. Reprint 1994. Cologne.

Doorn-Harder, P. van. 1995. *Contemporary Coptic Nuns.* Columbia, S.C.

Drioton, E. 1953. "Les Origines pharaoniques du nilomètre de Rodah." *BIE* 34:291–316.

Evetts, B.T.A., and A.J. Butler, eds. 1895. *The Churches and Monasteries of Egypt and Some Neighbouring Countries Attributed to Abu Salih, the Armenian.* Oxford (Reprint Piscataway NJ 2001).

Fuks, A. 1953. "The Jewish Revolt in Egypt (AD 115–17) in the Light of the Papyri." *Aegyptus* 33:131–58.

Gabra, G. 1990. "Ein Block Ptolemaios V. Epiphanes aus Babylon," in *Festschrift Jürgen von Beckerath,* eds. A. Eggebrecht and B. Schmitz. *Hildesheimer Agyptologische Beiträge* 30:49–51. Hildesheim.

———. 1993. *Cairo: The Coptic Museum and Old Churches.* Cairo.

———. 1995. "Zu einem Opferständer eines Hohenpriesters von Heliopolis des Mittleren Reiches." *Varia Aegyptica* 10/2–3:101–103.

———. 1999. "The Story of the Coptic Museum," in *Ägypten und Nubien in spätantiker und christlicher Zeit. Akten des 6. Internationalen Koptologenkongresses, Münster 20.–26. Juli 1996,* eds. S. Emmel et al., vol. 1. *SKCO* vol. 6, part 1: 147–51.

———. 2002. "Jews, Copts and Muslims in Medieval Old Cairo," in *Regionale Systeme koexistierender Religionsgemeinschaften,* eds. W. Beltz and J.

Tubach. Leucorea Kolloquium 2001. *Hallesche Beitrage zur Orientwissenschaft* 34, Halle (Saale): 167–75.

———. 2008. *Historical Dictionary of the Coptic Church*. Cairo.

———. 2010. "Once More: Nabis, Bishop of 'Aidhab/Berenike," in *Christianity and Monasticism in Upper Egypt*, eds G. Gabra and H. Takla. Vol. 2: Nag Hammadi–Esna, 45–48. Cairo.

———. 2012. "Ein vergessener Naos Nektanebos I. in Alt-Kairo." *SAK* 41:137–38

Gabra, G., and M. Eaton-Krauss. 2007a. *The Illustrated Guide to the Coptic Museum and Surrounding Churches*. Cairo.

———. 2007b. *The Treasures of Coptic Art in the Coptic Museum and the Churches of Old Cairo*. Cairo.

Gabra, G., and G.J.M. van Loon. 2007. *The Churches of Egypt: From the Journey of the Holy Family to the Present Day*. Cairo.

Gardiner, A. 1947. *Ancient Egyptian Onomastica* 2. Oxford.

Gayraud, R.-P. 1991. "Istabl-Antar (Fostat). Rapport de fouilles." *AI* 22 (1986): 1–26; 25 (1991); 27 (1993): 225–32; 28 (1994): 1–27; 29 (1995): 1–24. Collection in one issue of previously published articles.

Goitein, S.D. 1964. *Jews and Arabs: Their Contacts through the Ages*. New York.

———. 1967–88. *A Mediterranean Society: The Jewish Communities of the Arab World as Portrayed in the Documents of the Cairo Geniza*, vols. 1–5. Berkeley.

———. 1971. "Side Lights on Jewish Education from the Cairo Geniza," in *Gratz College Anniversary Volume*, eds. I.D. Passow and S.T. Lachs, 83–110. Philadelphia.

———. 1975. "Parents and Children: A Genizah Study on the Medieval Jewish Family." *Gratz College Annual of Jewish Studies* 4:47–50.

———. 1983. *A Mediterranean Society: The Jewish Communities in the Arab World as Portrayed in the Documents of the Cairo Geniza*. Vol. 4: *Daily Life*. Berkeley.

Goitein, S.D., and M.A. Friedman. 2008. *India Traders of the Middle Ages. Documents from the Cairo Geniza ('India Book')*. Leiden.

Goitein, S.D., and J. Hacker. 1980. *Ha-yishuv be-ereṣ yisrael be-reshit ha-islam uvi-tequfat ha-ṣalbanim le-or kitve ha-geniza*. Jerusalem.

Gomaa, F. 1982. "Per-Hapi," in *Lexikon der Agyptologie*, eds. W. Helck and W. Westendorf, vol. 4, 931. Wiesbaden.

Grebaut, S. 1927. "Le Synaxaire ethiopien: Mois de Tahsas." *PO* 15:543–798.

Grossmann, P. 1982. *Mittelalterliche Langhauskuppelkirchen und ihre verwandte Typen in Oberagypten*. Abhandlungen des Deutschen Archäologischen Instituts Kairo. Koptische Reihe 3. Gluckstadt.

———. 1991. "Babylon." *CE* 2:317–23.

———. 2002. *Christliche Architektur in Ägypten*. Handbook of Oriental Studies, section 1: The Near and Middle East, 62. Leiden.

———. 2006. "Neue Beobachtungen zur Sergioskirche von Alt-Kairo." *BSAC* 45:9–24.

Grossmann, P., M. Jones, H.-C. Noeske, C. Le Quesne, and P. Sheehan. 1998. "Zweiter Bericht uber die Britisch-Deutschen Grabungen in der romischen Festung von Babylon, Alt-Kairo." *Archaologischer Anzeiger* 1:173–207.

Grossmann, P., C. Le Quesne, and P. Sheehan. 1994. "Zur romischen Festung von Babylon-Alt-Kairo." *Archaologischer Anzeiger* 2:271–87.

Guirguis, M. 2008. *An Armenian Artist in Ottoman Egypt: Yuhanna al-Armani and His Coptic Icons*. Cairo.

El-Habashi, A., and N. Warner. 1998. "Recording the Monuments of Cairo: An Introduction and Overview." *AI* 32:81–99.

Habib, R. 1967a. *The Ancient Coptic Churches of Cairo: A Short Account*. Cairo.

———. 1967b. *The Coptic Museum: A General Guide*. Cairo.

al-Hamawi, Yaqut. c.1959. *Mu'jam al-buldan* III, translated and annotated by Wadie Jwaideh. Leiden.

Hartung, U. 2007. "Maadi: Eine pradynastische Siedlung am Stadtrand von Kairo," in *Begegnung mit der Vergangenheit: 100 Jahre in Agypten. Deutsches Archaologisches Institut Kairo 1907–2007*, eds. G. Dreyer and D. Polz, 120. Mainz am Rhein.

Heide, B., and A. Thiel, eds. 2004. *Sammler, Pilger, Wegbereiter: Die Sammlung des Prinzen Johann Georg von Sachsen. Mainz, Landesmuseum 5.12.2004–10.4.2005*. Mainz.

Heiden, D. 2002. "Die Stele des P3-dj-Pp." *SAK* 30:187–201.

Heijer, J. den. 1993. "The Composition of the 'History of the Churches and Monasteries of Egypt': Some Preliminary Remarks,' in *Acts of the Fifth International Congress of Coptic Studies, Washington D.C., 12–15 August 1992*, eds. T. Orlandi and D.W. Johnson, vol. 2-1, 209–19. Rome.

———. 1994. "The Influence of the 'History of the Patriarchs of Alexandria' on the 'History of the Churches and Monasteries of Egypt' by Abu'l-Makarim (and Abu Salih?)." Actes du 4ᵉᵐᵉ Congrès international d'études arabes chrétiennes, Cambridge, September 1992, vol. 2, ed. S.K. Samir. Parole de l' Orient 19:415–39.

———. 1996. "Coptic Historiography in the Fatimid, Ayyubid and Early Mamluk Periods." Papers from the Second Woodbrooke-Mingana Symposium on Arab Christianity and Islam, Woodbrooke College, Selly Oak Colleges, Birmingham, 19–22 September 1994. *Medieval Encounters* 2:67–98.

———. 2004. "Les patriarches coptes d'origine syrienne," in *Studies on the Christian Arabic Heritage in Honour of Father Prof. Dr. Samir Khalil Samir S.I. at the Occasion of his Sixty- Fifth Birthday*, eds. R. Ebied and H. Teule, 45–63. Leuven, Paris, and Dudley. Eastern Christian Studies 5.

Heikal, M. 1983. *Autumn of Fury: The Assassination of Sadat*. London.

Heinen, H. 1991. "Egypt, Roman and Byzantine Rule." *CE* 3:942–48.

Herz, M. 1914. *Index general des bulletins du Comite des annees 1882 a 1910*. Cairo.

HPC II-ii = Atiya, A.S., Y. 'Abd al-Masih, and O.H.E. Khs-Burmester, eds. 1948. *History of the Patriarchs of the Egyptian Church known as the History of the Holy Church*, vol. II-ii. Publications de la Societe d'archeologie copte, Textes et Documents 4. Cairo.

HPC II-iii = Atiya, A.S., Y. 'Abd al-Masih, and O.H.E. Khs-Burmester, eds. 1959. *History of the Patriarchs of the Egyptian Church known as the History of the Holy Church*, vol. II-iii. Publications de la Societe d'archeologie copte, Textes et Documents 5. Cairo.

HPC III-ii/iii = Khater, A., and O.H.E. Khs- Burmester, eds. 1970. *History of the Patriarchs of the Egyptian Church known as the History of the Holy Church*, vol. 3-ii and iii. Publications de la Societe d'archeologie copte, Textes et Documents 12–13. Cairo.

HPC IV-ii = A. Khater and O.H.E. Khs-Burmester, eds. 1974. *History of the Patriarchs of the Egyptian Church known as the History of the Holy Church*, vol. IV-ii, Cairo (Publications de la Société d'Archéologie Copte, Textes et Documents XV).

HPE III = Evetts, B.T.A., ed. 1910. "History of the Patriarchs of the Coptic Church of Alexandria," vol. 3. *PO* 5:1–215.

HPE IV = Evetts, B.T.A., ed. 1915. "History of the Patriarchs of the Coptic Church of Alexandria, vol. 4." *PO* 10:357–551.

Hunt, Lucy-Anne. 1998. *Byzantium, Eastern Christendom and Islam: Art at the Crossroads of the Medieval Mediterranean*. 2 vols. London.

Ibn 'Abd al-Hakam. 2002. *Futuh Misr wa'l-Maghrib: The History of the Conquest of Egypt, North Africa, and Spain*, edited from the manuscript in London, Paris, and Leiden by Charles C. Torrey. Piscataway, N.J.

Ibn Duqmaq, S. 1893. *Kitab al-intisar li-wasitat 'Iqd al-Amsar*, vol. 4, ed. Vollers. Cairo.

Isaacs, H.D., and Baker, C.F. 1994. *Medical and Para-Medical Manuscripts in the Cambridge Genizah Collections*. Cambridge UK.

Ishaq, E.M. 1991. "Metropolitan Sees." *CE* 5:1612–14.

al-Jabarti. 1880. *Aja'ib al-athar fi-l-tarajim wa-l- akhbar*. 4 vols. Cairo.

Jeudy, A. 2004. "Icones et ciboria: Relation entre les ateliers coptes de peinture d'icones et l'iconographie du mobilier liturgique en bois." *ECA* 1:67–87.

———. 2007a. "From Domestic Architecture to Religious Places of Worship: The Case of Deir al-Banat and Its Sanctuary Door," in *Actes du huitieme Congres international d'etudes coptes, Paris, 28 juin–3 juillet 2004*, eds. A. Boud'hors and N. Bosson, vol. 1, 217–18. Orientalia Lovaniensia Analecta 163. Louvain.

———. 2007b. "Masterpieces of Medieval Coptic Woodwork in Their Byzantine and Islamic Context: A Typological and Iconographical Study," in *Interactions: Artistic Interchange between the Eastern and Western Worlds in the Medieval Period*, ed. C. Hourihane, 120–32. Princeton, N.J.

Johann Georg, Duke of Saxony. 1914. *Streifzuge durch die Kirchen und Kloster Agyptens*. Leipzig and Berlin.

———. 1930. *Neue Streifzuge durch die Kirchen und Kloster Agyptens*. Leipzig and Berlin.

———. 1931. *Neueste Streifzuge durch die Kirchen und Kloster Agyptens*. Leipzig and Berlin.

Jomer, J. 1965. "al-Fustat." *EI* 2:957–59.

Jones, A.H.M. 1964. *The Later Roman Empire 284–602: A Social, Economic, and Administrative Survey*. 2 vols. Oxford.

327

Jullien, M. 1887. "Une visite au Vieux Caire: Souvenirs de la Sainte Famille." *Les Missions Catholiques* 19:536–38, 544–46, 557–60, 570–72, 584–86.

———. 1889. *L'Egypte: Souvenirs bibliques et chrétiens.* Lille.

Kakósy, L. 1977. "Heliopolis," in *Lexikon der Ägyptologie,* eds. Wolfgang Helck and Wolfahrt Westendorf, vol. 2, 1111–13. Wiesbaden.

Kautzsch, R. 1936. *Kapitellstudien: Beiträge zu einer Geschichte des spätantiken Kapitells im Osten vom vierten bis ins siebente Jahrhundert.* Leipzig and Berlin.

Kees, H. 1977. *Das alte Ägypten: Eine Kleine Landeskunde.* Vienna, Cologne, and Graz.

Khater, A., and O.H.E. Khs-Burmester. 1973. *Catalogue of the Coptic and Christian Arabic Mss. Preserved in the Library of the Church of the All-Holy Virgin Mary Known as Qasriat ar-Rihân at Old Cairo.* Bibliothèque de manuscrits 2. Cairo.

Köhler, C. 2008. "The Helwan Cemetery." *Archéo-Nil: Revue de la Société pour l'étude des cultures prépharaoniques de la vallée du Nil* 18:113–30.

Koptische Kunst: Christentum am Nil. 1963. Exh. cat., Villa Hugel, Essen.

Kraemer, J.L. 1991. "Spanish Ladies from the Cairo Geniza." *Mediterranean Historical Review* 6:247–48.

Kratchkowsky, I., and A. Vasiliev. 1924. "Histoire de Yahya ibn Sa'id d'Antioche, continuateur de Sa'id ibn Bitriq." *PO* 18:699–833.

Kubiak, W.B. 1987. *Al-Fustat: Its Foundation and Early Urban Development.* Cairo.

Lambert, P., ed. 1994. *Fortifications and the Synagogue: The Fortress of Babylon and the Ben Ezra Synagogue, Cairo.* London.

Leroy, J. 1974. *Les manuscrits coptes et coptes-arabes illustrés.* Institut Français d'Archéologie de Beyrouth, Bibliothèque Archéologie et Historique 96. Paris.

Lev, E., and Z. Amar. 2008. *Practical Materia Medica of the Medieval Eastern Mediterranean according to the Cairo Geniza.* Leiden.

Lézine, A. 1972. "Les salles nobles des palais mamelouks." *AI* 10:63–148.

Lim, T.H., and J.J. Collins, eds. 2010. *The Oxford Handbook of the Dead Sea Scrolls.* Oxford.

Loon, G.J.M. van. 1999. *The Gate of Heaven: Wall Paintings with Old Testament Scenes in the Altar Room and the Khurus of Coptic Churches.* Uitgaven van het Nederlands Historisch-Archeologisch Instituut te Istanbul/Publications de l'Institut historique- archéologique néerlandais de Stamboul 85. Leiden.

MacCoull, L.S.B. 1996. "A Note on the Career of Gabriel III, Scribe and Patriarch of Alexandria." *Arabica* 43:357–60.

Mann, J. 1931–35. *Texts and Studies in Jewish History and Literature.* 2 vols. Cincinnati and Philadelphia.

al-Maqrizi, T. 1959. *Kitab al-khitat al-maqriziya al-musammah bi-l-Mawa'iz wa-l-I'tibar fi Dhikr al-Khitat wa-l-Athar.* 2 vols. al-Shayyah, Lebanon.

Marcel, J.J. 1848. *Egypte, depuis la Conquête des Arabes jusqu'à la domination française.* Paris.

Maspero, J., and G. Wiet. 1919. "Matériaux pour servir à la géographie de l'Egypte." *MIFAO* 36.

Mayeur-Jaouen, C. 1992. "Un jésuite français en Egypte: Le père Jullien," *Itinéraires d'Egypte: Mélanges offerts au Père Maurice Martin S.J.,* ed. C. Décobert, 213–47. Bibliothèque d'études 107. Cairo.

McKenzie, N.D. 1992. *Ayyubid Cairo: A Topographical Study.* Cairo.

Meinardus, O.F.A. 1972–73. "St. Barbara in the Coptic Cult." *SOC-Collectanea* 15:123–32.

———. 1977. *Christian Egypt, Ancient and Modern.* 2nd rev. ed. Cairo.

———. 1994. *The Historic Coptic Churches of Cairo.* Cairo.

———. 2002. *Coptic Saints and Pilgrimages.* Cairo.

Meulenaere, H. de. 1975. "Babylon," in *Lexikon der Ägyptologie,* eds. W. Helck and E. Otto, vol. 1, 592. Wiesbaden.

Middeldorf Kosegarten, A. 2000. "Die mittelalterlichen Ambonen aus Marmor in den koptischen Kirchen Alt-Kairos." *Marburger Jahrbuch für Kunstwissenschaft* 27:29–81.

Milward Jones, A. 2006. "Conservation of the Mediaeval Wall Painting in the Church of Sts. Sergius and Bacchus (Abu Serga)." *BARCE* 190:9–13.

Montet, P. 1957. *Géographie de l'Egypte ancienne.* Paris.

Moorsel, P.P.V. van. 1991. "Ein Thron für den Kelch," in *Tesserae: Festschrift für Josef Engemann,* 299–303. Jahrbuch für Antike und Christentum— Ergänzungsband 18. Münster.

Moorsel, P.P.V. van, M. Immerzeel, and L. Langen. 1994. *Catalogue général du Musée copte: The Icons.* Cairo.

Motzki, H. 1991. "Ibrahim al-Jawhari." *CE* 4:1274.

Munier, H. 1943. *Recueil des listes épiscopales de l'Egypte copte.* Publications de la Société d'archéologie copte. Textes et documents 2. Cairo.

al-Muqaddasi. 1967. *Ahsan al-taqasim fi ma'rifat al-aqalim,* ed. M.J. de Geoje. Leiden.

Mustafa, M., and H. Jaritz. 1984–85. "A Roman Fortress at Nag' el-Hagar: First Preliminary Report." *ASAE* 70:21–31.

Muyser, J. 1935. *Maria's heerlijkheid in Egypte: Een studie der Koptische Maria-literatuur.* Leuven and Utrecht.

Nasir-i-Khusraw. 1881. *Safar Nameh, Relation du Voyage de Nasiri Khusraw.* Paris.

O'Kane, B. 2000. "Domestic and Religious Architecture in Cairo: Mutual Influences," in *The Cairo Heritage: Essays in Honor of Laila Ali Ibrahim,* ed. D. Behrens-Abouseif, 149–82. Cairo.

Ormos, I. 2001. "Max Herz (1856–1919): His Life and Activities in Egypt," in *Le Caire—Alexandrie: Architecture européenne, 1850–1950,* ed. M. Volait, 161–74. Cairo.

Panckoucke, C.L.F., ed. 1829. *Description de l'Égypte ou Recueil des observations et des recherches qui ont été faites en Égypte pendant l'Expédition de l'armée française,* vol. 18-2: État moderne. Paris.

Papaconstantinou, A. 2001. *Le culte des saints en Égypte, des Byzantins aux Abbassides: L'apport des sources papyrologiques et épigraphiques grecques et coptes.* Paris.

Patricolo, A., U. Monneret de Villard, and H. Munier. 1922a. *La chiesa di Santa Barbara al vecchio Cairo.* Florence.

———. 1922b. *The Church of Sitt Burbara in Old Cairo.* Florence.

Pococke, R. 1743–45. *A Description of the East, and Some Other Countries.* 2 vols. London.

Porcher, E., ed. 1914. "Vie d'Isaac, patriarche d'Alexandrie de 686 à 689, écrite par Mina, évêque de Pchati." *PO* 11:300–80.

Porten, B. 1968. *Archives from Elephantine: The Life of an Ancient Jewish Military Colony.* Berkeley.

Posener, G. 1936. "Première domination perse en Egypte." *Bibliothèque d'Etude* 11. Cairo.

———. 1938. "Le Canal du Nil à la Mer Rouge avant les Ptolémées," *CdE* 13:258–73.

al-Qalqashandi, A. 1913–19. *Subh al-a'sha fi sina'at al-insha'.* Vol. 3. Cairo.

Raue, D. 1999. *Heliopolis und das Haus des Re: Eine Prosopographie und ein Toponym im Neuen Reich.* Abhandlung des Deutschen Archäologischen Instituts Kairo, Ägyptologische Reihe 16. Berlin.

Raymond, A. 2000. *Cairo.* Trans. W. Wood. Cairo.

Redmount, C.A. 1995. "The Wadi Tumailat and the 'Canal of the Pharaohs.'" *JNES* 54:127–35.

Reid, D.M. 1992. "Cultural Imperialism and Nationalism: The Struggle to Define and Control the Heritage of Arab Art in Egypt." *International Journal of Middle East Studies* 24:57–76.

———. 2002. *Whose Pharaohs? Archaeology, Museums and Egyptian National Identity from Napoleon to World War I.* Cairo.

Reif, S.C. 2000. *A Jewish Archive from Old Cairo: The History of Cambridge University's Genizah Collection.* Richmond, Surrey.

———., ed. 2009. *Charles Taylor and the Genizah Collection.* Cambridge, UK.

———. 2010. "Reviewing the Links Between the Dead Sea Scrolls and the Cairo Genizah," in Lim and Collins, eds., ch. 27.

Revault, J., and B. Maury. 1977. *Palais et maisons du Caire du XIVᵉ au XVIIIᵉ siècle,* vol. 2. MIFAO 100. Cairo.

Richler, B. 1994. *Guide to Hebrew Manuscript Collections.* Jerusalem.

Rowlandson, J. 1996. *Landowners and Tenants in Roman Egypt: The Social Relations of Agriculture in the Oxyrhynchite Nome.* Oxford.

Rufayla, Y. 1899. *Tarikh al-ummah al-qibtiyia* (History of the Coptic Nation; reprinted by the Saint Mark Foundation for Coptic History Studies, Cairo 2000), Cairo.

el-Saghir, M., J-C. Golvin, M. Reddé, E. Hegazy, and G. Wagner. 1986. *Le Camp romain de Louqsor.* MIFAO 83.

Salmon, G. 1903. "Un texte arabe inédit pour servir à l'histoire des chrétiens d'Égypte." *BIFAO* 3:25–68.

Sanders, P. 2008. *Creating Medieval Cairo: Empire, Religion, and Architectural Preservation in Nineteenth-century Egypt.* Cairo.

Scanlon, G.T. 1974. "The Pits of Fustat." The Egypt Exploration Society. *Journal of Egyptian Archeology* 60:60–78.

Scanlon, G.T., and W. Kubiak. 1964–78. "Preliminary Reports: Excavations at Fustat." *Journal of the American Research Center in Egypt*, 4–21.

Scanlon, G.T., and R. Pinder-Wilson. 2001. *Fustat Glass in the Early Islamic Period: Finds Excavated by the American Research Center in Egypt (1964–1980)*. London.

Sellheim, R., and D. Sourdel. 1978. "Katib." *EI* 4, 754–57.

Severin, H-G. 1977. "Frühchristliche Skulptur und Malerei in Ägypten," in *Spätantike und frühes Christentum*, ed. B. Brenk. Propyläen Kunstgeschichte Supplement, vol. 1., 243–53. Frankfurt, Berlin, and Vienna.

———. 1998. "Zur Skulptur und Malerei der und spätantiken und frühmittelalterlichen Zeit in Ägypten," in *Ägypten in spätantik- christlicher Zeit: Einführung in die koptische Kunst*, ed. M. Krause. *SKCO* 4:295–338. Wiesbaden.

Sheehan, P. 1994. "The Roman Fortifications," in P. Lambert 1994, 49–63.

———. 2010. *Babylon of Egypt: The Archaeology of Old Cairo and the Origin of the City*. Cairo.

Sidebothman, S.E., and W.Z. Wendrich. 2001–2002. "Berenike: Archaeological Fieldwork at a Ptolemaic–Roman Port on the Red Sea Coast of Egypt 1999–2001." *Sahara* 13:23–50.

Simaika, M. 1930. *Dalil al-mathaf al-qibti*. Cairo.

———. 1937. *Guide sommaire du Musée copte et des principales églises du Caire*. Cairo.

———. 1939. *Catalogue of the Coptic and Arabic Manuscripts in the Coptic Museum, the Patriarchate, the Principal Churches of Cairo and Alexandria and the Monasteries of Egypt*. Vol. 1: *The Coptic Museum*. Cairo.

Skálová, Z., and G. Gabra. 2003. *Icons of the Nile Valley*. Cairo.

———. 2006. *Icons of the Nile Valley*. 2nd ed. Cairo.

Snelders, B., and A. Jeudy. 2006. "Guarding the Entrances: Equestrian Saints in Egypt and North Mesopotamia." *ECA* 3:103–40.

Somers Clarke. 1896. "Notes on the Roman Fortress of Babylon at Kasr-ash-Shammah, Near Cairo, in Egypt." *Proceedings of the Society of Antiquaries of London 1895–1897*, Second Series, vol. 16, 58–68.

St. George's Convent, Old Cairo. 1992. *Saint George's Nunnery, Old Cairo*. Cairo.

———. 1997. *Saint George's Convent in Photos*. Cairo.

Stillman, N.A. 1979. *The Jews of Arab Lands*. Philadelphia.

al-Suryani, S. 1992. *Abu al-Makarem, History of the Churches and Monasteries in Lower Egypt in the 13th Century*. Cairo.

———. 1996. *Ancient Coptic Churches and Monasteries in Delta, Sinai, and Cairo*. Cairo.

Török, L. 2005a. *After the Pharaohs: Treasures of Coptic Art from Egyptian Collections* (exh. cat.; Museum of Fine Arts, Budapest). Budapest.

———. 2005b. *Transfigurations of Hellenism: Aspects of Late Antique Art in Egypt AD 250–700*. Probleme der Ägyptologie 23. Leiden and Boston.

Toussoun, O. 1922. *Mémoire sur les anciennes branches du Nil: Mémoires présentés a l'Institut d'Egypte*, vol. 4/1. Cairo.

———. 1925. *Mémoire sur l'histoire du Nil: Mémoires présentés a la Société archéologique d'Alexandrie*, vol. 3. Cairo.

Van Esbroeck, M. 1991. "Michael the Archangel, Saint." *CE* 5:1616–20.

Vansleb (Wansleben), J.M. 1671. *Relazione Dello Stato Presente Dell'Egitto: Nella quale si da esattissimo ragguaglio delle cose Naturali del paese: Del Gouerno Politico, che vi è: Della Religione de'Copti: Dell'Economia delli Egizij, e delle magnifiche Fabriche, che ancor'hoggidi visi ci veggeno*. Paris.

———. 1677. *Nouvelle relation en forme de journal d'un voyage fait en Egypte en 1672 & 1673*. Paris.

———. 1678. *The Present State of Egypt or, A New Relation of a Late Voyage into That Kingdom: Performed in the Years 1672 and 1673*. London.

Vliet, J. van der. 2007. "Perennial Hellenism! Lásló Török and the al-Mo'allaqa Lintel (Coptic Museum inv. no. 753)." *ECA* 4:77–80.

Wissa Wassef, C. 1971. *Pratiques rituelles et alimentaires des Coptes. Bibliothèque d'études coptes* 9. Cairo.

———. 1991. "Calendar, Months of Coptic," "Calendar and Agriculture," "Calendar, Seasons, and Coptic Liturgy." *CE* 2, 440–44.

Wüstenfeld, F., trans. 1845. *Macrizi's Geschichte der Copten*. Göttingen (reprint Hildesheim 1979).

Yeomans, R. 2006. *The Art and Architecture of Islamic Cairo*. Reading, UK.

Yoyotte, J. 1954. "Prêtres et sanctuaires du nome héliopolite à la Basse Epoque." *BIFAO* 54:83–115.

———. 1973. "Réflexions sur la topographie et la toponymie de la région du Caire." *BSFE* 67:27–35.

Zanetti, U. 1995. "Abu'l-Makarim et Abu Salih." *BSAC* 34:85–138.

Zosimus. 1887. *Historia nova*, ed. L. Mendelssohn. Leipzig.

INDEX

ACKNOWLEDGMENTS

MOST IMPORTANTLY, WE ARE MOST GRATEFUL to the late Pope Shenouda III, who made it possible for Sherif Sonbol to work in the churches taking the amazing photographs that document this important part of Old Cairo's history. It has been a pleasure once again collaborating with the same team that created *The Churches of Egypt: From the Journey of the Holy Family to the Present Day*—Gawdat Gabra, Gertrud van Loon, Sherif Sonbol, Morris Jackson, Bruce Ludwig, Ola Seif at the American University in Cairo (AUC) Rare Books and Special Collections Library, and the AUC Press. Gawdat Gabra's efforts in bringing distinguished scholar Stefan Reif at Cambridge, and Tarek Swelim, to this project was brilliant. We thank especially Dr. Zahi Hawass and all of the Department of Antiquities inspectors in Old Cairo, for without their input and cooperation this work could not have been accomplished.

Mohamed Nazmy and Hassan Eid of Quest Travel put together the accommodations again, as they did for *The Churches of Egypt*. Gregory Dillon (in memoriam) and Jean-Pierre Minardi of Hilton Hotels for their grand hospitality and staff. Michael Saad of Watani International opened many opportunities, making this publication much more interesting and complete. Elliott Woodruff for his initial work in editing the book. Susana Funsten for immeasurable knowledge and support. Roger Wong for his expert technical assistance and Sonia Hernandez for her care. Timi Loomis Freshman and Father John Bakas, Dean of St. Sophia Greek Orthodox Cathedral in Los Angeles. Cambridge University Library, and the Head of its Genizah Research Unit, Dr. Ben Outhwaite, for the complimentary photographs and manuscript images, and Dr. Reif for his assistance. Carmen Weinstein, JCC Cairo, who opened the Ben Ezra Synagogue to us and added so much to the history there. Ambassador and Mrs. Daniel Kurtzer for their introductions and support. Dr. Samir Simaika for the courtesy of the portrait of Marcus Simaika Pasha.

We are most grateful to Dr. Peter Grossmann for his gift of sharing his research and drawings. Without his dedication to the study of Coptic churches, we would not have the ground plans of the churches included in this edition. Dr. Grossmann spent more than forty years in Egypt and discovered many churches in addition to the execution of the ground plans of nearly all Egypt's ancient and medieval churches. The value of these precise eleven ground plans cannot be overestimated.

Acknowledgments from Sherif Sonbol

Mary from St. George Greek Orthodox Church; Sinout Shenouda for his never-ending patience in making appointments with the bishops and priests; Ayman Karim, who helped us with permits in the churches; Mr. Mahgoub, head of the Old Cairo area; Ahmed Abd El Aty; Mrs. Hend, in charge of the Abu Sayfayn compound; Father Youhannah Fouad at the Church of the Virgin 'al-Damshiriya'; Hannah Sonbol for her support and photographic talents.